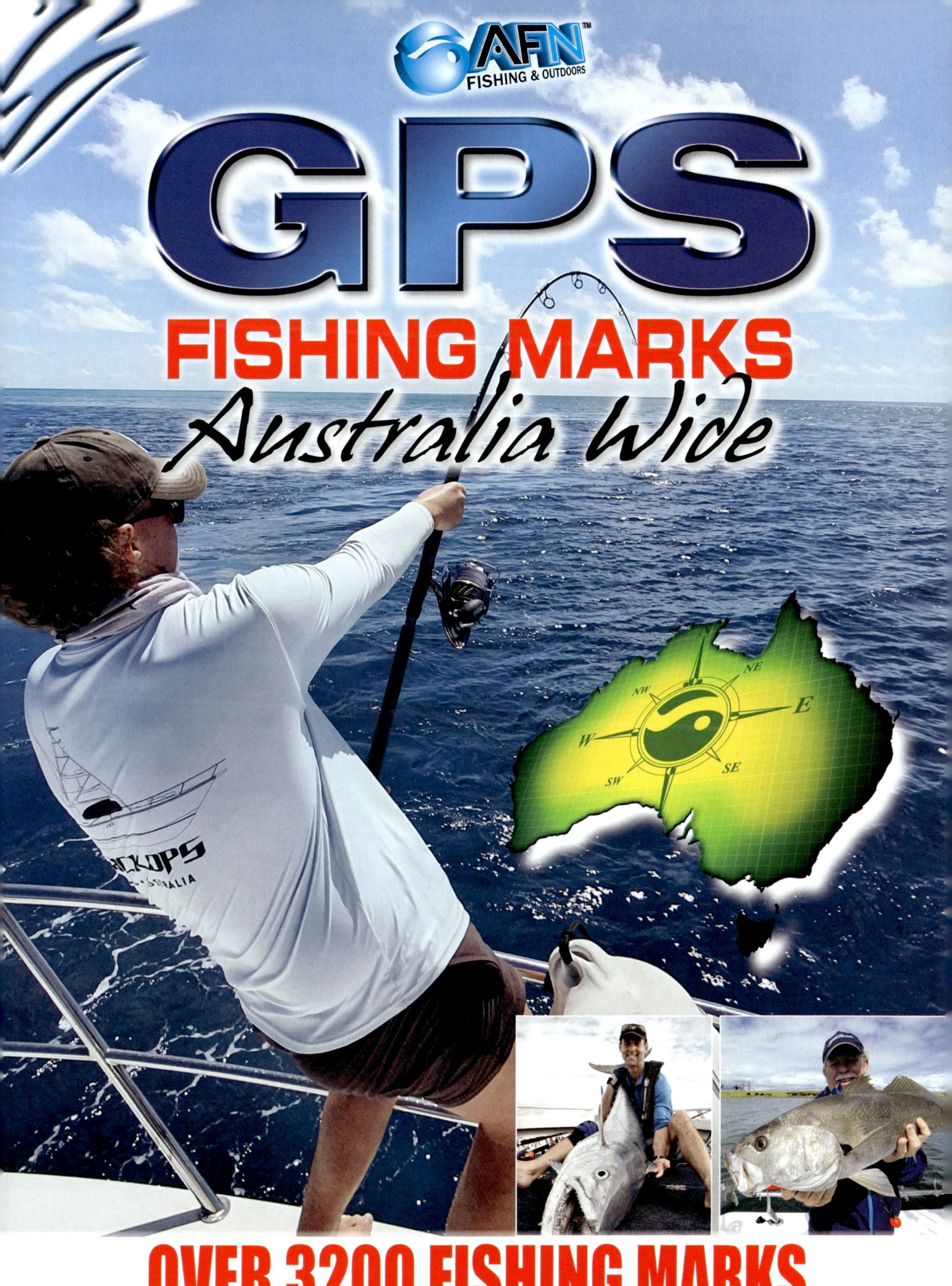
AFN
FISHING & OUTDOORS
GPS
FISHING MARKS
Australia Wide
NE
NW
E
W
SE
SW
OVER 3200 FISHING MARKS

ACKNOWLEDGEMENTS

In accumulating the information within this book we acknowledge the members of the general fishing population around Australia who, over the years, have recorded GPS marks and passed their knowledge to their peers through a myriad of mediums. This book is a compilation of their efforts.

Special thanks are offered to Peter McGrath and Julian Patino for their expert assistance.

DISCLAIMER

All care has been taken in the compilation of these fishing marks and all have been verified as well as possible, but AFN takes no responsibility for any effects either indirectly or directly from their use. AFN also takes no responsibility for any errors in the GPS marks in this book and all marks must be double-checked on a marine chart before proceeding.

CAUTION

Any individual navigating a craft must take total responsibility for the safety of the craft and those on board. Before moving to any GPS co-ordinate the skipper MUST double-check the co-ordinates on a marine chart to determine it is safe to proceed there. Some GPS fishing marks are close to shore, reefs and other hazards and the skipper of the craft must take responsibility to ensure they are not putting their craft or occupants in danger by heading to, or positioning on, a particular mark.

Navigating at night is always dangerous and it is always recommended that skippers have an intimate knowledge of the area before navigating anywhere at night, in fog or in any adverse weather conditions.

MARINE PARKS AND MARINE SANCTUARIES

Not every point in this book is meant as a fishing spot. Some are for reference, for use as landmarks and others are included for interest.

Also note that State Governments are continually forming and reviewing marine parks and sanctuaries and their boundaries. While at the time of publication all efforts to identify such areas had been made, there may be some inadvertent inclusions and exclusions. Additionally, some points may be within close proximity to MP or MS boundaries and accidental incursion into these areas is possible. It is the reader's responsibility to be aware of and to abide by the regulations associated with individual marine parks and marine sanctuaries.

At the time of publication State Governments, especially the South Australian and West Australian Governments, are reviewing the access and use rules in the areas they have gazetted as Marine Parks. These areas and conditions are unavailable at this time and may well include points included in this book. Check each point before you use it.

First published 2004
Revised and Updated, 2006
Revised and Updated 2007
Revised and updated 2010
Revised and updated 2021
Australian Fishing Network,
PO Box 544, Croydon, Vic 3136
Telephone: (03) 9729 8788, Fax: (03) 9729 7833
Email: sales@afn.com.au Website: www.afn.com.au

ISBN: 9781 8651 3365 2

TABLE OF CONTENTS

PREFACE

Almost every angler who fishes on the water either uses a GPS (Global Positioning System) or wishes they did! The GPS enables anglers to determine their latitude and longitude out on the water, but more than that it can steer them to any particular co-ordinate within their boats physical ability to get there and get home.

In years past the noting of fishing marks was restricted to lined up landmarks and perhaps cross-referencing with depth. With a GPS anglers can now navigate to any co-ordinate without the need for line of sight reference. Gone are the days when pulling down the church spire meant losing your favourite snapper mark!

Now the angler with a GPS unit can electronically log a mark to return there at any future time using that GPS unit as the navigation tool. For anglers with a GPS and few recorded marks this book or for anglers going to unfamiliar fishing destinations this book is for you! The aim of this book is to present the co-ordinates of known and pre-mapped fishing locations. For the experts it will provide alternative locations to those they normally fish. For all travelling anglers it will give some great starting points to fishing in areas with which they are not familiar. Anyone can get a head start using these GPS hot spot marks when fishing a new locality.

The co-ordinates have been compiled from regular contributors to the Australian Fishing Network, from readers' submissions and from the public domain. All spots have been presented in a consistent WGS84 format for ease of use.

As most anglers will want to keep a record of new spots and favourite locations we have included areas in this book where such new entries can be made so that the risk of the loss of your hot spots through the loss of your GPS unit is minimised.

A chapter by noted electronics columnist Fred Studden contains information that will enable the newcomer to understand how the GPS system works and will help all users to get the most from their GPS units.

A GPS plotter will put an angler accurately on to an offshore mark time after time.

INTRODUCTION

Since the 1990's when the Global Positioning System (GPS) first became fully available to recreational boaters, there have been incredible advances made in the design and production in this arena, and today's units have a degree of sophistication undreamed of even a decade ago. Due to the advances made in mass production technology of electronic equipment and the huge world wide market for GPS the cost in real terms has fallen considerably, and modern GPS units are cheaper than they have ever been, and yet have more features and facilities than ever before.

As a result of these technological advantages, there would be few serious recreational fishing boats not equipped with a GPS receiver, and yet to many users this equipment represents 'black box' technology and its use is still shrouded in mystery. Due to this attitude, many owners are not realising anywhere near the full potential of their equipment and others are reluctant to purchase new gear because of the fear they may not be able to use it properly.

With these thoughts in mind this book is aimed at dispelling the myths surrounding the complexity of modern GPS, and by doing so help owners to get the best performance from their equipment.

My background is a technical one, having owned and operated a marine electronics business for 20 years, which specialised in sales, service and installation of marine electronics. However I am also a keen angler, fishing mainly offshore for most of my life, and regularly use all types of marine electronics, giving me the unique advantage of understanding both the technical and practical side of the equipment described in this book. I have kept the text, wherever possible, to a non-technical level, only straying into specialised terminology, when absolutely essential to understand an important point of the operation of the equipment. The content has also been purposely kept as 'generic' as possible so as to be applicable to all brands and models of GPS. On occasions, particular brands may be mentioned, however this is to draw attention to a special feature or function and is not intended as a personal recommendation of any one brand.

I would like to thank the following suppliers of GPS equipment for their assistance, Bob Litter Agencies (Humminbird), Lowrance Australia (Lowrance and Eagle), and Navman Australian (Navman), Oceantalk Australia (Raymarine).

Images used were made by using screen download software, Snapshot (Lowrance), Navision (Navman) and photographs of actual screen displays.

While the chapters dealing with the history and basic description of the operating principals of GPS are not, strictly speaking, necessary to know how to operate, or to install the equipment, I hope you will find them both interesting and informative.

Fred Studden

Snapper are one of the most popular and sought after fish species, and GPS marks are fast becoming synonymous with successful captures.

CHAPTER ONE

HISTORY AND BASIC PRINCIPLES

THE SATELLITES

The Global Positioning System became fully operational in the early 1990's, although partial coverage was provided for some years before (the first satellite was launched in February 1989 and the most recent March 31 2003.) The system now consists of 28 satellites in a high polar orbit, some 20,000 kilometres above the earth (fig 1.) The orbit design was developed to guarantee that at least four satellites are always in view at every point on the earth's surface twenty-four hours a day. In many instances, however, as many as twelve or thirteen satellites will be visible to the earth based user. Each satellite in the constellation orbits the earth twice a day. The satellites continually transmit a unique coded sequence, which allows identification of the satellite, precise time correction signals, as well as almanac data for all the satellites in the constellation.

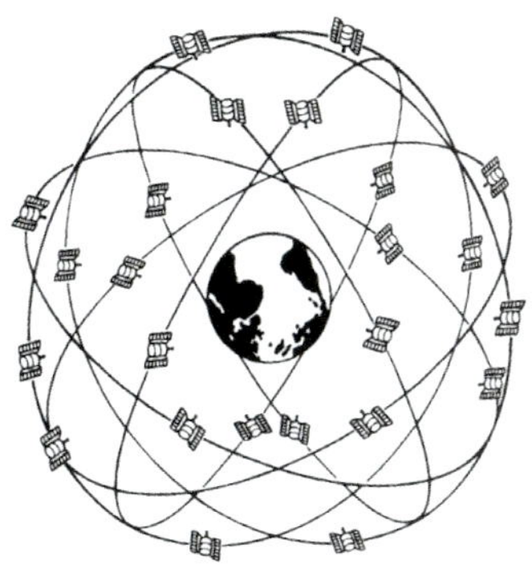

Figure 1
GPS Satellite Constellation

GPS RECEIVERS

The GPS receiver measures the time of arrival of each signal and then calculates the range (distance) of each satellite. Once the range of the satellites is known, the position of the receiver can be determined by triangulation. If it were possible to measure 'true satellite ranges' directly it would only be necessary to track data from two satellites to obtain your latitude and longitude. The range measurement depends on accurately measuring the time taken for the radio signal, which is travelling at the speed of light, to reach the receiver. Unfortunately these transmissions are affected by the ionosphere as well as by timing errors in the receiver's own internal clock, so a minimum of three satellites is required to cancel out these errors to obtain an initial fix.

GPS TIME

Accurate time is critical to the operation of GPS and to this end each satellite has four atomic clocks on board and the performance of these clocks is regularly monitored and adjusted by earth stations. As you would appreciate, time is of prime importance in GPS and the satellites refer to UTC (Universal Time Coordinates) time, which for all practical purposes is the same as GMT (Greenwich Mean Time). (For the purest, UTC is about 5 seconds ahead of GMT.) Each satellite's time is checked and corrected on a weekly basis by the earth stations.

SATELLITE CODES AND SELECTIVE AVAILABILITY

The satellites transmit on two frequencies, 1575.42 MHz and 1227.60 MHz, which are known as the 'L-band'. Each signal has sequence codes superimposed on the carrier frequency by modulation.

These codes are a Precision Code (P) and a Course Acquisition Code (C/A). The P code is reserved for the military and the C/A code for civilian use. It was originally intended that the P code would be considerably more accurate than the C/A code, yet when implemented, the difference was not as significant as the system designers had expected. To deny the unexpected accuracy of the system to anyone other than the United States military and friendly allies, a deliberate degrading of the system was introduced in early 1991.

This intended error was called Selective Availability (S/A), also know as dithering of the signal, which reduced the civilian accuracy to about 100 metres. In May 2000 S/A was removed and the accuracy of the system improved to around 10–15 metres. The reasoning behind this change was improvements to the satellites now in service, which enabled the US Department of Defence to selectively degrade the accuracy of the satellite signals in any particular region. If, for instance, the US wished to render the system virtually useless in the Persian Gulf region to users of the C/A code, it only required re-programming of the satellites for that region. The rest of the world would still be able to enjoy the full accuracy of the system. Without S/A the accuracy of the system has improved dramatically, however there are a number of factors which can still effect the overall accuracy of the fix. Factors such as the satellites geometry, component tolerances, chart datum etc. The degree of accuracy that the average user can expect will be looked at later in full detail.

DILUTION OF PRECISION

All GPS receivers are designed to select a configuration of satellites with the best geometry and by doing so provide optimum position accuracy. Thus the greater number of satellites in view, from which the GPS receiver can select, the greater the accuracy. To present the user with a realistic measure of the quality of the satellite configuration a factor know as Dilution of Precision (DOP) is available on all receivers. A DOP can refer to several types of precision; the main ones are Geometric Dilution of Precision (GDOP), Positional Dilution of Precision (PDOP) and Horizontal Dilution of Precision (HDOP.)

GDOP refers to the expected precision of a three dimensional fix, that is length, breadth and height, and includes a calculation for time. PDOP is also a three dimensional factor but does not include time. HDOP is two dimensional—length and breadth—and is the factor used for marine positioning since height measurements are meaningless as the boat will always be at sea level. While some GPS receivers display all of these factors, most only show the HDOP reading. It should be remembered that HDOP is only a relative number, a multiplier in other words, which is used to calculate the error of a fix in cases when it is important to determine the probable error of any readings. The smaller the HDOP number the better the fix, a figure of three is considered very good, five is good and any readings greater than ten are going to have an appreciable effect on the accuracy of the system. Having said this it is rare today to see HDOP figures of greater than three (fig 2.) Some GPS units display HDOP as a real measurement, either in feet or metres, which refers to a circle of accuracy around the boat, in other words if the display indicates an estimated error of 15 metres the true position will be within 15 metres of the boat's position.

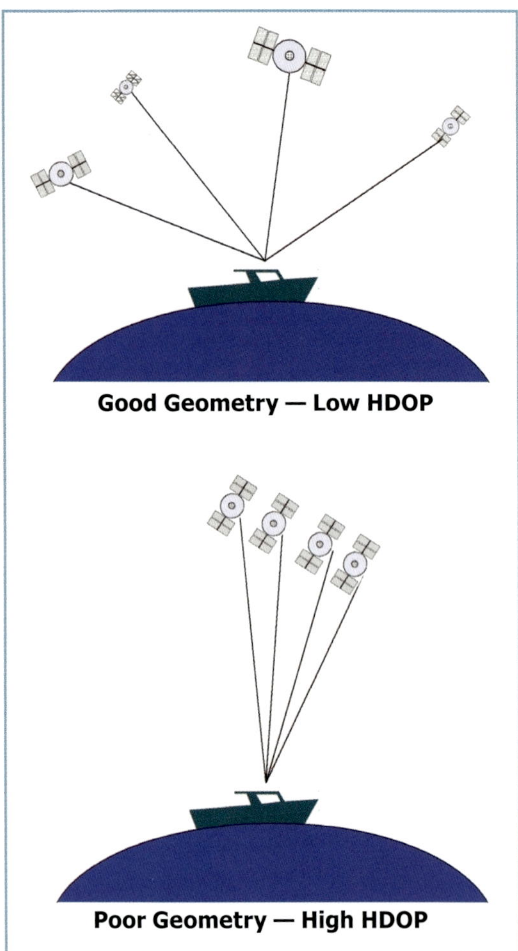

Figure 2 *Geometry Effects*

LINE OF POSITION

When a receiver is first switched on it must obtain an initial position fix. To do this the receiver uses three satellites and, by comparison, the internal processor can determine the amount of clock error in each range calculation. The receiver subtracts

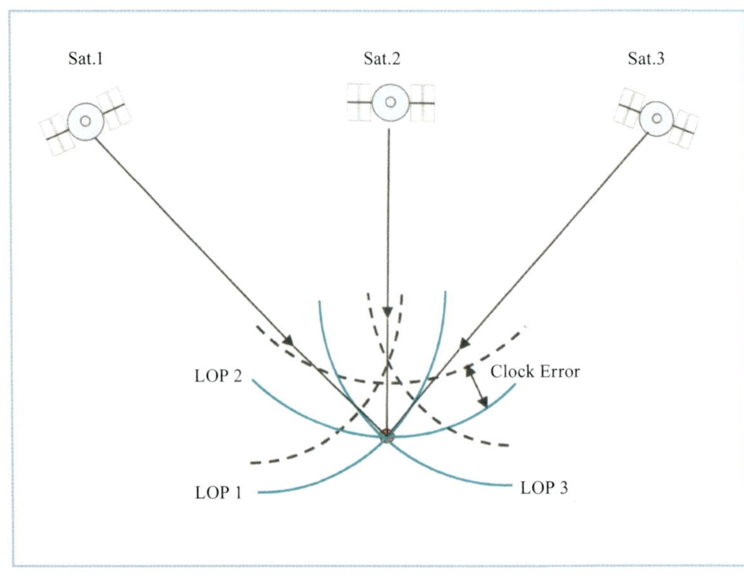

Figure 3 *Intersecting Satellites LOPs*

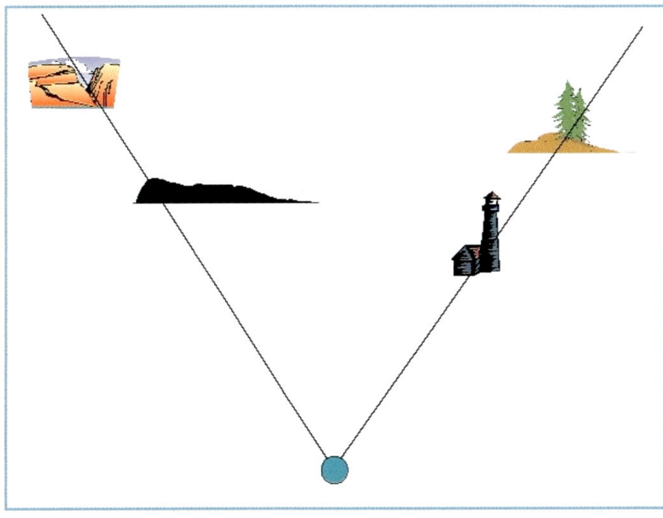

Figure 4 *Visual Line of Position*

the error from each range solution until the Lines of Position (LOP) intersect at one point, this then is the fix (fig 3.) LOP are used in all types of navigation, for example, when you use visual marks to locate a fishing spot you are using LOP. When two objects are lined up, you know the location must lie somewhere along that line. When a second set of marks is lined up, the point where the two lines intersect is the location of your fishing spot (fig 4.)

SATELLITE NUMBERS

All satellites are identified by numbers and these numbers are shown on the receiver's status screen, usually the number has a prefix either PRN (Pseudo-Random Number) or SVID (Space Vehicle IDentity).

DIFFERENTIAL GPS

During the years when S/A was active, a system know as Differential GPS (DGPS) was introduced. DGPS consists of a GPS receiver permanently located at a known reference point. Positional errors at the reference GPS are corrected for each satellite and these corrections are broadcast over a radio link. A DGPS set receives these radio corrections and mixes them in the standard GPS receiver greatly enhancing its accuracy (fig 5.)

The limitations of such a system are the distance from the base station, radio interference and cost. Depending on the frequency of the radio data link and the distance from the base, accuracy was improved to 10 metres or less. A number of commercial (user pays) DGPS bases were set-up and use radio links in the VHF and UHF band, giving users in close proximity to the base accuracy of a couple of meters.

Of main interest to the recreational user was a DGPS system established by the Commonwealth using HF frequency transmitters—this service was free to users. While VHF and UHF are almost line-of-sight frequencies, HF is long range. Initially the Government commissioned DGPS stations as a navigation aid to cover high-risk areas, such as the North West Shelf and Bass Strait oil fields, and the Great Barrier Reef passage. Later, more stations were established along the coast, particularly in areas of high commercial marine traffic.

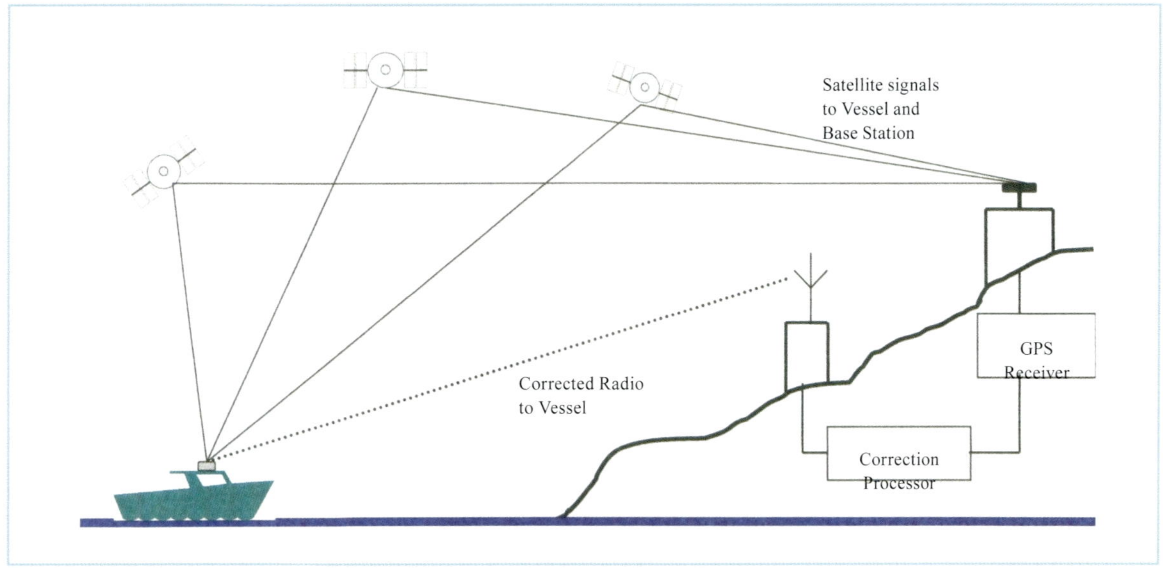

Figure 5 *Differential GPS*

The RF system of DGPS provided users as far away as 60 nautical miles (n miles) from the base station with accuracy's of 10–15 metres, however with the dropping of S/A by the United States Department of Defence in 2000, few recreational users found they could justify the cost of a Differential Receiver for the small increase in accuracy it offered.

FUTURE DIFFERENTIAL DEVELOPMENTS

Two systems based, rather loosely, on DGPS technology are expected to become operational overseas within the next couple of years. However they are unlikely to be seen in Australian waters for quite some time, if ever. The North American system, called Wide Area Augmentation System (WAAS), which offers greater accuracy without many of the problems associated with DGPS—including only requiring one receiver as the correction signals are transmitted on the same frequency as the GPS signals and has less interference due to weather. The European equivalent is to be known as EGNOS an abbreviation for European Geostationary Navigation Overlay Service. (Both systems use geostationary satellites as well as base stations.)

CHART AND MAP DATUM

Since the earth is not a true sphere, but a spheroid with the diameter at the equator greater than at the poles, to create marine charts and land maps it is necessary to have a fixed, geodetic, point on the earth's surface against which all other positions are measured. This point is called the geodetic datum. But as would be expected, there is a number of different datum in use, often changing from country to country. For the navigator it is obviously critical that the position from the GPS receiver is the same datum as that of the navigation chart, or that a GPS mark being entered was recorded using the same datum as in the GPS receiver. Most electronics charts used in chart plotters these days are WGS84 datum.

Fortunately there is a degree of uniformity appearing and the World Geodetic System of 1984 (WGS84) is fast becoming standard. Most of the Admiralty charts produced in recent years are based on WGS84 and all of the older charts printed during the last few years carry the corrections which need to be made to bring positions derived from the paper chart to agree with the GPS positions obtained if the GPS receiver's datum has been set to WGS84. For example, this is a type of notice that would appear on an Australian Chart.

SATELLITE — DERIVED POSITIONS

Positions obtained from satellite navigation systems are referred to the WGS datum; such positions should be moved 0.09 minutes SOUTHWARD and 0.06 minutes WESTWARD to agree with this chart.

Most GPS receivers have provision to change their datum to match that used on your paper chart of the area. By default the receiver usually uses WGS84. However be aware, if the datum has been changed to suit a local chart, and another chart is used, make sure the datum of the GPS receiver is checked to see that it agrees with the new chart's datum.

If you are using a paper chart to plot your position from GPS coordinates or are transferring positions from a chart to your GPS it is VITAL that you be aware of both the datum used when the chart was drawn and the datum that the GPS is using. Similarly, you must be aware that the datum of a GPS mark that you enter into your GPS receiver must be the same as that of the GPS receiver to accurately represent the intended position.

Land maps also carry notices of the datum used in their production. If there is no notice displayed on the chart or map as to the datum, use WGS84. Other than WGS84 the main datum used in Australia is Australian Geodetic Datum 1966 (AGD66) and Australian Geodetic Datum 1984 (AGD84).

An aspect of chart datum and it's effect on the accuracy of the system, which is often overlooked, is transferring of coordinate data between GPS receivers. If a position fix is recorded, using the Australian AGD84 datum and this data is then transferred to a unit operating on the default WGS84 then the error will be considerable.

To correct this type of datum error a correction is applied to the coordinates to convert them to the required datum. This correction factor is obtained by setting up a GPS receiver at a fixed location and recording the coordinates and the Geodetic Datum used. Without moving the receiver, change the datum to the required one and record the coordinates. It now becomes a simple matter to calculate the correction factor. As an example the following is the correction for my location which is on the NSW Central Coast;

WGS84: S32 57.273 E151 37.556

AGD84: S32 57.370 E151 37.488

Correcting WGS84 to AGD84 add 0.097 to latitude and subtract 0.068 from longitude.

Correcting AGD84 to WGS84 subtract 0.097 from latitude and add 0.068 to longitude.

The difference between the two datum is about 0.1 of a nautical mile, about 200 metres.

It is important to remember the correction factor will vary according to the location, so if you change your location more than about 60 nautical miles from the location where the correction was calculated it is advisable to calculate a new factor.

Fortunately this type of error is not common as most GPS receivers have WGS84 as a default datum and few operators ever find the need to alter this configuration.

Chart datum is only of importance when transferring data to, or from, a chart or map. There are other factors, which could effect the accuracy of a position plotted from a paper chart, or plotted to a paper chart. The wise navigator will always take heed of the disclaimer published in all GPS instruction books and displayed at the start-up of the GPS receivers warning uses to exercise common prudence and navigational judgement and the device should not relied on as the only source of navigation. The rule for pilots also applies to navigators: 'There are old navigators and bold navigators, but few old, bold navigators'.

Big yellowtail kingfish live on reefs, and GPS plotter will enable you to find the same spot despite the size of the ocean!

CHAPTER TWO

GPS INSTALLATION

CONSIDERATIONS

After reading all about the System and how it all works, now is the time to get your hands dirty and install the unit in the boat. The installation of a GPS receiver is generally a straightforward job, which should present no problems for the average handyman.

The first step is to sit down and read the installation instructions supplied with the unit, this will not only make the job easier but probably save a lot of heartache later.

LOCATING THE DISPLAY UNIT

The display unit can be fitted either as a flush mount or bracket mounting. GPS receivers that are suitable for flush mounting are generally supplied with hardware to mount the unit and a template for cutting the correct sized hole in the bulkhead. Points to be checked before starting to cut are to make sure that there is sufficient room behind the bulkhead to comfortably take the unit, that there are no obstructions, such as cabling, behind the bulkhead and the bulkhead itself is strong enough to support the display. Remember, when the boat is pounding in a sea there are considerable inertia forces placed on the mounting. Check, and then check again, that the selected location is the correct one before cutting the hole in the panel.

I have found one of the best methods for determining the right spot for both bracket and flush mounted installations is to temporarily attach the power lead to the unit and 'fire it up'. Assume your normal driving position and move the display around until all of the controls are in easy reach and you are getting a good view under all conditions. If the unit is to be bracket mounted, ensure there is enough room to swing the display through its range of adjustments. It is often advantageous to be able to swing the display so that if you are fishing from just about anywhere in the boat you can still see the display. By doing this it is possible to check—if you have anchored—that the anchor has not dragged and you have moved off the mark, or if you are drift fishing you can verify your rate and direction of drift and your current position. If all is well, temporarily mount the unit.

Bracket or gimbal mounting is much the same as for flush mounting. Check that there is room for the brackets, that the panel chosen to mount the bracket is strong enough to support the unit even in rough seas (it may be an advantage to fit a reinforcing plate under the panel if there is any doubt), and that there is space to run the cabling.

Time spent on selecting the right location is well worth the extra effort. Remember that you will use the GPS more than any other instrument on the boat, so make its location comfortable and convenient to use.

MOUNTING THE ANTENNA

While the position of the antenna is not critical there are a couple of rules to be observed. The antenna should have an uninterrupted, clear view of the whole of the sky, however glass, Perspex, fibreglass, and fabrics will not impede the signal, wood or metal will.

GPS antennas should be kept away from radio transmitter antennas. Three metres is a safe distance from high power antennas such as VHF and HF radios, but if room is tight you can creep up a little closer to the 27 MHz, which has a fairly low output. Radars are a definite no no, they radiate large amounts of radio frequency and the antenna should be kept well out of the radar beam.

On most runabouts the antenna is mounted on the foredeck, which in many ways is an ideal site. It is usually easy to find space on the deck and in this location the antenna is generally protected from the bumps and knocks that are to be expected in day to day fishing. Wiring the antenna back to the display unit is usually simple too. Many of today's antennas are compact units, which can be fitted, almost flush, straight onto the deck (fig 6.) The antenna should always be mounted as near to horizontal as possibly to enable it to 'see' the sky from horizon to horizon, however when one considers the movement of the boat in a seaway, a few degrees doesn't matter. If the deck is steeply sloped it will be necessary to make up a wooden packing piece to bring the antenna back to the

Figure 6 *Deck mounting the antenna is the simplest method where room permits.*

horizontal. Another option is to use a fully adjustable radio antenna base, which are available at most chandler supplies.

While the foredeck is a common location, there are plenty of other equally suitable sites. The antenna does not have to be mounted out in the open. If there is room it can be successfully placed on the dash provided there are no metal frames close by to mask the antenna, the windscreen will not interfere with the signal strength. The antenna can also be mounted below decks, provided the hull material is fibreglass—this is a favourite spot on yachts.

If it is more convenient the antenna can be fitted to an overhead rod rack or targa bar (fig 7.) The extra height above the water is no advantage, nor is it a disadvantage, although do not mount the antenna at the top of a high mast, the swinging about of the mast in anything of a sea will lead to errors in the received data. If you are having a rod rack or targa made up and intend to have a stub fitted at the time of manufacturer to mount the GPS antenna—be warned—the standard thread in the bases of both radio and GPS is 1 inch diameter, 14 threads to the inch. This is American thread, not the common 1 inch Whitworth thread used in Australia.

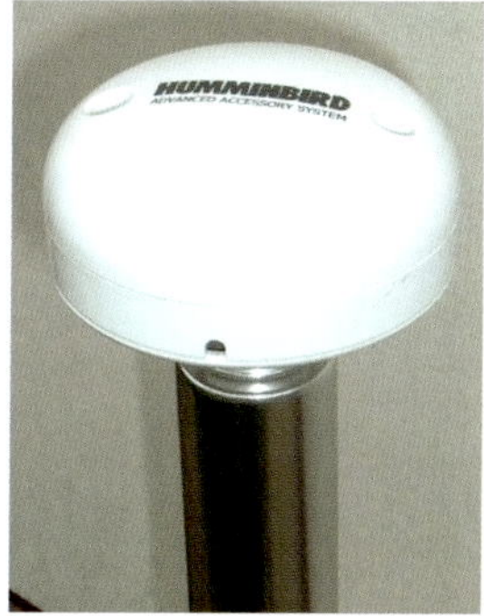

Figure 7 *Antenna mounted on a pole or post. This type of mounting is ideal for a rod rack or to position the antenna clear of obstructions.*

Route the antenna cable back to the display unit, making sure the cable is well secured and cannot move about and chaff on the hull. The majority of antennas are supplied with a long connecting cable, up to 6 metres to cater for remote antenna installations, but the average runabout usually only requires 1–1.5 metres. This lead may be cut; it is not a tuned circuit like a radio antenna lead. Some units have moulded plugs which cannot be opened, and even those plugs which can be serviced have small connectors, which require a certain level of skill to un-solder and re-solder the connections to shorten the lead. If you do not feel confident in attempting this job, just coil up the lead and stow it neatly in some out of the way location.

Connect the power lead from the display unit to a convenient power supply point in the boat's electrical system. LCD units draw very little current, but it still pays to ensure the connection point has a good clean supply. Make sure you fit the fuse supplied with the unit and if the GPS has a ferrite suppression block supplied, also fit this around the power cable.

Attach the antenna cable to the unit and switch it on, if everything checks out okay install the display permanently and tidy up the cables.

VOLTAGE SPIKES

All electronic equipment is subjected to voltage spikes and fluctuations in the boat's power supply, but a GPS is particularly prone to problems from this type of interference. These spikes can create serious problems in electronic equipment, although they can usually be overcome with a little care, planning and knowledge.

Spikes are spurious fluctuations in the power supply from the battery, generated by other equipment operating from the same supply at the same time. Spikes can take two forms, high voltage spikes, when the voltage jumps up to very high values, or low voltage spikes when the voltage drops low. Spikes are generally of very short duration, sometimes lasting only milliseconds (a millisecond is 1/1000th. of a second), and can have varying effects on electronic equipment.

High voltage spikes are generally caused by equipment such as engine starter motors, electric motors, ignition systems etc, with the starter motors creating the main problems. These spikes are usually of very short duration but can reach levels as high as 300 volts from a 12 volt supply. Low voltage spikes, more correctly called a negative going pulse, are caused by the battery supply being subjected to a very heavy load for a short time, such as when an engine starter motor first cuts in. Negative going pulses are generally of a much longer duration, and the voltage can drop as low as six volts for short periods of time.

High voltage spikes tend to do more permanent damage to electronic equipment, while the low voltage drops tend to play havoc with electronic memories. Most modern equipment, including GPS, is safeguarded to a degree by it's own internal protection circuitry, but can still suffer damage from severe spiking. Many unexplained failures of equipment are caused by a constant barrage of high voltage spiking. Components may be able to take spiking for some time, but continual abuse will shorten their life and cause premature failure. Today most equipment consists of a number of printed circuit boards (PCB), these boards are assembled by machine and are almost impossible to repair, which means if one component fails — for any reason — it generally means a replacement board, which can mean big money.

Negative going pulses are seldom associated with component failure, however they can scramble the electronic memory. The highly sophisticated memory of a GPS is used to retain the original calibration setting, the satellite configuration from the last time it was used and all the waypoints that have been entered into storage. Negative going pulses can cause a catastrophic memory failure severe enough to return the unit to it's original factory setting, or more subtle effects when only a few numbers may be corrupted. Whatever the effect, the result is usually the same—the whole of the data in the memory has to be checked, and more often than not, re-entered. Sometimes the effect on the equipment is not immediately apparent, and goes unnoticed until a waypoint's location is obviously wrong, or the indicated distance to a selected waypoint is shown as hundreds of miles when you know it is only a couple of miles away. While a negative going pulse seldom causes component breakdown, it creates much frustration and, if they are lost, hours of work re-installing waypoints into the memory.

Remembering spikes, both positive and negative, are caused by Interference by other equipment on the same power supply, the obvious answer is to have a separate power supply for the electronic equipment —a so-called 'dedicated supply'. Fitting a separate battery to only run the GPS and all of the other electronic equipment certainly solves the problem, but like so many things in life it does come with it's own problems. While the total amount of current drawn will be generally small, the battery will still need recharging at regular intervals. It is a simple matter to fit a voltmeter to this battery and trickle charge it at home as soon as the voltage shows signs of dropping, but this can be a real pain, and you must remember to put the charger on before the battery drops too low. The battery cannot be directly hooked up to the boat's motor charging system, for this simply connects it back into the loop. While it is possible to connect the electronics battery to the main battery and the charging circuit via a switch, you must remember to open the switch, to isolate the battery, before switching on your equipment. Human nature being what it is, you will eventually forget, and the first time you forget is when the most damage will be done.

ELECTRONICS BATTERY

The simplest method of keeping a special battery, dedicated as a power supply for electronic equipment, fully charged is to use a simple circuit which incorporates a circuit breaker (fig 8.)

Referring to the illustration, the principle of operation is that the electronics battery is connected to the main battery via a 5 amp circuit breaker. During normal operations the electronics battery is kept charged from the motor's alternator through the main battery. If during starting the drain of the starter motor drags the main battery voltage down and the current drawn from the electronic battery exceeds 5 amps, the circuit breaker will trip and isolate the electronics battery (and the electronics connected to it), from the voltage drop in the main battery.

It is a simple matter to reset the circuit breaker when the motor is running.

Depending on the state of charge in the main battery, the circuit breaker will only trip occasionally, but when it does, it will guarantee your equipment will be protected from the negative going pulse.

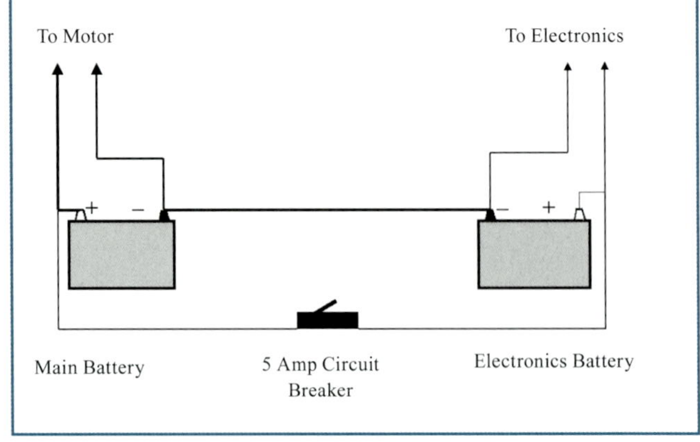

Figure 8 *Electronic Battery*

CHAPTER THREE

GPS RECEIVER

The initial GPS receivers were known as navigators and simply provided numerical data such as position, waypoint information etc, however today all units, with the exception of sets for very specialised applications, are plotters. Plotters consist of a number of display screens each of which has a unique function, making up a very powerful navigation tool.

THE PLOTTER SCREEN

The plotter screen represents an area of the earth's surface with the receiver's current position shown in the centre, commonly by a flashing cursor. Imagine the plotter screen to be like a section of a map without any details showing.

The size of the area represented on the screen can be varied from a very large area, typically 300 n miles or more across the screen, down to about 0.1 miles. (The units of measure can be programmed to read in statute miles, (land miles), nautical miles or kilometres. This will be covered in more detail later). The screen can display the position of waypoints, represented by icons or numbers and names, or both. As the boat moves across the plotter screen a track or trail is laid down (sometimes called a 'snail trail'), this is the history of where the boat has been. This track is composed of dots or points, which are joined together to give the appearance of a continuous line.

The GPS has a limited amount of memory for drawing the dots so when all of the memory has been used the unit removes one from the beginning of the track and uses it at the current position.

The method by which the track is updated can be varied, it can be laid down at a fixed time interval (generally at one second up to one minute or more) or at a predetermined distance (usually one per 0.01 units of distance to 10 units of distance.) For normal fishing use the shortest update time.

All modern units have very large memories, typically 2000 points or more, and when fishing it is rare to run out of track memory. Many units delete the track when switched off or even when plotter scales are changed, however plotter trails can be named and saved in the unit's permanent memory. This is a useful feature; for instance if you have navigated your way out through a tricky channel you may save the track as an aid for navigating the same channel at a later date.

When a waypoint is selected a dotted line is drawn from the boats position to the waypoint. If the scale is too small to show the waypoint, the line is extended beyond the edge of the screen.

The plotter screen can be orientated in several ways, North Up, Track Up or Bearing Up. Orientation will be fully dealt with later.

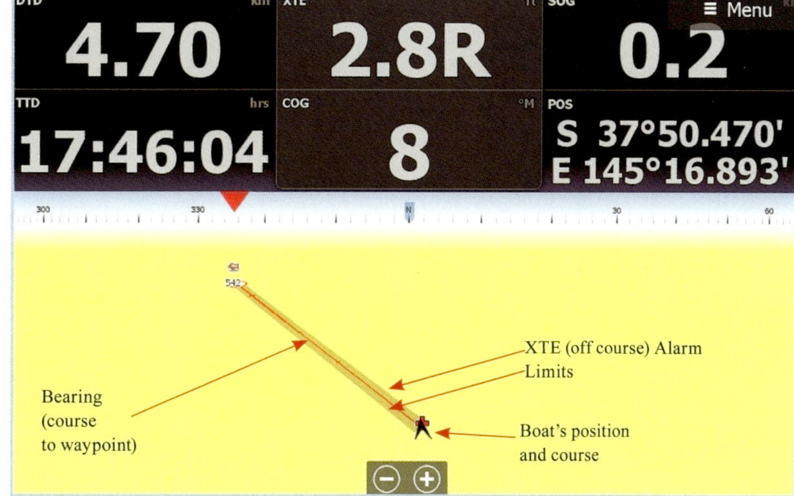

Figure 9 *Highway Screen*

HIGHWAY SCREEN

An alternative to using the plotter for navigating to the destination waypoint, is the Highway display. This is somewhat like a bird's eye view of the boat tracking down a highway towards the waypoint (fig 9.) There are almost as many names for this type of display and ways to present this screen as there are manufacturers.

In their latest models Lowrance have a circular display indicating the boat's course surrounded by a compass rose (fig 10) which graphically illustrating the boats direction. The width of the 'road' is the cross track error range. A number of boxes on the left of the screen show the vital navigation data, Humminbird use a unique 3-dimensional view which can be rotated to view the boats progress from any angle, Navman use the classic road presentation which grows shorter as the boat approaches the waypoint.

Figure 10 *Combination Highway and Compass Rose*

SATELLITE STATUS SCREEN

This screen displays the functions associated with the satellite data that is being received and processed by the unit. It includes the number of satellites in view of the unit's antenna, the satellites being tracked, which satellites are providing data to the receiver, the signal strength, signal to noise ratio (SNR), the position, time, and the accuracy of the current fix (fig 11.) Many of these parameters can be expressed in different ways, depending on the brand of the GPS, again check the owners manual. The accuracy of the fix in particular can be specified in a number of different ways, American manufactured units (Lowrance, Hummingbird) tend to show the error as a distance, that is the error to be expected at the actual location, while units of Japanese origin use the Dilution of Precision (DOP) method, usually the HDOP.

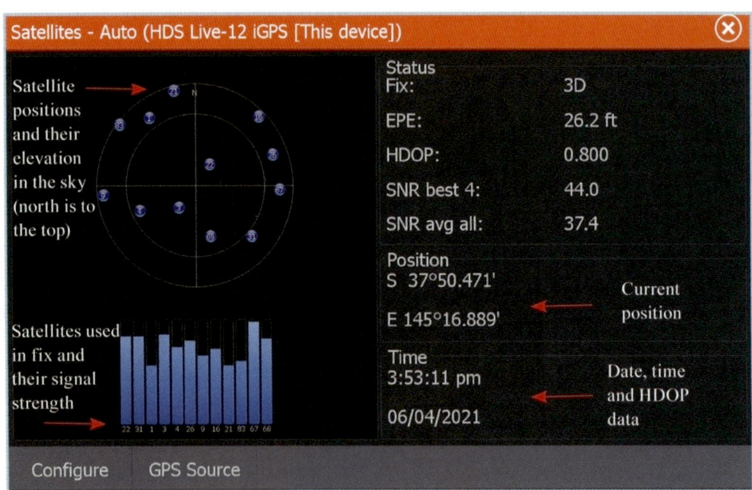

Figure 11 *Satellite Status Screen*

NAVIGATION DISPLAY

Depending on the brand of plotter, this screen (fig 12) is also called a data display or a position screen. The display typically has a number of large numeric displays, indicating important navigation data such as, SOG (Speed Over Ground), COG (Course Over Ground),

Distance and Bearing to the Waypoint, XTE (Cross Track Error) and TTG (Time To Go). This display is really designed for large vessel operations, particularly when using autopilots, and has very little application for small boats.

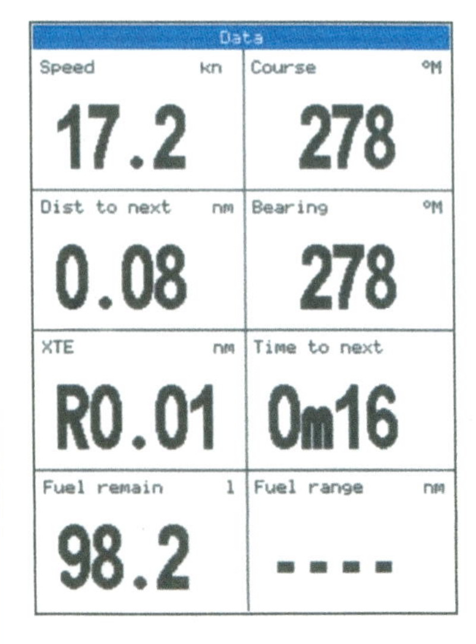

Figure 12 *Navigation Display*

CHART PLOTTERS

Chart plotters were a natural progression from GPS plotters. In all respects they are the same as GPS plotters but with the added advantage of being able to overlay an electronic chart on the screen. Chart plotters have, as standard, a world map installed, however when zoomed-in to useable size the detail is too coarse to be of practical use. To realise the full potential of chart plotters, cartridges are available which contain detailed, up-to-date charts for the Australian coast and offshore waters. The actual area covered by

Figure 13 Lowrance Chart Plotter and Sounder Display

the charts varies from place to place but catalogues are obtainable from the chart suppliers and from GPS dealers.

The chart display can, if necessary, be turned off; the chart plotter then becomes a simple GPS plotter. This may be required in areas that have limited chart coverage and a large degree of zoom is required.

Chart plotters provide another wonderful dimension to GPS receivers, they give informative data on features such as navigation aids, lights, buoys, channel markers, depth contours, safety hazards etc (fig 13, 14, 15.) They display waypoint symbols in the correct relationship to landmasses and when a waypoint is selected the bearing line on the chart will indicate if there are any obstructions such as islands or headlands in the course to the destination.

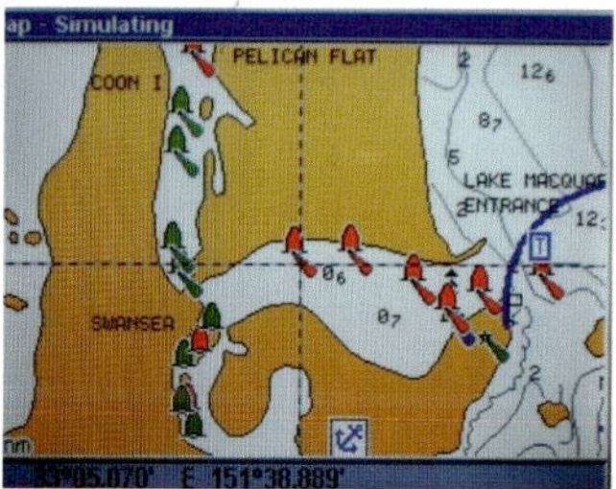

Figure 15 Chart overlaid with with lights and buoy for channel entrance

Using a chart of your local area in which you are probably totally familiar may be a case of gilding the lily, however when plying strange waters such as when on holidays or on that voyage amatically over the last few years, do not trust them implicitly, cross check with admiralty paper charts and heed the warnings with these charts and the warnings in your owners manual.

Another feature is the inclusion of tide and moon phase tables in the chart cards. These tables can be called up (fig 16) for any of the ports included on the chart and display the tidal information for current date. This information is commonly displayed in both numeric and graphic forms, the moon phase and sunrise and sunset times are similarly displayed. If desired the date can be changed to give predictions for other times.

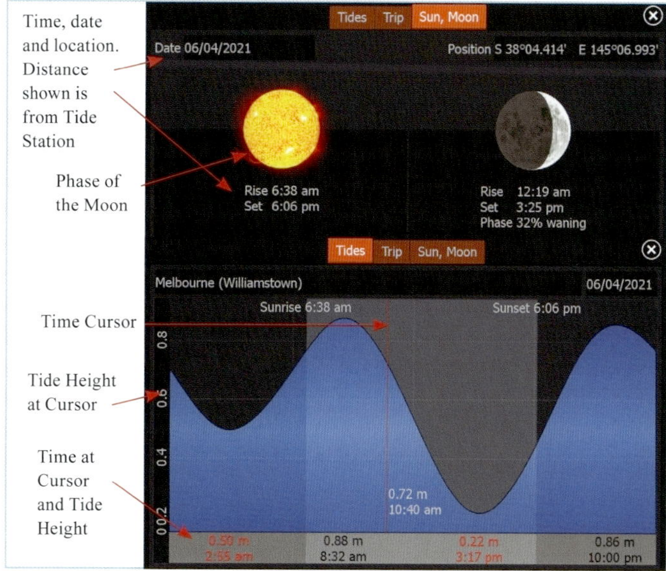

Figure 16 Tide and Moon Phase

HANDHELD GPS

The concept of handheld GPS receivers appeals to a lot of fishermen. They are small, have an in-built antenna, installation is simple (in most cases nothing more than mounting a holding bracket), and they are portable—so if you fish from a mates boat you can take your GPS with you. The greatest disadvantage of the handheld GPS is their size, particularly the screen size. The small handheld screens are difficult to see, particularly when the boat is moving about in a seaway and the number and size of the data boxes is restricted.

If you have an overriding reason for choosing a handheld unit, such as dual use in bushwalking, shooting etc then the disadvantages when using it in a boat are an acceptable trade-off, however in normal circumstances I would always recommend a full size unit.

As an alternative, data from a handheld receiver can be linked to a full sized plotter via a cable connection. The handheld then becomes, in effect, the plotter's antenna, consequently saving on the cost and giving the user the best of both worlds.

COMBO UNITS

The ideal instrument setup is to have a sounder and a plotter as separate dedicated units, this enables each unit to function independently providing the best possible results from each. However, for reasons of space, or perhaps cost, at times a combination sounder/GPS plotter will be chosen. These combo units, particularly in the larger screen sizes, are ideal for smaller boats and suffer very little in comparison to dedicated units.

OFFSETS

Offsets, also called correction factor or map shift, is used to bring the GPS position to correspond with that of a paper chart. For instance, you may regularly use a particular buoy as a turning point, however the physical position of the buoy does not agree with the chart display on your plotter, or the buoy's position plotted on a paper chart. This can be caused by various reasons, such as incorrect chart datum, incorrect original plotting of the buoy, HDOP errors in the system, etc.

Using offsets, which are corrections applied to all latitude and longitude readings within the receiver, it is possible to make the chart display and the GPS agree. Offsets are usually decimal minutes either added or subtracted from the latitude and longitude readings of the GPS receiver. Offsets should be approached with extreme caution. Offsets are actually an intentional error and effect all functions of the GPS, including navigation and recording waypoints. While offsets are a legitimate function of the GPS receiver they should be given a great deal of thought and consideration before employing them.

Often, if the GPS has been spiked (see Voltage Spikes), it is the offset menu which is corrupted by the addition of error corrections. If your unit has been spiked this is one of the areas of the unit's memory, which should be checked and corrected if found to be corrupted.

WAYPOINT LIST

This screen display contains your library of all your waypoints. Here the list can be sorted into any convenient order, individual entries edited, re-named, re-numbered or deleted. The waypoint list represents many hours of work, either through adding waypoints by latitude and longitude coordinates or by going to the spot. Due to the limited size of the GPS receiver's keyboard, it is a laborious task to enter a large number of waypoints. Many units have the ability to interface with a personal computer (PC) and upload and download data, usually waypoints but specialised charts can also be uploaded from the PC. A full size computer keyboard makes it much quicker to type in the waypoints and then upload them than it would be using the GPS input system.

One very important point, which cannot be over stressed, NEVER TRUST AN ELECTRONIC MEMORY! It is Murphy's Law that sometime, somehow the memory will fail, be it in a GPS or a computer. Always have some type of backup, be it electronic or hard copy, or both. There is too much time and effort put into a waypoint list to lose it cold, as many have found out over the years.

Depending on the brand and model of the GPS you have purchased, the initialisation, set-up and operation may differ slightly from the descriptions in the text, but a quick check in the owner's manual should tell you what is needed for your particular unit. The owner's manual is a valuable document, take the time to read it and store it in a safe place for reference in the future.

CHAPTER FOUR

INITIALISATION AND SETUP

INITIALISATION

Initialisation is not strictly necessary for the unit to operate correctly, but it does speed up the first 'fix'. A fix is when the GPS receiver has decoded all the data from the satellites and determined its correct position.

If the unit is turned on, straight out of the box—this is know as a cold start—the receiver will eventually obtain a fix but this could take as long as 20 minutes. Initialising will reduce this to a few minutes.

The first step is to input your current position as latitude and longitude. The dealer may supply this information, or you can take it from a chart, or a mate who has a GPS can give it to you. This data does not need to be absolutely accurate about 100 km is close enough, however it is important to make sure you change the 'N' latitude, which will be displayed for a 'S' to indicate the unit is now operating in the southern hemisphere. Similarly make sure you change the 'W' to 'E' in the longitude setting to program the unit for operating in Australian longitudes. Latitude and longitude is expressed in degrees, minutes and points of a minute (not seconds) e.g. S 32° 57.25 for latitude and E 152°37.52 for longitude or sometimes it may be written, as S 32 57.25 for latitude and E 152 37.52 longitude if the typewriter or printer cannot show the degree sign, also sometimes three decimals places are shown. The actual entry of the position will be straightforward, with menus prompting you when and where to input the data.

The date and time are the next entries to be made. Again, depending on where the unit was manufactured, this could be expressed in different formats. The date may be required in year, month, day sequence (know as YY,MM,DD format) or month, day and year (MM,DD,YY) or even the one we use, day, month, year (DD,MM,YY.) The owner's manual will tell you what format is needed. Next comes the time. Again this may be entered as 'UTC' time (basically Greenwich Mean Time), or it may be in local time, which should present no problems as this does not need to be absolutely accurate either. If it is UTC time, on the east coast of Australia time is 10 hours ahead, or 11 hours during daylight saving time, the west coast is 8 hours ahead of UTC. There is one point to keep in mind when working on UTC dates and times, if you are initialising your GPS before 10 a.m., (8 a.m. West Coast), the date you are to enter will be yesterdays date, because 10 a.m. is midnight yesterday in Greenwich. Few GPS receivers have provision for half-hour corrections, so if you are in South Australia or the Northern Territory you will just have to compromise.

All of this may seem confusing, but if you take your time and do one step at a time you should have few problems. One of the most important points to remember, you cannot harm the GPS in any way by pressing the wrong key. If you do enter the wrong data just go back to the beginning and start over. Normally the initialisation process only needs to be undertaken once, when the unit is new, however if you have not used the unit for longer than three months the almanac will be out of date and the unit will need to update the satellites data—in effect a cold start. Also if you have moved the unit over 100 km from it's last fix position, it will cold start. To avoid cold starting a partial initialisation can be performed, only changing any parameters that may have altered, i.e. date or position.

This completes the initialisation and your unit should obtain its first fix in a matter of a minute or less. By accessing the status screen you will be able to see the receiver locate and begin tracking the first satellite, then as it downloads the data other satellites will be selected and tracked and then the unit will establish it's initial fix.

SET-UP

Setting-up customises the unit to best suit your needs by programming the receiver with the units of measure you wish to use. Units such as speed units e.g. miles per hour, kilometres per hour or knots, distance units e.g. statute miles, kilometres or nautical miles, compass values, either true or magnetic. Other settings that may require attention are the alarm settings e.g. cross track alarm, arrival alarm and anchor alarm. Most of these options are self explanatory, but for those setting up a GPS for the first time the following may be helpful.

UNITS OF MEASURE

Units of measure will probably be either nautical miles or kilometres. Nautical miles have the advantage of being the same units as measured on a marine chart and have a direct relationship with latitude. One degree of latitude is equal to 60 n miles and one minute of latitude equals one n mile. Kilometres have the advantage of being the units of distance we are most familiar with and have the advantage of easily converting to multiples of metres used in search patterns and anchoring techniques (more about these in the practical sections.) If the unit of distance is set to kilometres, the speed will be kilometres per hour (kph) or if nautical miles it will be knots.

COMPASS HEADINGS

Compass heading would normally be set to magnetic, but if you intend to do a lot of reference work with nautical charts, then true readings may be worth considering.

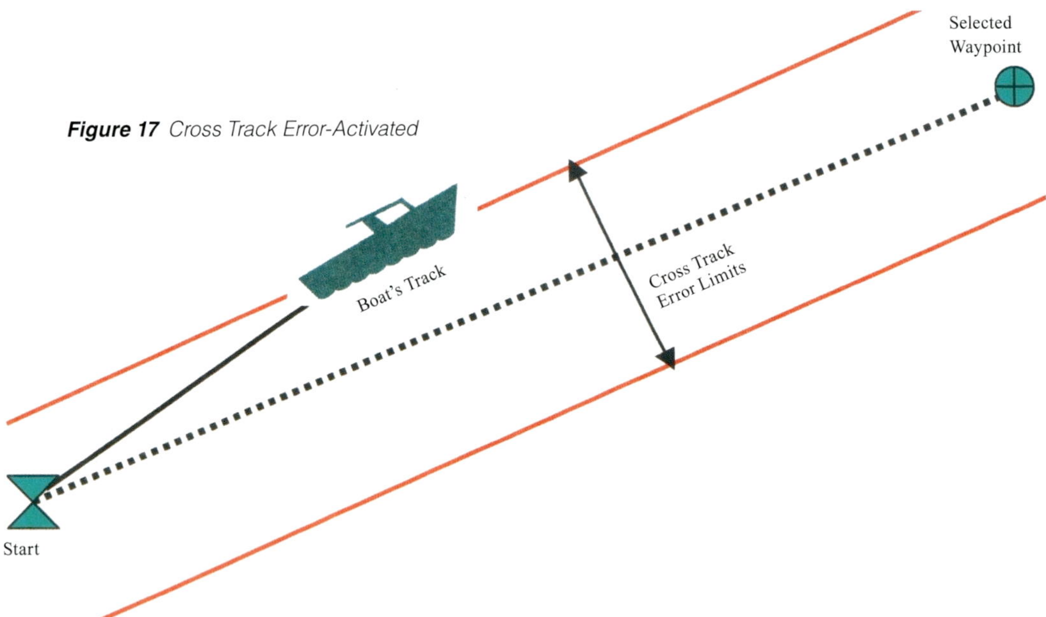

Figure 17 *Cross Track Error-Activated*

ALARMS

Alarms have a somewhat limited application for the angler, cross track error (XTE) activates when the boat is off the course to the selected waypoint (fig 17.) This alarm (fig 18) is provided mainly for auto pilot operation, when hand steering the helmsman is aware of his course and does not need this feature. The arrival alarm (fig 19) is also autopilot orientated, again the helmsman's knows his position in relationship to the waypoint. If this alarm is used it will continue to sound whenever the boat is within the selected distance of the waypoint and will need to be de-activated as soon as possible after arriving, to save the sanity of the crew. While cross track and arrival alarms have little application for fisherman, the anchor alarm (fig 20) is most useful. Once the boat has settled back onto it's anchor this alarm is activated, if the boat drags anchor and moves out from the pre-set zone, the alarm will sound. This alerts the crew that the boat has moved off the mark — a very handy feature, particularly at night.

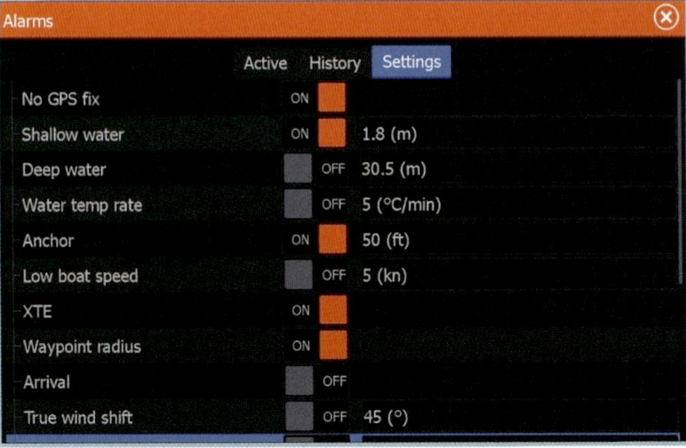

Figure 18 *Cross Track Erroror and other alarms setup*

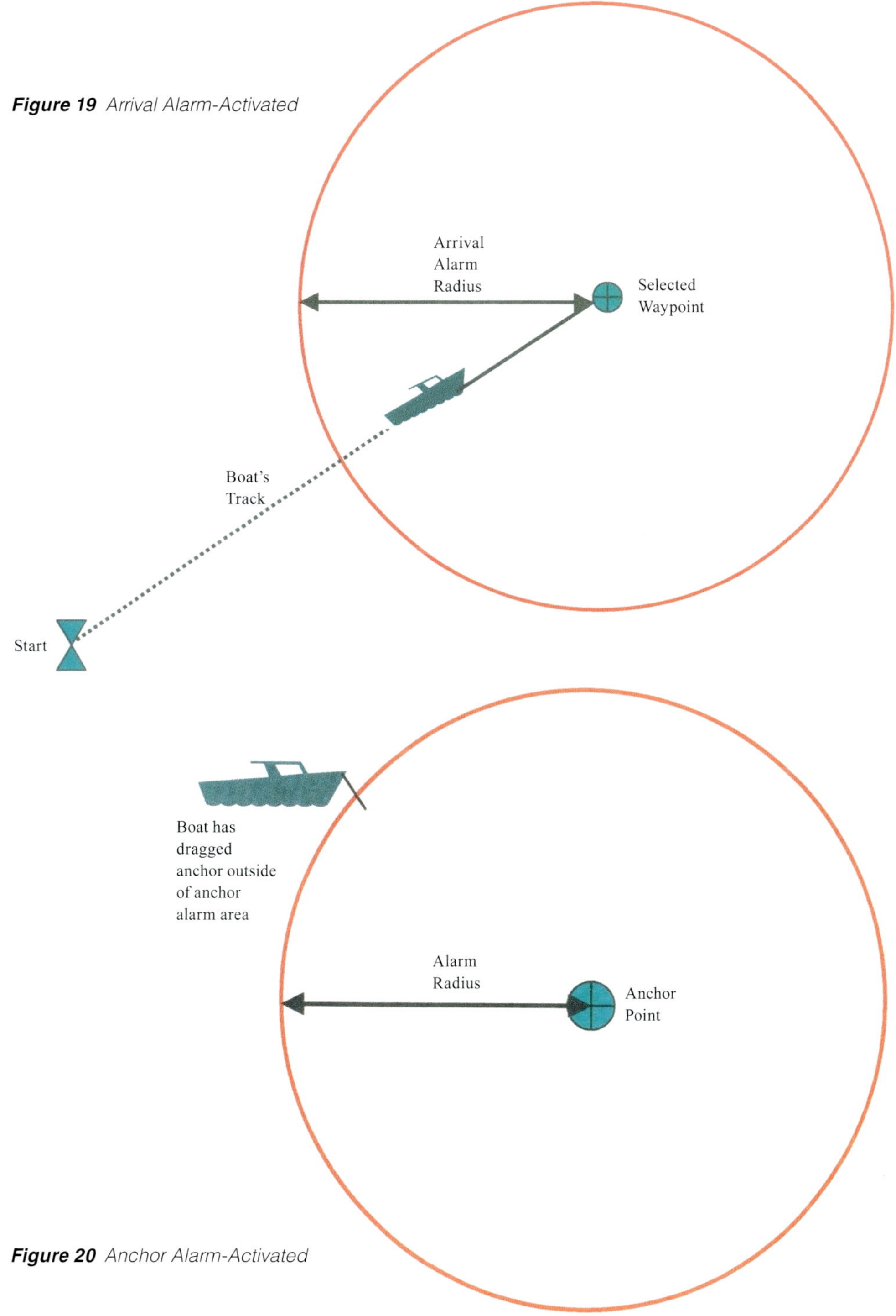

Figure 19 *Arrival Alarm-Activated*

Figure 20 *Anchor Alarm-Activated*

CHAPTER FIVE

PRACTICAL APPLICATIONS

WAYPOINTS

With the GPS receiver initialised and operating parameters set, the next step is to program some waypoints into the unit. In GPS jargon, waypoints are just another way of saying, 'places I may need to go to'. They are usually fishing spots, entrances to ports and other navigation features. These are entered into the unit's memory as latitude and longitude coordinates.

There are several ways to obtain coordinates for your waypoints. Your mates who own GPS will usually give you a set for your local area, (perhaps not their secret spots). Waypoint coordinates are also becoming more common in magazine articles, (Saltwater Sportfishing, Freshwater Fishing Australia) and they are available on the internet at a number of sites, and last but not least you can enter the waypoint into the memory by physically going to the spot.

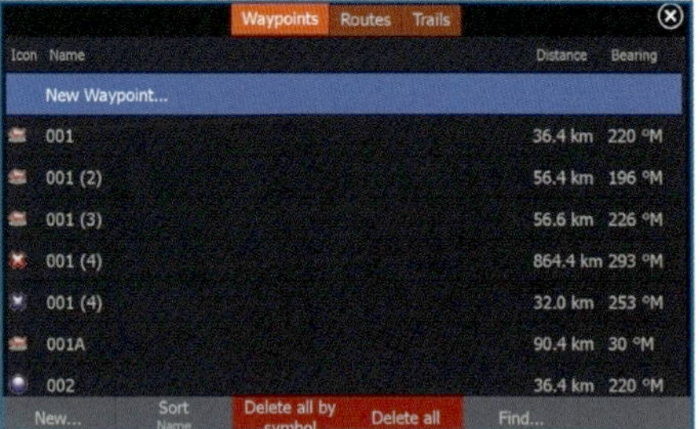

Figure 21a *Weightpoint List*

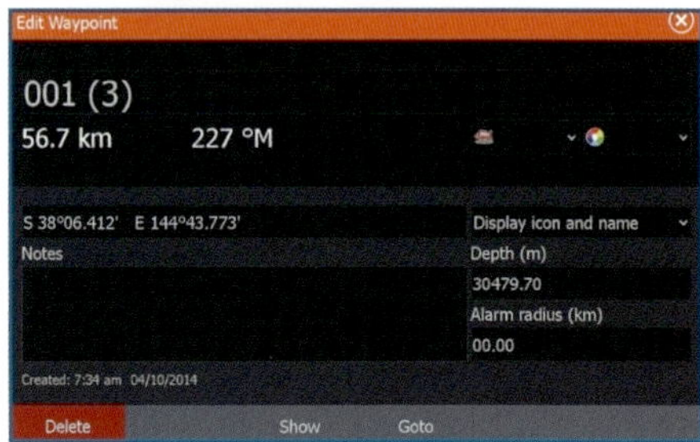

Figure 21b *WEditing a weighpoint*

Assuming you have some waypoint coordinates to enter, access the unit's waypoint memory. Again, this will vary from brand to brand but is usually a prominently marked button, check you manual for details for your set.

Once you are into this memory menu, the unit will display a list of waypoints (fig 21), in our case this will be empty. The first step is to give your waypoint an identification number. While there is no electronic reason you should not give the first waypoint any number you like, it is probably a good move to allocate number one waypoint to the entrance to the port from which you fish the most. It does not matter where you go in a day's fishing, you will always wish to return to the port and if this is number one it is easiest to remember.

If you have a orderly mind and like to keep everything nice and neat, then allocate blocks of numbers for each port you fish, even separate them into north and south of the port. This keeps all of the locations you are likely to need in a days fishing grouped around the same numbers, making it easier to find a waypoint when you need it. If you choose to enter them in a random fashion, this will have no effect whatsoever on the operation of the unit.

Almost all modern units have a facility to name your waypoints, earlier machines did not have this and it was a pain having to carry a list of your waypoints and their numbers. You will probably be limited to eight letters or numbers with spaces, even though spaces are blank they will still be counted as a letter, but you should have little trouble giving your fishing spots a meaningful name, even with this limitation. Usually the waypoint can be allocated a symbol or icon; this will vary from unit to unit but are self-explanatory. Another feature of modern sets is you will be able to sort the waypoint list, either by name or by number. The choice is entirely up to you. If you have allocated groups of numbers to specific locations then numbers will probably be best, if the waypoints have been entered randomly, alphabetically may be a better way to go. While it is of little importance how you number or sort your waypoint list, it is vitally important you be extremely careful when you are entering the coordinates of a waypoint.

A 'small' error of even a single digit when entering the data can put you many miles away from the desired spot. Another trap for new players is to overlook the north, south, east and west prefixes. Since all of the GPS available in Australia were designed for sale in the northern hemisphere, they will automatically default to showing an 'N' in the latitude. If you fail to correct this, your waypoint will be many thousands of miles away from where it should be. The longitude prefix may not default to a 'W' reading, the chances are if your set was made in Japan or one of the other Asian countries, it will show 'E' for longitude, however be aware and check and double check your entries.

If your GPS is operating and has given you a fix, it cannot be incorrect (within the limitations of the system). If you call up a waypoint which you know is about five miles away and the display tells you it is hundreds, or even thousands of miles away, it will invariably be operator error and not a faulty unit. If this happens, blame yourself and check the numbers, or better still get somebody else to check.

At times you can look at an error a dozen times, and not 'see' it. Another person can come along and pick it up first off. Incorrect data entry has happened to all of use at some time and is part of being human in an electronic world. To correct the error simply go into the edit menu and update it.

CUSTOMISING DISPLAY

During normal day-to-day operation the most common display screen will be the plotter screen, or the 'highway' screen. Both of these screens illustrate, in graphic form, the progress of the boat towards the selected waypoint. These screens can display data boxes, which contain important facts about the navigation status of the GPS (fig 22). Data such as speed over ground (SOG), bearing (to waypoint), distance (to waypoint), course over ground (COG), cross track error (XTE), time to go (to waypoint at current speed) (TTG), latitude and longitude (current position), time of day etc. The number, position and the data displayed in these boxes can be customised to suit your individual taste. My choice is to keep the boxes to a minimum to see more of the plotter screen, using only the important data e.g. speed over ground, bearing, course over ground and distance.

Figure 22 *RIGHT: Analogue and Digital Display.*

BELOW: A GPS plotter can be useful on pelagic fish as they often feed over reef.

CHAPTER SIX

PRACTICAL GPS FISHING

While this chapter is about using your GPS as a general navigation tool, particular emphasis has been placed on the needs of fishermen and the use of techniques to enhance the operation of the system in everyday fishing situations. Most of these practical methods have been developed out on the water fishing during the last fifteen years or so.

RECORDING WAYPOINTS

Entering waypoints by using latitude and longitude coordinates has been covered in detail in a previous chapter but waypoints can also be entered by being on the actual spot. Most units have a simple, one key stroke operation for storing the current location as a waypoint, the name and procedure varies from brand to brand—refer to the instruction manual for details of your unit. Once you are over the spot you wish to record, simply press the waypoint key and a notice will appear on the screen notifying you that the waypoint has been saved along with its memory location and number. While it is quite practical at this time to go into the waypoint edit menu and give the spot a meaningful name, this job is much easier when the boat is back on the trailer or in the marina. Keep in mind that if you enter more than a couple of waypoints, it pays to jot down a brief description and the number, otherwise when the time comes to edit and name the waypoints it can be difficult remembering the order in which they were recorded.

A method I have found useful, particularly when recording reef areas rather than single isolated points, is to place a mark on the plotter screen as soon as the sounder indicates the start of the reef. A mark, as distinct from a waypoint, is a symbol placed on the plotter screen. The mark is stored in the unit's memory, but unlike a waypoint, which can be named, moved around in the memory and called-up as a destination to go to, marks can only be displayed on the screen and are primarily designed as a temporary indicator. They are stored in a memory and will remain on the plot (even if the unit is switched off) until such times as you physically remove them. By placing a mark on the screen you give yourself a reference point to work around to survey the reef. As I sound over the reef, I place a mark on any significant feature. Later I will convert one of these marks to a waypoint for the reef. If the reef complex is large I will use two waypoints to mark both ends of the reef.

The boat should be stopped, or at least only moving slowly, when saving a waypoint. Even though the update time on modern GPS receivers is one second, if the boat is travelling at an appreciable speed the actual spot recorded could be some distance away from the spot when you pressed the waypoint save key. If the saved waypoint were of a large area like a reef, this would be of little consequence, but if it is a tiny spot it could be significant. This is particularly so if you are recording waypoints of buoys or channel markers to be used in a route sequence to navigate a narrow channel.

MAN OVER BOARD

One of the most frightening incidents that can happen on a boat is to lose a crewman overboard. Without exception, all GPS receivers have a man over board (MOB) feature, which is generally activated by single keystroke, and places a special waypoint in the memory. Once MOB is in operation, all normal navigation functions are suspended, Goto, Bearing, DTG etc all refer to the spot in the water where the key was pressed. If the MOB key is pressed again, all the data is changed to refer to the new MOB waypoint. Depending on the unit, the MOB function must be cancelled before normal navigation can be resumed.

GOTO WAYPOINT

To call up a waypoint to go to is generally no more complex than finding the waypoint in the units memory, highlighting it and selecting the Goto command. If you are using the plotter screen the boat's position will be shown in the centre of the screen and a dotted line will extend to the waypoint (fig 23) if the map's scale is sufficiently large to cover the waypoint's position. If the scale is not sufficiently large the line, called the bearing line, will disappear off the side of the screen. The data boxes at the side of the screen will show the distance to the waypoint (DTG) and the bearing (in compass degrees).

When I call up a waypoint I adjust the scale to show the selected waypoint, that is if the DTG display indicates 8.5 n mile, the scale would be 20 n mile This enables me to check that I have called up the right number for the waypoint and the waypoint is about where it should be, and has thus been entered correctly. When I start to navigate to the location, I will bring the scale back to 5 n mile, which I find is a comfortable range to travel on. Once the boat is tracking down the dotted bearing line, I look ahead and try and find a point towards which to steer the boat. If the land is in sight this is easy, but if there is only sea, I may use a convenient cloud, if there are no clouds then I take note of the direction the sea is meeting the boat and use this to steer by.

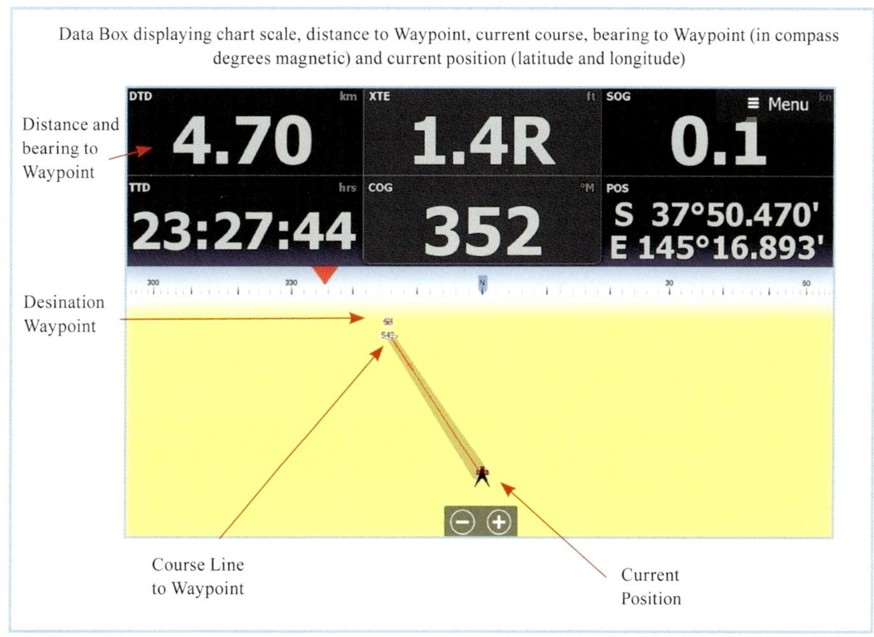

Figure 23 *Plotter Screen*

At night I choose a star. Every few minutes check your progress on the plotter and make any adjustments to your aiming point. This is much easier than attempting to steer directly from the plotter screen alone or by the compass.

When the DTG display indicates 0.5 n mile slow the boat to sounding speed and check that the sounder settings are right for the depth. Change the plotter screen to the largest magnification, usually 0.1 n mile, and warn the crew to have the anchor ready, and by this time you should be just about ready to pass over the waypoint. On their latest models, Lowrance have an auto zoom feature which, when a waypoint is selected, adjusts the plotter scale (zooms out) until the whole of the course is visible, from the present position to the waypoint. As the boat moves the unit automatically zooms in, always keeping the waypoint on the screen but always at the maximum scale size.

The alternate method of navigating to a waypoint is to use the highway screen.

GPS COMPASS

The GPS receiver has no in-built compass. Compass readings are generated by the unit knowing where it was a second ago and where it is now and thus the direction the boat has moved to reach this position. It is important to realise a GPS compass reading indicates which direction the boat is moving, a compass indicates which direction the boat is pointing. At very low speed the GPS compass can be misleading and in conditions of strong cross winds or current there may be a discrepancy between the two systems (fig 24.)

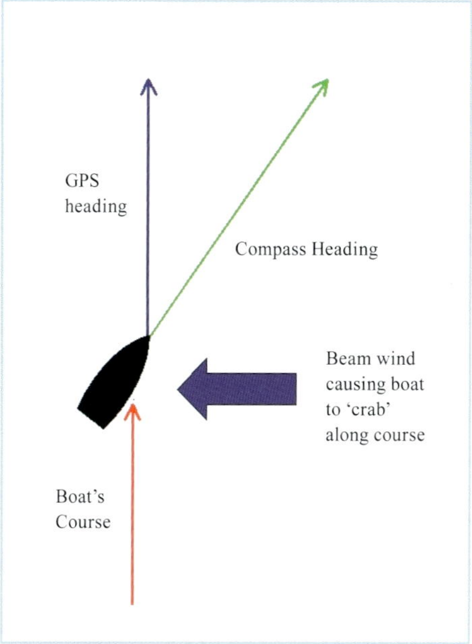

Figure 24 *GPS and Compass Headings*

ROUTES

Routes, sometimes called a 'route sequence', are a string of waypoints linked together to mark a course of travel (fig 25.) Routes have been likened to a string of beads, the beads representing the waypoints and the string representing the course connecting waypoint to waypoint. In GPS jargon the course from one waypoint to the next is a 'leg' and routes are composed of any number of legs. The legs are based on straight lines between waypoints. This is an important fact to keep in mind whenever dealing with routes.

Routes provide the automatic capability to navigate through a number of waypoints without having to program the GPS each time a waypoint is reached, when the boat arrives at a waypoint the GPS automatically selects the next waypoint in the sequence. Routes are stored in the memory, usually under a name or a number, often both, and can be navigated forward through the group or in the reverse order, also you can start navigating, either forward or back from any point in the sequence.

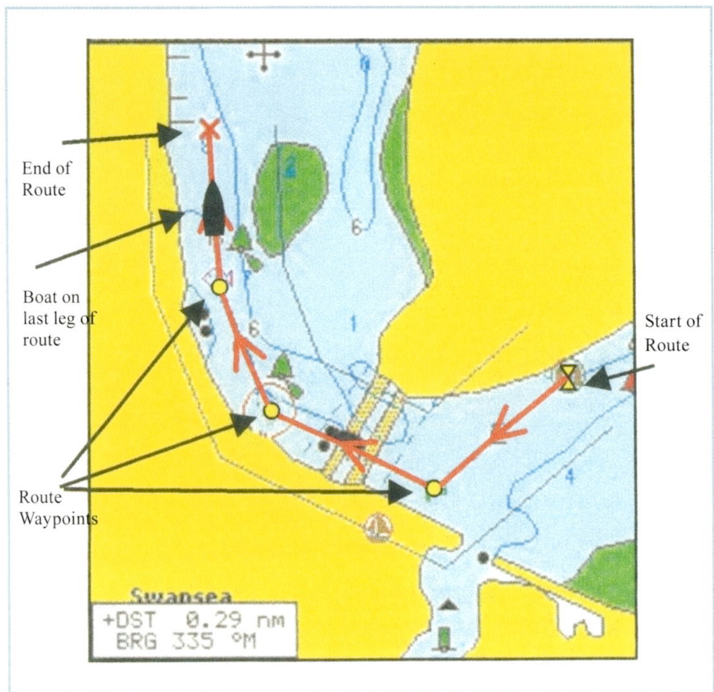

Figure 25 *Route Sequence*

Routes are a very powerful feature of GPS plotters, providing a means of easy progress through tricky navigation situations, such as narrow channels etc. and makes long trip planning a breeze. Routes can be created by several methods, travelling along the planed course and making waypoints at each point it is necessary to change the boat's direction, from a list of waypoints already stored in the plotter's memory or from the chart display on the plotters screen. If you elect to create a route using the plotter chart display and the route is through some narrow waters or among obstructions, it is worthwhile checking the route under good conditions to verify it's accuracy.

A few points to keep in mind about routes are first, always confirm that any leg does not cross land or dangerous waters. Second, any waypoint can be used in a route and can be used more than once in that route and using a waypoint in a route sequence does not preclude it from being used in normal navigation. Third, while it is possible to skip a waypoint when travelling along a route, be very careful if you do so, as this action may change the whole complexion of the route and give rise to a dangerous situation.

Routes can be a little fiddling to set-up but are well worth the effort, such as when you have to find your way back into harbour on a dark, wet night.

PLOTTER ORIENTATION

The plotter screen may be orientated in several ways, north-up, track-up or course-up. North-up is usually the default orientation (fig 26), that is north is always at the top of the plotter screen, just as it is in paper charts and maps. When you are navigating to a waypoint which is to the north, everything is fine, if you drift off to the left of the bearing line just move to the right and you come back on course. In other words what you see on the left side of the screen is on your left, and so on. However when travelling on any other bearing, the plotter screen no longer agrees with your view of the world. If for example your are travelling south and drift off course to the left and you adjust by bringing the boat back to the right, the error will increase. The trick is not to think as left and right but as compass directions. If, when moving north the error is to the left, it is actually to the west and is corrected by moving to the east, similarly when moving south and the error is to the left, it is actually to the east and a westerly correction is required.

This may, at first, sound complicated but your mind will quickly adapt and the correction becomes almost automatic.

To overcome this problem many of the modern plotters have a track-up mode (fig 27) which rotates the display to keep the top of the plotter in the direction the boat is moving, thus left is left etc. Another alternative

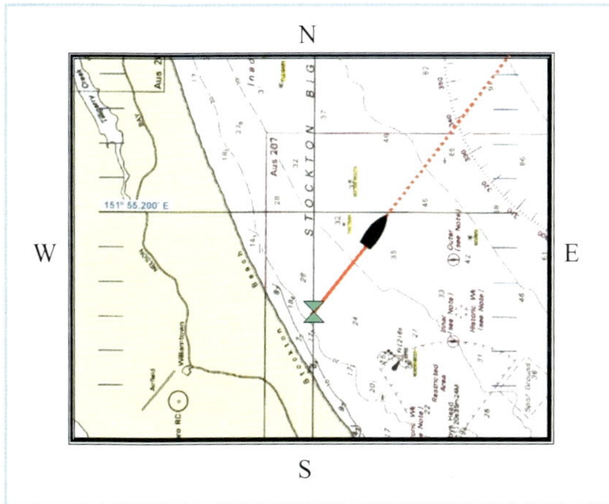

Figure 26 *North-up Orientation*

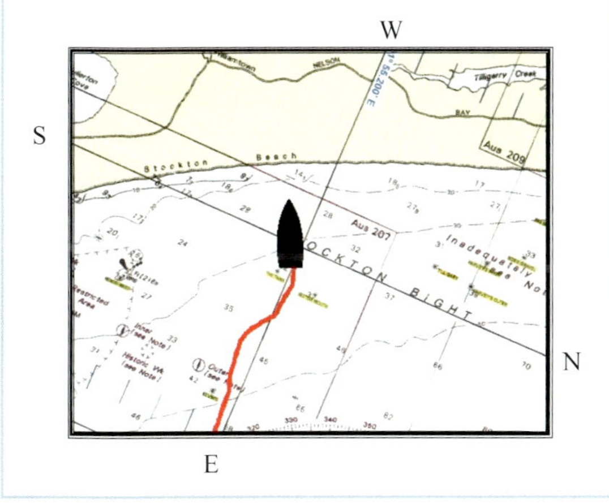

Figure 27 *Track-up Orientation*

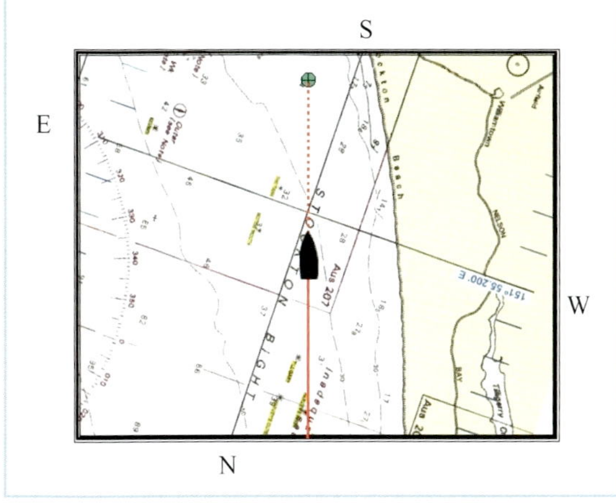

Figure 28 *Course-up Orientation*

is course-up orientation (fig 28), which presents the bearing to the waypoint always at the top of the screen. (Of course a waypoint must be selected for this orientation to operate).

I have found the track-up mode to be somewhat disconcerting with the plotter screen re-positioning every time the boat's heading changes, even if it is only a slight change in direction. Course-up is an excellent orientation, particularly for new users who have difficulty coming to grips with the traditional north-up orientation. (This is the orientation that Highway displays use).

PRACTICAL ACCURACY

Accuracy theory of the GPS system was covered earlier, however there are other factors that effect accuracy that you can expect from your unit in the field. These are defined as 'repeatable accuracy' and 'relative accuracy'. Repeatable accuracy is the precision that can be expected when the GPS is navigating back to a waypoint that has been created by that particular unit. This is usually totally accurate within the limits of the system. Relative accuracy refers to the degree of accuracy, which can be expected from waypoints made with other units or coordinates from charts. Due to component tolerances, latitude and longitude readings can exhibit error as great as 100 metres. Another point to keep in mind when using waypoint lists is that many of these waypoints were recorded when S/A was operating and these will contain the inherent positional errors of that system.

SEARCH PATTERNS

Accepting that, unless the waypoint was created by your GPS, there will be every chance you will need to search for the correct mark. If, after running down your selected waypoint, and accurately passing through the waypoint symbol on the plotter screen, the sounder does not show the spot you are looking for, then a pattern search should be undertaken. While it is easy and human nature to just have a quick look around the mark to see if you can find it, this usually leads to wandering all over the place and creating snail tracks all over the screen, and still not finding the spot. Then once a proper pattern search is used the spot shows up, not all that far away. Take my word for it, I have done it. A search is easy to implement and will quickly put you bang onto the spot, however there are a few facts, which will make understanding a pattern search quite a little easier.

The first factor to keep in mind is the area of bottom your echo sounder is covering. Unless you are in very deep water you will probably be using a 20 degree

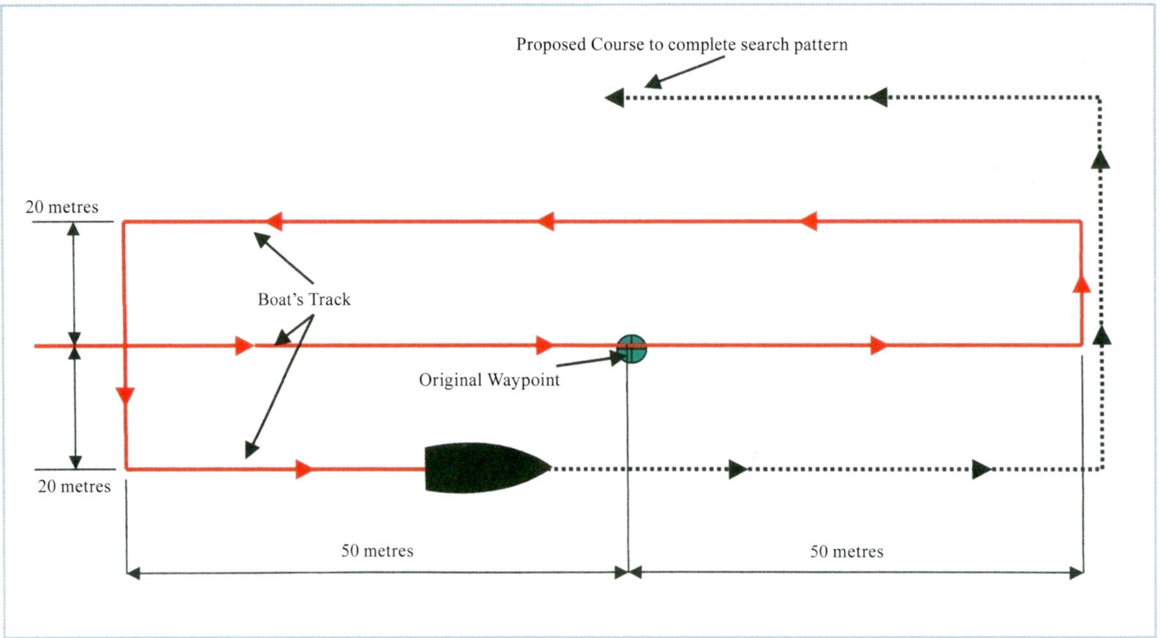

Figure 29 *Search Pattern*

cone angle transducer which covers an area about one third of the depth. Supposing the depth of water over the selected waypoint is 30 metres, the sounder will be sounding a 10 metre circle, which as the boat moves along will become a ten metre wide strip, five metres either side of the boat's track. Now take into consideration the probable error of the fix, if it is a location from a waypoint list or from another unit it could be as bad as 100 metres. Bearing all of this in mind, if you do a grid pattern search, with each leg about 20 metres apart, and 50 metres long you will cover the possible location of the spot in a maximum of six or seven legs (fig 29), in practice, usually a lot less. This theoretical case assumes you will sweep the bottom with your sounder, with the possibility of missing any one spot by a maximum of five metres. However since the spot you are looking for is unlikely to be that small and, in practice, the transducer's beam wanders over a much wider area than theory suggests, due to wave motion rocking the boat from side to side. This search method works extremely well in practice.

To start the search pattern just continue on the course you were using to get to the waypoint, travelling through the waypoint icon by about 50 metres. The obvious question is how far is 50 metres on the plotter screen? If you are using nautical miles for distance measurements and knots for speed then a rule-of-thumb type of calculation assumes a nautical mile is 2,000 metres, 0.1 n mile is then 200 metres and 0.01 n mile is twenty metres. Remember these simple figures for you will find them very handy in doing a number of quick calculations on the water in a day's fishing. If you are using kilometres then the calculations are even simpler. But back to our search pattern, what you must do now is to work out what an actual measurement on the screen represents in metres on the water. Measure the plotter screen in millimetres, just the actual plotter screen, do not include the area covered by the information boxes. For this example, suppose the screen is 100 mm by 100 mm, and we are using a scale of 0.25 n mile. It is simple arithmetic to work out 0.25 n mile (500 metres) equal 100 mm or 5 metres equals 1 mm on the screen. So on this scale of 0.25 n mile, 50 metres would be represented on the plotter screen by 10 millimetres. Had the scale been 0.1 n mile, (200 metres), 50 metres would be represented by 25 millimetres.

While all of this may seem a little complicated you only need to do it once and then remember it, or better still, jot it down in your marks book for future reference. If you always use the same scale it quickly becomes second nature to estimate distance on the screen. I always use 0.25 n mile scale for my close searching work, and I know that 10 mm represents about 50 metres on the screen. Humminbird's latest models, Matrix models 55 and 65, have a grid feature (fig 30), which can be overlaid on the waypoint, this is called a trolling grid and makes setting up a search pattern simplicity itself. Once the spot is located record it as a waypoint and then when you have the time replace the original one with the new, corrected one.

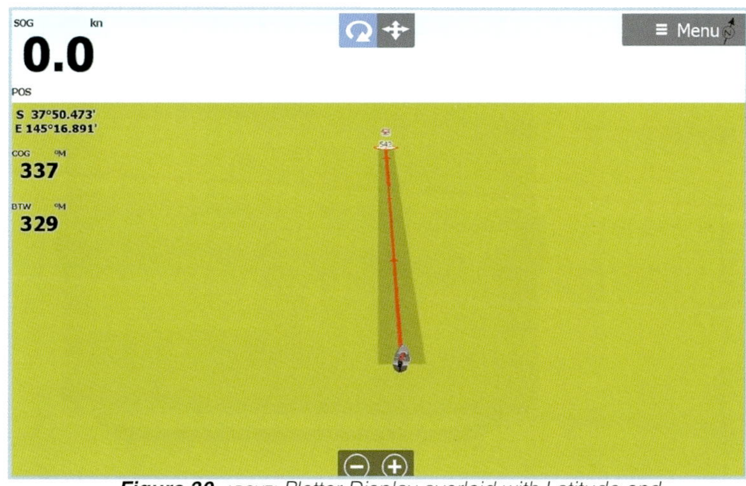

Figure 30 ABOVE: *Plotter Display overlaid with Latitude and Longitude Grid.*

GPS ANCHORING

The DTG and BRG displays are handy for those occasions when, after locating the fishing spot, you have anchored but have not laid over the spot you wish to fish, because of current or wind, or a combination of both. Once you have settled on the anchor, check the displays, the DTG will tell you how far off the spot you are, and the BRG will tell you in which direction it is. Often, from this data, it is possible to swing the boat over to the spot, or if you must go and re-anchor, you will have a pretty good idea what correction needs to be made as to where to drop the pick. On occasions, particularly when anchoring in deep water, another more sophisticated method needs to be employed. The illustrations (fig 31), which are actual downloads from the plotter, are pretty much self-explanatory. This plot was made in a depth of 100 metres off Swansea on the NSW central coast. The first screen shows the boat's position after it has laid back on the anchor. Due to the unknown direction and strength of the current when the anchor was first dropped, the boat has finished up about 180 metres off the mark. While this may seem a large distance, errors of this magnitude are common in deep water when there is up to 300 metres of anchor rope in the water.

The distance and the direction the boat is out of position are used to estimate the point where the anchor should be re-positioned. This system is simple and quite accurate and saves a lot of time and effort in deepwater fishing.

Figure 31 BELOW: *GPS Anchoring*

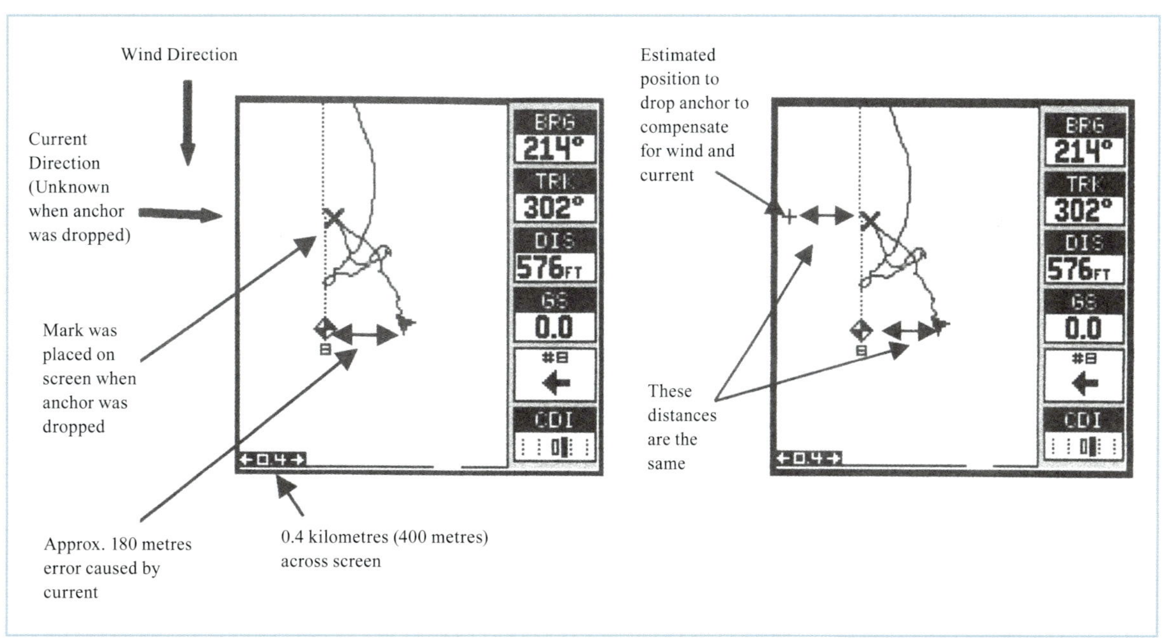

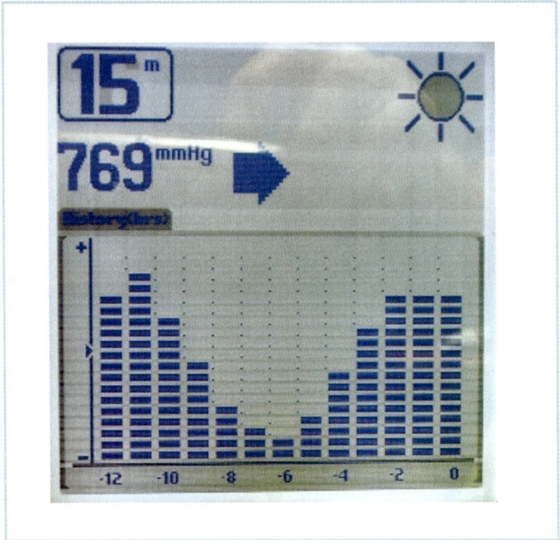

Figure 32 *Integration.*
Barometer reading for 12 hour period incorporated in Humminbird plotter.

Figure 33 *Integration*
Chart Plotter Display with Radar.

THE FUTURE

While it is a risky business trying to prophesise the future path of marine electronics, (as I have found out in the past), it is a pretty fair bet to expect integration to play a big large part of that future. Today a number of the major manufacturers have already started on that path with tide and moon predictions an integral part of chart plotters, fuel flow meters are available, as well as barometric displays (fig 32) and radar images (fig 33) overlaid onto chart displays are now available. More engine monitoring displays incorporated into plotters are already in the planning stages and as the price of colour screens fall, we will see more and more colour used in the cheaper price-ranged units. More data is being stored into smaller and smaller packages. As an example look at the size of the current electronic chart chips, smaller than a postage stamp (fig 34) and yet containing more data than the old cards of only a few years ago which were three times the size. Data exchange between units and home computers, (PC's), already available on some models will become more commonplace, as will navigation data available on the Internet. Whatever happens in the future, it will be an exciting time for users of Global Position System.

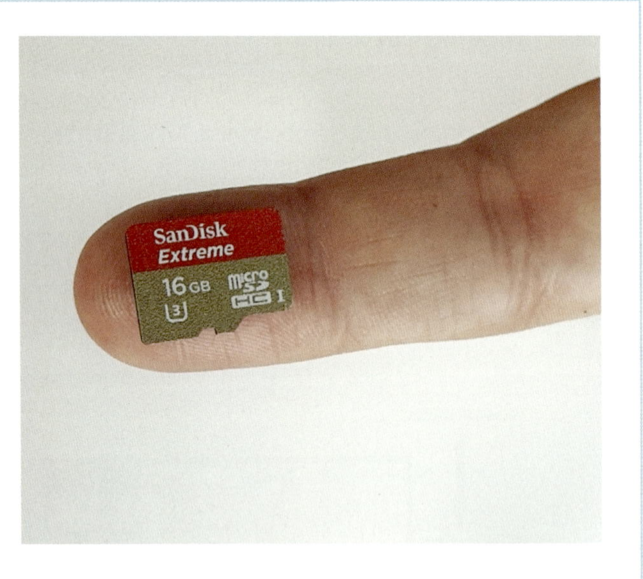

Figure 34 *Multi Media Cards and postage stamp*

CHAPTER SEVEN

GLOSSARY

AGD66	Australian Geodetic Datum 66 (see Datum.)
AGD84	Australian Geodetic Datum 84 (see Datum.)
BRG	Compass Bearing to the destination waypoint.
CDI	Course Deviation Indicator. The distance the boat has deviated from the straight line course to the waypoint. Also called Cross Track Error (XTE.)
CHART CARD	A plug-in card which stores chart data for an area.
CHART DATUM	see Datum.
COG	Course Over Ground. The compass direction the boat is moving over the ground, not necessarily the direction it is pointing.
CTS	Course To Steer. The optimum compass course to steer to bring the boat back to the plotted course to the waypoint.
CURSOR	A symbol on the display screen indicating the entry position or the boat's position.
DATUM	A fixed, geodetic, point on the earth's surface against which all other positions are measured for drawing maps and charts. World Geodetic System (WGS84) will slowly replace all other systems (see also AGD Australian Geodetic Datum 66 and 84).
DD,MM,YY	Day, Month, and Year date format.
DGPS	Differential Global Positioning System. A supplementary navigation system to correct errors in the GPS.
DOP	Dilution Of Precision. A measure of the quality of a satellite configuration and it's effect on the accuracy of the fix (see also HDOP Horizontal Dilution Of Precision).
DTG	Distance To Go the distance from the boat's present position to the waypoint.
EGNOS	European Geostationary Navigation Overlay Service. The European system of DGPS using satellites as well as base stations (see also WASS Wide Area Augmentation System.)
ETA	Expected Time of Arrival at the waypoint (see also Time To Go (TTG).)
GOTO	A simple method of navigating to a waypoint.
GPS	Global Positioning System. A global navigation system based on a satellite constellation.
HDOP	Horizontal Dilution Of Precision. A length and breadth measurement of satellite configuration and it's effect on accuracy of the fix (see also DOP Dilution Of Precision.)
HF	High Frequency. Radio frequencies used to transmit Differential Global Positioning System (DGPS) data (see also VHF Very High Frequency and UHF Ultra High Frequency.)
LEG	The straight segments of a route between waypoints. A route with four waypoints will have three legs.

LOP	Line Of Position are used in all types of navigation and refer to a number of points, including position, which lie in a straight line.
MM,DD,YY	Month, Day and Year date format.
MOB	Man Over Board. A function that starts navigating back to the spot where the person fell overboard.
NMEA	National Marine Electronics Association (United States.)
NMEA0183	A standard for interfacing marine electronic devices.
OFFSET	Also called, correction factor or map shift, is used to bring the GPS position to correspond with that of a paper chart.
PRN	Pseudo-Random Number. A method of numbering GPS satellites. (see also SVID Space Vehicle Identity.)
ROUTE	Two or more waypoints linked in sequence to form a course for the boat to automatically follow.
SNR	Signal to Noise Ratio A measure of radio signal strength compared to background noise.
SOG	Speed Over Ground. The boat's speed over the ground, which may not be the boat's speed through the water because of current, wind etc.
SVID	Space Vehicle Identity a method of numbering GPS satellites (see also PRN Pseudo-Random Number.)
TTG	Time To Go. The estimated time to reach the waypoint at current speed (see also ETA Estimated Time of Arrival.)
UHF	Ultra High Frequency. Radio frequencies used to transmit Differentia Global Positioning System (DGPS) data (see also VHF Very High Frequency and HF High Frequency.)
UTC	Universal Time Coordinated which is the standard world time (formally known as Greenwich Mean Time (GMT).)
VHF	Very High Frequency. Radio frequencies used to transmit Differential Global Positioning System (DGPS) data (see also UHF Ultra High Frequency and HF High Frequency.)
WAAS	Wide Area Augmentation System. An American system of DGPS using satellites as well as base stations (see also EGNOS European Geostationary Navigation Overlay Service.)
WAYPOINT	A user-defined navigation location store in the GPS Receivers Memory.
XTE	Cross Track Error. The distance the boat has deviated from the direct course to the waypoint (see also CDI Course Deviation Indicator.)
YY,MM,DD	Year, Month and Day date format.

VICTORIA GPS MARKS

Locality	Description	Comments	Latitude	Latitude
Apollo Bay	Blanket Bay		38 48 450	143 37 050
Apollo Bay	Cape Patton	Drift	38 42 240	143 49 350
Aspendale	East pallet ball	Snapper	38 02 168	145 04 636
Aspendale	North pallet ball	Snapper	38 02 152	145 04 616
Aspendale	South pallet ball	Snapper	38 02 184	145 04 615
Beaumaris	Gaso	Snapper	38 02 110	144 58 605
Beaumaris	Wedding Ring	Snapper	38 03 114	145 01 019
Beaumaris		Pinkies	38 00 165	145 01 917
Beaumaris		Snapper	38 01 269	145 02 700
Beaumaris		Snapper	38 01 617	145 02 967
Black Rock	Clock tower	Whiting Pinkies snapper	37 58 843	145 00 693
Black Rock		Whiting Pinkies snapper	37 58 464	145 00 226
Blairgowrie	Artificial reef	Squid	38 21 139	144 47 217
Brighton	Artificial reef	Whiting	37 55 018	144 58 982
Cape Otway	Blanket Bay 1	drift between 2	38 52 600	143 34 040
Cape Otway	Blanket Bay 2	drift between 1	38 53 080	143 33 040
Cape Otway	Deep Ground		38 56 730	143 27 000
Cape Otway	No name	Gummies	38 53 240	143 29 750
Cape Otway	Opp Blanket Bay 1	Drift snapper	38 51 830	143 34 940
Cape Otway	Opp Blanket Bay 2	Drift snapper	38 52 200	143 34 410
Carrum	Artificial reef	Snapper	38 05 318	145 06 855
Carrum	Artificial reef	Snapper	38 05 777	145 03 940
Carrum	Artificial reef	Snapper	38 07 387	145 04 593
Carrum		Snapper	38 06 065	144 57 490
Frankston	East pallet ball	Snapper	38 08 483	145 05 500
Frankston	North pallet ball	Snapper	38 08 467	145 05 480
Frankston	South pallet ball	Snapper	38 08 499	145 05 479
Frankston		Snapper	38 08 686	145 02 262
Frankston		Snapper	38 09 063	145 01 975
Geelong Area	Arthur the Great	Snapper	38 05 000	144 33 000
Geelong Area	Avalon	7 m. Snapper	38 06 000	144 24 456
Geelong Area	Black Stick	Snapper	38 06 206	144 24 743
Geelong Area	Corio Quay	Snapper–winter mark. June, July, August work best, Trevally, bream	38 06 350	144 22 000
Geelong Area	Lagoon—Geelong Grammar	Snapper	38 04 450	144 24 210

Locality	Description	Comments	Latitude	Latitude
Geelong Area	Nine Foot Bank	7 m. Snapper	38 05 884	144 27 486
Geelong Area	Oyster beds	Snapper reef	38 05 653	144 23 814
Geelong Area	Paddock	Snapper	38 06 800	144 23 400
Geelong Area	Point Lillias—Bird Rock	Snapper	38 05 450	144 27 000
Geelong Area	Point Wilson West	Snapper	38 05 790	144 30 700
Geelong Area	Quarries	Snapper	38 06 200	144 30 620
Geelong Area	Shell North	5 m. Snapper reef	38 05 100	144 23 900
Geelong Area	Shell North 5 m.	Snapper reef	38 05 101	144 23 903
Geelong Area	Silos	10 m. Snapper	38 07 017	144 22 714
Geelong Area	Spoil Ground	Snapper–Fish here when the snapper have been worked over inshore	38 08 500	144 23 880
Geelong Area	Spoil Ground—drop off	4–7 m. Snapper	38 08 114	144 23 432
Geelong Area	St Leonards Inshore	5 m. Snapper	38 10 177	144 43 608
Geelong Area	Steam Packet Channel	Snapper	38 04 890	144 37 448
Geelong Area	Turning Buoy	10 m. Snapper	38 07 287	144 22 961
Geelong Area	Western Beach Bombie	10 m. Snapper	38 08 017	144 21 709
Geelong Area	Western Beach Yachts	Snapper	38 08 059	144 21 595
Geelong Area	Wilson Mud	Snapper	38 05 690	144 32 680
Gippsland	Front	Snapper	37 59 421	148 00 016
Gippsland	Grange	Snapper	37 58 051	147 48 071
Gippsland	Lakes Entrance. 6 Mile Reef	Snapper, morwong, mulloway	37 58 840	147 59 882
Gippsland	Rock	Snapper	37 58 935	147 58 408
Mallacoota	Goodwin Sands	Navigation mark	37 31 480	149 45 430
McLoughlin's	Big red		38 31 510	147 12 100
McLoughlin's	Jack Smith's 1		38 32 460	147 05 830
McLoughlin's	Jack Smith's 2		38 32 520	147 06 200
McLoughlin's	Jack Smith's 3		38 34 710	147 05 800
McLoughlin's	Kilcunda	Sharks, yellowtail, snapper, trumpeter, silver whiting, flathead, blue nose wrasse	38 33 900	145 26 900
McLoughlin's	Magaurens 1		38 29 450	147 13 390
McLoughlin's	Magaurens 2		38 30 950	147 05 220
McLoughlin's	Magaurens 3		38 31 780	147 06 760
McLoughlin's	McLoughlin's Beach 1	Snapper	38 44 539	146 51 109
McLoughlin's	McLoughlin's Beach 2	Snapper	38 34 946	147 02 248
McLoughlin's	McLoughlin's Beach 3	Snapper	38 36 865	147 02 946

Locality	Description	Comments	Latitude	Latitude
McLoughlin's	McLoughlin's Beach 4	Entrance	38 38 857	146 53 001
McLoughlin's	McLoughlin's Beach 5	Snapper	38 40 762	146 55 833
McLoughlin's	McLoughlin's Beach 6	18 m. Early season snapper point	38 42 370	146 58 020
McLoughlin's	McLoughlin's Beach main Reef	21m. Snapper especially early season bait schools and other fish	38 40 460	146 56 190
McLoughlin's	McLoughlin's Reef 1		38 38 790	147 01 270
McLoughlin's	No name		38 34 410	147 02 320
McLoughlin's	No name		38 35 390	146 58 920
McLoughlin's	No name	Gummies and sharks at night	38 35 400	146 57 050
McLoughlin's	No name	Deep drift for snapper and gummies	38 41 200	147 05 530
McLoughlin's	Omega tower		38 32 060	147 06 620
McLoughlin's	Seaspray		38 29 550	147 15 900
McLoughlin's	Woodside		38 33 290	147 01 330
McLoughlin's	Woodside Hole		38 35 280	147 02 970
McLoughlin's	Yakmasters snapper mark		38 39 740	147 05 770
Mordialloc		Whiting	38 01 056	145 05 086
Mud Island	Artificial reef	Whiting	38 16 459	144 48 564
Parkdale	Artificial reef	Whiting	38 00 394	145 04 641
Phillip Island	Cape Patterson	Gummy	38 31 747	145 09 339
Phillip Island	Cape Patterson	Gummy	38 40 802	145 34 555
Phillip Island	Cape Shank	Gummy	38 29 572	144 52 308
Phillip Island	Flinders Bank	Gummy	38 32 891	145 04 429
Phillip Island	Penguin Parade	Gummy	38 34 749	145 05 655
Phillip Island	San Remo	Silver Whiting (for bait)	38 34 363	145 25 304
Port Albert	Big gum		38 48 470	146 37 770
Port Albert	Blackbird Wreck		38 44 500	146 41 800
Port Albert	Chris Reef		38 52 800	146 49 150
Port Albert	Cliffy Is	Flathead	38 56 300	146 43 090
Port Albert	Deeper gummy mark		38 53 940	146 47 780
Port Albert	Entrance Fairway Buoy		38 46 250	146 42 210
Port Albert	Flathead ground		38 50 250	146 47 360
Port Albert	Gummy hole		38 40 360	146 56 540
Port Albert	Joe's		38 39 430	147 01 140
Port Albert	Joe's 2		38 39 520	147 00 970
Port Albert	Kate Kearney	Entrance	38 42 334	146 44 369

Locality	Description	Comments	Latitude	Latitude
Port Albert	Kernies drifting		39 43 010	146 48 680
Port Albert	Lippy's	Deep, gummies	38 51 610	146 51 480
Port Albert	Magaurens 4		38 27 440	147 07 720
Port Albert	Magaurens 5		38 27 530	147 08 540
Port Albert	Magaurens 6		38 29 670	147 08 880
Port Albert	Manns 1		38 42 840	146 54 300
Port Albert	Manns 2		38 42 920	146 54 490
Port Albert	Manns 3		38 43 010	146 50 190
Port Albert	Manns 4	Whiting and pinkies	38 43 240	146 53 750
Port Albert	Manns 5		38 43 480	146 48 290
Port Albert	Manns 6	Snapper, squid, sharks	39 42 940	146 53 490
Port Albert	Manns Beach 1		38 39 350	146 57 900
Port Albert	Manns Beach 2	3.6 miles	38 42 660	146 52 270
Port Albert	Manns Beach 3		39 43 240	146 51 480
Port Albert	Mann's Beach–Offshore 1	Snapper	38 41 980	146 50 100
Port Albert	Mann's Beach–Offshore 2	Snapper	38 42 940	146 54 190
Port Albert	Manns Entrance		38 41 270	146 49 560
Port Albert	May Bee Reef		38 50 530	146 55 610
Port Albert	McLoughlin's Beach Entrance		38 38 460	146 53 110
Port Albert	McLoughlin's Reef 2		38 43 390	146 54 300
Port Albert	Mervs snapper mark		38 38 550	147 01 730
Port Albert	Micks Reef		38 39 350	147 01 030
Port Albert	Murray's afternoon spot	Snapper and gummies	38 42 200	146 54 670
Port Albert	Murray's mixed	Snapper and gummies	38 41 950	146 54 750
Port Albert	Murray's spot	Snapper	38 42 200	146 54 340
Port Albert	Near 043-044		38 39 570	147 00 960
Port Albert	Near gummy hole	Snapper	38 39 290	146 58 980
Port Albert	No name		38 36 657	147 01 258
Port Albert	No name	Snapper	38 37 905	147 00 682
Port Albert	No name		38 38 870	147 01 230
Port Albert	No name	16 m	38 39 032	146 55 765
Port Albert	No name		38 39 451	146 57 693
Port Albert	No name		38 39 530	147 01 030
Port Albert	No name	Flathead	38 40 311	146 42 300

Locality	Description	Comments	Latitude	Latitude
Port Albert	No name	Whiting	38 40 362	146 38 551
Port Albert	No name	Big flathead	38 40 571	147 05 925
Port Albert	No name	Squid	38 40 780	146 56 230
Port Albert	No name	Flathead	38 40 824	146 41 767
Port Albert	No name	Whiting	38 41 875	146 40 769
Port Albert	No name	Snapper	38 42 001	146 35 255
Port Albert	No name	Snapper	38 42 008	146 35 249
Port Albert	No name	Snapper	38 42 648	146 34 726
Port Albert	No name		38 42 800	147 00 960
Port Albert	No name		38 42 940	147 03 050
Port Albert	No name		38 43 038	146 52 241
Port Albert	No name		38 43 493	146 53 954
Port Albert	No name	Whiting	38 44 079	146 36 165
Port Albert	No name	Flatties between cliffs and Port Albert–flathead	38 50 460	146 41 330
Port Albert	Off White Rock	Flathead and gummies	38 54 710	146 38 730
Port Albert	Past Snows Reef		38 50 750	146 49 140
Port Albert	Port Albert	Entrance	38 45 113	146 41 445
Port Albert	Port Albert Reef		38 49 490	146 48 270
Port Albert	Reef 1		38 38 300	146 59 260
Port Albert	Reef 2		38 41 480	146 58 680
Port Albert	Reef Entrance	1.5 miles off	38 45 600	146 43 450
Port Albert	Whiting hole 2		38 41 360	146 56 560
Port Albert	Whiting hole1		38 39 360	147 01 200
Port Albert	Woodside		38 38 620	147 01 400
Port Albert	Wreck off Port Albert		38 44 700	146 40 600
Port Lonsdale	Artificial reef	Kingfish	38 17 529	144 35 361
Port Phillip	18 meter reef	Carrum. Snapper	38 06 650	145 00 801
Port Phillip	19 meter Carrum	Snapper	38 06 116	145 00 653
Port Phillip	AB gutter—Mornington	Snapper	38 11 200	145 00 700
Port Phillip	Aeroplane	Carrum Snapper	38 06 004	145 00 714
Port Phillip	Aircraft		38 05 992	145 06 830
Port Phillip	Aircraft 1		38 05 997	145 00 683
Port Phillip	Aircraft Carrum	Snapper	38 05 980	145 00 692
Port Phillip	Altona Reef	Snapper	37 52 761	144 51 515

Locality	Description	Comments	Latitude	Latitude
Port Phillip	Ansett's	Good right through season. Can produce big fish	38 11 313	145 00 346
Port Phillip	Ansett's 1	20 m. Snapper	38 11 300	145 00 500
Port Phillip	Ansett's 2	Snapper	38 10 255	145 01 595
Port Phillip	Ansett's 3	18 m. Snapper	38 10 220	145 01 590
Port Phillip	Aquarium Hole	Snapper, flathead, whiting, salmon	38 17 450	144 47 542
Port Phillip	Arthurs Seat	Snapper	38 17 340	144 55 600
Port Phillip	Artificial Carrum 1	Snapper	38 04 635	145 02 160
Port Phillip	Artificial Carrum 2	Snapper	38 04 706	145 02 476
Port Phillip	Artificial reef	Snapper	37 56 180	144 57 630
Port Phillip	Barny		38 01 660	144 58 373
Port Phillip	Black Rock	Can fish well any time of day. Mostly school fish—snapper, whiting and bream	37 58 425	144 58 558
Port Phillip	BMYS—Beaumaris	Snapper	37 59 500	145 02 800
Port Phillip	Boofa 1		38 06 398	144 57 670
Port Phillip	Boofa 2		38 09 219	145 05 125
Port Phillip	Brighton 1	Mid Nov to Christmas cunje beds, best in afternoon	37 54 902	144 57 431
Port Phillip	Brighton 2	Similar area Brighton 1 but closer in	37 54 556	144 57 775
Port Phillip	Carrum	Snapper	38 04 608	145 06 849
Port Phillip	Carrum	Snapper	38 07 175	145 05 605
Port Phillip	Carrum	20 m. Snapper	38 07 900	145 02 800
Port Phillip	Carrum 14 m	14 m. Snapper	38 08 753	145 03 374
Port Phillip	Carrum No1	Snapper–All season mark. Water depth 18 m	38 04 478	145 02 126
Port Phillip	Carrum Outer Artificial 1	Snapper	38 04 510	145 06 963
Port Phillip	Carrum Outer Artificial 2	Snapper	38 04 560	145 02 340
Port Phillip	Carrum Outer Artificial 3	Snapper	38 04 800	145 02 100
Port Phillip	Carrum reef	Snapper	38 06 384	145 00 464
Port Phillip	Carrum Wide	20 m. Snapper	38 05 500	145 01 450
Port Phillip	Chelsea	Snapper	38 03 199	145 06 099
Port Phillip	Chelsea Reef 1	Snapper	38 02 174	145 05 578
Port Phillip	Chelsea reef 2	Snapper	38 03 534	145 05 273
Port Phillip	Chelsea wedding ring	Snapper	38 03 109	145 01 010
Port Phillip	Chinamans Hat	Snapper, flathead, whiting, salmon	38 17 385	144 43 515
Port Phillip	Cod hole 1		38 04 930	145 04 410
Port Phillip	Cod Hole 2	Snapper	38 05 866	145 03 539

Locality	Description	Comments	Latitude	Latitude
Port Phillip	Cody Bank 1		38 47 265	145 31 242
Port Phillip	Cody Bank 2		38 47 410	145 31 310
Port Phillip	Dead Mans—Williamstown	Snapper	37 53 092	144 52 319
Port Phillip	Deep hump		38 01 001	145 02 627
Port Phillip	Deep Rye	Snapper	38 16 650	144 52 000
Port Phillip	Deep Seaford	20 m. Snapper	38 06 740	145 04 100
Port Phillip	Dodkins Hovell Mark	Snapper	38 17 296	144 55 543
Port Phillip	Drain	Whiting	38 00 464	145 04 154
Port Phillip	Dumb Joe—Pt Cook	Snapper	37 55 800	144 50 300
Port Phillip	Eliza Ramsden	Snapper	38 17 434	144 40 300
Port Phillip	Faulko	Jan mark	37 57 677	144 56 792
Port Phillip	Fawkner Beacon	Snapper	37 57 000	144 51 800
Port Phillip	Fawkner Beacon old	Snapper	37 57 000	144 55 750
Port Phillip	Finger	20 m. Snapper in late season	38 02 731	144 47 777
Port Phillip	Footy Ground—Williamstown	9 m. Snapper reef	37 53 284	144 53 960
Port Phillip	Foul bottom		38 03 080	145 04 645
Port Phillip	Frankston	20 m big numbers of mixed size	38 07 693	145 01 237
Port Phillip	Frankston 1	15 m	38 07 994	145 03 474
Port Phillip	Frankston Boat Ramp		38 08 658	145 06 866
Port Phillip	Frankston Bombie		38 07 980	145 05 803
Port Phillip	Frankston deep	20+ m. Snapper	38 08 300	145 01 300
Port Phillip	Frankston Mile Bridge 1	12 m. Snapper	38 07 370	145 05 810
Port Phillip	Frankston Mile Bridge 2	12 m. Snapper	38 06 500	145 05 400
Port Phillip	Frankston Mile Bridge 3	Snapper	38 07 068	145 06 587
Port Phillip	Frankston Mile Bridge 4	Snapper	38 07 120	145 05 275
Port Phillip	Frankston Reef	Snapper	38 07 939	145 05 924
Port Phillip	Frankston wide	Snapper–one of my favourite marks Nov to Christmas	38 06 458	144 59 881
Port Phillip	Gas pipeline area off Ricketts Point	Snapper	38 00 428	145 00 008
Port Phillip	Gasometer—Mordialloc	19 m. Snapper	38 02 690	144 58 520
Port Phillip	Gasso	Snapper	38 02 679	144 58 693
Port Phillip	Gasso Four	15 m. Snapper	38 02 785	145 03 181
Port Phillip	Graeme's 1	Snapper	38 05 870	145 02 240
Port Phillip	Graeme's 2	Snapper	38 07 620	145 03 930

Locality	Description	Comments	Latitude	Latitude
Port Phillip	Green Point—Brighton	Snapper	37 55 662	144 57 147
Port Phillip	Gummy /Gill 29m	Early and late season, new moon phase best	38 18 300	144 51 725
Port Phillip	HJs		38 01 505	145 03 360
Port Phillip	Hospital Frankston	20 m snapper	38 09 762	145 01 211
Port Phillip	Hovell Pile	Snapper	38 18 342	144 54 218
Port Phillip	Indented Head	Snapper	38 08 200	144 45 340
Port Phillip	Inner Artificial 1	Snapper–Productive early season mark. Water depth 12 m, best at night	38 03 090	145 04 630
Port Phillip	Inner Artificial 2	12 m. Snapper at night	38 03 100	145 04 500
Port Phillip	Inner Rip	Plot a course between Inner and Outer Rip marks for safe passage through the heads	38 17 320	144 38 170
Port Phillip	Inner Seaford		38 06 250	145 06 170
Port Phillip	Jeff's spot		38 04 173	144 58 352
Port Phillip	Jeff's spot 2		38 07 055	145 04 043
Port Phillip	Jimmy's	Mid season first light	38 03 918	145 01 224
Port Phillip	Lenny's	Late November on any tide change	38 03 621	144 56 072
Port Phillip	Little River Wedge	Snapper	38 01 100	144 40 000
Port Phillip	Mordialloc	Snapper late Nov to late Jan, also chance of mulloway any time of day, morning best	38 01 233	145 02 479
Port Phillip	Mordialloc	10 m. Snapper	38 00 432	145 03 132
Port Phillip	Mordialloc Deep	Good pre-Christmas any time of day	38 02 071	144 58 505
Port Phillip	Mordialloc Long	Reef, snapper	38 01 808	144 35 494
Port Phillip	Mordialloc reef		38 02 385	145 02 627
Port Phillip	Mordialloc Reef	14 m. Snapper	38 01 338	145 03 574
Port Phillip	Mornington	Snapper, flathead.	38 11 459	145 00 843
Port Phillip	Mornington #1	Kingfish, snapper, calamari, flathead, whiting, garfish, slimy mackerel, yelloweye	38 10 970	144 57 540
Port Phillip	Mornington #2	Kingfish, snapper, calamari, flathead, whiting, garfish, slimy mackerel, yelloweye	38 15 836	145 00 388
Port Phillip	Mornington #3	Kingfish, snapper, calamari, flathead, whiting, garfish, slimy mackerel, yelloweye	38 10 980	145 02 459
Port Phillip	Mornington #4	Kingfish, snapper, calamari, flathead, whiting, garfish, slimy mackerel, yelloweye	38 15 846	145 00 430
Port Phillip	Mornington #5	Snapper, calamari, flathead, whiting, garfish, slimy mackerel, yelloweye	38 09 480	145 03 571
Port Phillip	Mornington #6	Kingfish, snapper, calamari, flathead, whiting, garfish, slimy mackerel, yelloweye	38 11 291	145 01 842
Port Phillip	Mornington #7	Kingfish, snapper, calamari, flathead, whiting, garfish, slimy mackerel, yelloweye	38 11 660	145 00 724

Locality	Description	Comments	Latitude	Latitude
Port Phillip	Mornington #8	Kingfish, snapper, calamari, flathead, whiting	38 07 987	145 01 425
Port Phillip	Mornington 15 m line	Snapper	38 06 690	145 03 830
Port Phillip	Mornington Boat Ramp		38 12 883	145 02 113
Port Phillip	Mornington Jetty	Navigation Mark	38 12 440	145 01 560
Port Phillip	Mornington Paddock	Snapper	38 08 910	145 02 180
Port Phillip	Mornington Wide	21–23 m. Snapper later in season	38 06 200	144 55 800
Port Phillip	Morrisons Fault Line	Snapper	38 14 262	145 00 466
Port Phillip	Mt Eliza	Snapper	38 10 660	145 02 245
Port Phillip	Mt Martha 20	20 m. Snapper	38 17 425	144 55 607
Port Phillip	Mt Martha Artificial	Snapper	38 17 337	144 58 192
Port Phillip	Mt Martha dropoff	21 m. Snapper	38 17 207	144 55 383
Port Phillip	Mt Martha gutter	Snapper	38 16 500	144 52 350
Port Phillip	Mt Martha Weed	Snapper and gummy	38 15 650	144 57 250
Port Phillip	Mud flats		38 05 652	145 00 136
Port Phillip	Muscle Beds	Frankston. Snapper	38 08 085	145 02 212
Port Phillip	No name	Snapper	37 55 295	144 52 884
Port Phillip	No name	Snapper, gummy	37 59 861	144 53 572
Port Phillip	No name		38 00 420	145 01 066
Port Phillip	No name		38 01 956	145 03 165
Port Phillip	No name		38 02 466	144 59 807
Port Phillip	No name		38 03 608	145 04 738
Port Phillip	No name		38 06 006	145 00 429
Port Phillip	No name		38 09 151	145 02 290
Port Phillip	No name		38 09 167	145 02 276
Port Phillip	No name		38 09 179	145 02 032
Port Phillip	Off Portsea Hole	snapper, kingfish, bream, sharks	38 18 370	144 42 410
Port Phillip	Oliver's Hill	18 m Nov to late Jan.	38 07 145	145 01 701
Port Phillip	Oliver's Hill Boat Ramp		38 09 099	145 06 469
Port Phillip	Outer Edge—St Kilda	Snapper	37 55 150	144 53 871
Port Phillip	Outer Footy Ground	12–13 m. Snapper	37 53 785	144 53 904
Port Phillip	Outer Reef Carrum	Snapper	38 07 319	145 05 780
Port Phillip	Outer Rip	Travel between Inner and Outer Rip marks for safe passage through the heads	38 18 170	144 37 260
Port Phillip	Outer Seaford	12 m.	38 06 190	145 02 530
Port Phillip	P2	Snapper reef	37 55 380	144 53 181

Locality	Description	Comments	Latitude	Latitude
Port Phillip	Patterson Lakes Boat Ramp		38 04 437	145 06 968
Port Phillip	Pier—Mornington	Snapper	38 11 849	145 01 479
Port Phillip	Pinky		38 00 398	145 04 199
Port Phillip	Pipeline		38 00 101	145 01 996
Port Phillip	Plane Wreck		38 06 091	145 00 627
Port Phillip	Portsea Deep		38 17 250	144 40 230
Port Phillip	P-special	Snapper	38 05 860	145 02 100
Port Phillip	Pt Cook Airfield	14 m. Snapper	37 57 776	144 49 401
Port Phillip	Pt Cook Deep	15 m. Snapper	37 57 162	144 51 309
Port Phillip	R2	Snapper	37 54 566	144 56 321
Port Phillip	Red Bluff—Hospital	18 m. Snapper	38 10 100	145 02 500
Port Phillip	Red Road	Frankston. Snapper	38 09 163	145 02 176
Port Phillip	Ricky and Baz		38 09 336	145 03 523
Port Phillip	Rubbish dump		38 00 119	145 02 296
Port Phillip	Rye Wreck	Snapper	38 20 543	144 52 309
Port Phillip	Safety Beach.	Snapper, flathead.	38 17 467	144 58 142
Port Phillip	Seaford 1	Kingfish, snapper, calamari, flathead, whiting.	38 05 752	145 04 878
Port Phillip	Seaford 16 metre	Snapper	38 06 300	145 02 900
Port Phillip	Seaford 2	Reef–Snapper	38 06 738	145 04 120
Port Phillip	Seaford 3	Snapper	38 06 821	145 06 658
Port Phillip	Seaford 4	16 m late Nov to Mar good chance of bigger fish	38 07 662	145 03 421
Port Phillip	Seaford reef	Snapper	38 06 731	145 05 289
Port Phillip	Seaford shallow	6–10 m. Snapper	38 06 100	145 05 500
Port Phillip	Shortland Bluff	Snapper	38 16 477	144 39 685
Port Phillip	Snapper Point	Snapper	38 12 005	145 01 112
Port Phillip	Snapper–Good early season	C Buoy Snapper	38 11 177	145 00 216
Port Phillip	Sorrento 1	Whiting	38 19 759	144 44 829
Port Phillip	Sorrento 2	Whiting	38 20 208	144 45 398
Port Phillip	Sorrento 3	Whiting	38 20 476	144 45 356
Port Phillip	Spit	Snapper	38 16 425	144 56 100
Port Phillip	Spoil Ground	Snapper	38 00 100	144 52 500
Port Phillip	St Kilda #1	Snapper, flathead, whiting	37 54 715	144 56 200
Port Phillip	St Kilda #2	Snapper, flathead, whiting	37 59 016	144 58 521
Port Phillip	St Kilda 1		37 54 964	144 54 243

Locality	Description	Comments	Latitude	Latitude
Port Phillip	St Kilda 2		37 54 964	144 56 992
Port Phillip	St Kilda Boat Ramp		37 52 319	144 58 415
Port Phillip	St Kilda night spot		37 54 886	144 57 043
Port Phillip	Sth Channel Wreck 1		38 17 627	144 40 432
Port Phillip	Sth Channel Wreck 2		38 17 410	144 40 960
Port Phillip	Symonds Channel	Snapper. Fish slack water	38 15 408	144 45 079
Port Phillip	Taig N Zeth Hump		38 03 173	145 03 374
Port Phillip	Tedesco Reef	Artificial reef	38 05 246	145 05 954
Port Phillip	The Stick	Reef, Depth 6–8m near Altona.	37 53 100	144 51 300
Port Phillip	The Well	10 m. Snapper	38 02 900	145 05 129
Port Phillip	Werribee	Whiting	37 56 669	144 45 760
Port Phillip	Werribee Hole	Snapper	37 58 250	144 50 100
Port Phillip	Westgate	Snapper–Late season mark	38 01 584	144 52 350
Port Phillip	Wide and South	Snapper	38 09 600	144 59 700
Port Phillip	Willi' Reef	Pinkies and gummies	37 52 985	144 54 775
Port Phillip	Williamstown	Snapper, whiting, garfish	37 52 518	144 54 151
Port Phillip	Wooley Reef		38 09 318	145 05 390
Port Phillip	Yacht marks 1		38 03 338	144 58 773
Port Phillip	Yacht marks 2		38 07 464	145 02 318
Port Phillip	Yacht marks 3		38 03 469	144 58 789
Port Phillip	Yakka Reef	Artificial reef	38 08 482	145 05 480
Port Phillip		Snapper	38 09 660	145 03 397
Port Phillip		Squid	38 21 085	144 48 459
Port Phillip			38 06 181	145 04 562
Port Welshpool	Behind Cliffy	Flathead and gummies	38 58 120	146 40 180
Port Welshpool	Bentley Harbour		38 47 590	146 32 590
Port Welshpool	Boydies Reef		38 57 250	146 36 550
Port Welshpool	Corner Inlet 02		38 49 131	146 31 432
Port Welshpool	Corner Inlet 04		38 48 087	146 30 060
Port Welshpool	Corner Inlet 05		38 50 491	146 33 481
Port Welshpool	Corner Inlet 06		38 47 042	146 28 793
Port Welshpool	Cornet Inlet 03		38 51 036	146 34 073
Port Welshpool	Crayfish Rabbit Reef		38 56 690	146 36 100
Port Welshpool	Crofties Reef		38 56 600	146 35 800

Locality	Description	Comments	Latitude	Latitude
Port Welshpool	Entrance	Snapper	38 47 500	146 30 150
Port Welshpool	Fair Way Entrance Buoy		38 51 110	146 35 650
Port Welshpool	Johnny Reef		38 57 230	146 36 470
Port Welshpool	Lewis Channel 07		38 43 737	146 25 552
Port Welshpool	Manns Channel	Gummies, china	38 47 260	146 25 970
Port Welshpool	Micks hot spot		38 47 700	146 30 240
Port Welshpool	Micks Marl		38 46 220	146 27 510
Port Welshpool	Near Singapore Deep		38 46 650	146 28 450
Port Welshpool	No name	Gummies wider	38 48 300	146 36 600
Port Welshpool	Off Buoy 2		38 49 170	146 31 800
Port Welshpool	Off Buoy 4		38 48 250	146 30 530
Port Welshpool	Pinkies Reef		38 57 860	146 36 100
Port Welshpool	Port Welshpool	Corner Inlet	38 46 801	146 29 111
Port Welshpool	Rabbit Is reef 1		38 56 570	146 36 660
Port Welshpool	Rabbit Is reef 2		38 56 590	146 36 100
Port Welshpool	Rabbit Is reef 3		38 56 920	146 36 680
Port Welshpool	Rag Is W		38 57 430	146 36 660
Port Welshpool	Refuge Cove		39 02 400	146 28 590
Port Welshpool	Sealer's Cove	Sharks	39 01 240	146 27 730
Port Welshpool	Singapore Deep		38 46 250	146 27 670
Port Welshpool	Under the hat		38 59 590	146 26 690
Port Welshpool	Warrens Flathead		38 59 120	146 33 620
Port Welshpool	Welshpool Entrance Johnny	Gummies	38 50 360	146 35 310
Port Welshpool	Welshpool Pinnacles		38 47 140	146 29 900
Port Welshpool	White Rock		38 54 250	146 30 240
Port Welshpool	White Rock, Cliffy Is W		38 57 350	146 36 680
Portland	Blacknose Point	5–10 m. Reef patches. Snapper, morwong, mulloway	38 22 798	141 38 727
Portland	Cod Splat	21 m. Reef. Snapper, morwong, mulloway	38 20 237	141 39 976
Portland	Maggoty Bay	9 m. Near Snapper Point. Snapper, morwong, mulloway	38 17 674	141 39 882
Portland	Narrawong	5 m. Snapper, morwong, mulloway	38 16 432	141 41 581
Portland	North Shore	10 m. Reef patches snapper	38 18 738	141 38 068
Sandringham	Shoal	Snapper, whiting, squid	37 57 506	144 59 478
Seaford	East pallet ball	Snapper	38 05 246	145 05 974

Locality	Description	Comments	Latitude	Latitude
Seaford	North pallet ball	Snapper	38 05 229	145 05 954
Seaford	South pallet ball	Snapper	38 05 261	145 05 953
Sorrento		Whiting	38 20 276	144 46 816
Torquay	Fad 1	Kingfish	38 19 828	144 22 500
Torquay	Fad 2	Kingfish	38 19 942	144 22 600
Torquay	Fad 3	Kingfish	38 20 184	144 22 320
Torquay	Fad 4	Kingfish	38 20 065	144 22 225
Western Port	.	Snapper, gummy and school shark	38 25 758	145 15 207
Western Port	.	Ram Island snapper, gummy, elephants	38 25 898	145 20 936
Western Port	.	Snapper, gummy and school shark	38 26 327	145 16 885
Western Port	Ace Fishing Charters . Middle Spit	Whiting, south of cut	38 21 080	145 14 965
Western Port	Ace Fishing Charters Whiting. Tortoise Head	Approx. 2.5 m	38 25 074	145 16 620
Western Port	Ace Fishing Charters. Bottom of Middle Spit	Whiting, approx. 2.5–6 m	38 22 352	145 15 404
Western Port	Ace Fishing Charters. Buoy 11	Snapper, approx. 21 m	38 26 660	145 11 694
Western Port	Ace Fishing Charters. Buoy 5	Snapper, approx. 23 m	38 28 529	145 08 318
Western Port	Ace Fishing Charters. Cowes	Snapper, gummies, approx. 30 m	38 26 153	145 13 072
Western Port	Ace Fishing Charters. Hanns Inlet	Pinkies and whiting, approx. 15 m	38 23 185	145 14 548
Western Port	Ace Fishing Charters. Hanns Inlet	Whiting, approx. 11 m	38 23 483	145 14 204
Western Port	Ace Fishing Charters. Hastings	Snapper, early season, flood and ebb, approx. 17 m	38 19 050	145 14 204
Western Port	Ace Fishing Charters. Hastings Middle Spit	5–7 m at low tide	38 19 308	145 15 139
Western Port	Ace Fishing Charters. Lysaghts	Snapper, pinkies flood tide, approx. 14.5 m	38 16 897	145 15 095
Western Port	Ace Fishing Charters. Lysaghts	Snapper, flood tide, approx. 18 m	38 17 407	145 14 807
Western Port	Ace Fishing Charters. Silver leaves	Mark approx. 16 m	38 26 135	145 17 169
Western Port	Artificial reef	Gummy Shark	38 19 158	144 34 527
Western Port	Artificial reef	Squid	38 19 432	144 46 408
Western Port	Artificial reef	Gummy Shark	38 20 061	144 52 846
Western Port	Artificial reef	Squid	38 20 344	144 49 091
Western Port	Blue Gum Point	Snapper	38 22 522	145 28 470
Western Port	Bouchiers Channel	Snapper	38 14 860	145 26 280

Locality	Description	Comments	Latitude	Latitude
Western Port	Bouchiers Entrance	Snapper	38 16 516	145 23 181
Western Port	Boultans Channel	Snapper	38 16 739	145 27 600
Western Port	Boulton Channel.	Snapper and gummy	38 16 201	145 25 924
Western Port	Boultons	Channel junction	38 16 450	145 23 550
Western Port	Bouy 1	Snapper and Gummy	38 30 063	145 06 302
Western Port	Bouy 1	Snapper and Gummy	38 30 064	145 06 240
Western Port	Bouy 12	Snapper and Gummy	38 26 318	145 11 555
Western Port	Bp.	Snapper	38 20 846	145 14 437
Western Port	Buoy 17	Gummy	38 24 116	145 15 304
Western Port	Buoy 17	Deep water	38 24 250	145 15 150
Western Port	Buoy 24	Whiting	38 21 788	145 14 153
Western Port	Cat Bay 1	Whiting	38 30 168	145 08 419
Western Port	Cat Bay 2	Whiting	38 30 255	145 08 619
Western Port	Cat Bay 3	Whiting	38 30 269	145 08 473
Western Port	Chilcott Channel		38 19 523	145 16 486
Western Port	Chris Halstead. Lysaghts	Snapper, good reef and cunje, approx. 14–15 m	38 17 504	145 14 826
Western Port	Churchill Island	Snapper	38 26 696	145 17 983
Western Port	Colin Gilmartin. Corals	Snapper, general area	38 27 150	145 20 550
Western Port	Colin Gilmartin. Middle ground	Gummy, school shark, pinkies, 4–9 m	38 26 882	145 21 186
Western Port	Colin Gilmartin. Nitts	Pinkies, Jan–March whiting, slack water	38 26 977	145 18 179
Western Port	Colin Gilmartin. Rhyll	Snapper, approx. 15 m, early season	38 27 270	145 19 285
Western Port	Colin Gilmartin. Silver leaves	Snapper, early season, ebb tide, approx. 20 m	38 26 504	145 16 719
Western Port	Colin Guilmartin Gardners. Channel exit	Elephants, snapper, gummies, approx. 10 m	38 25 556	145 19 560
Western Port	Colin Guilmartin. East Arm big snapper,	Gummy spring and summer, approx. 9 m	38 26 325	145 18 352
Western Port	Colin Guilmartin. Ram Is/Bird Rock	Elephants Mar–May, snapper early season, start of flood	38 25 642	145 20 212
Western Port	Colin Guilmartin. Ram Island	Elephants, mulloway, April–May, approx. 5 m	38 25 533	145 21 052
Western Port	Colin Guilmartin. Tortoise Head Bank	Snapper, early season, start of flood tide, gummy, school shark, Jan–March, elephants	38 25 689	145 17 995
Western Port	Coral	Pinkie snapper and big whiting	38 26 779	145 19 796
Western Port	Corinella	Snapper	38 22 758	145 26 499
Western Port	Coronet Bay	6–16 m. Snapper	38 26 450	145 23 190
Western Port	Crawfish Rock	Snapper all round.	38 16 200	145 17 850
Western Port	Crawfish Rock. Beacon		38 16 228	145 17 788

Locality	Description	Comments	Latitude	Latitude
Western Port	Eagle Rock	Snapper all round.	38 15 900	145 16 800
Western Port	Eagle Rock Isolated Danger Mark.		38 15 905	145 16 795
Western Port	East 7.	Whiting and pinkies	38 27 068	145 11 722
Western Port	East Entrance to The Cut.		38 20 905	145 15 582
Western Port	Elephant Mark	Elephant fish	38 24 770	145 16 510
Western Port	Elizabeth Island 1	Snapper	38 25 116	145 23 349
Western Port	Elizabeth Island 2	Location–highly productive area. Snapper all round	38 25 200	145 22 600
Western Port	ESSO	Reef, snapper	38 19 820	145 13 780
Western Port	Flinders 1	Whiting	38 27 768	145 02 347
Western Port	Flinders 2	Whiting	38 28 414	145 02 652
Western Port	Flinders 3	Whiting	38 28 675	145 02 234
Western Port	Flinders Pier.		38 28 570	145 01 709
Western Port	French Island	Whiting	38 16 636	145 16 877
Western Port	French Island North	Whiting	38 20 962	145 16 322
Western Port	Gardners Channel	Gummy	38 25 680	145 17 995
Western Port	Gummies		38 24 087	145 09 378
Western Port	Gummies		38 25 039	145 14 392
Western Port	Hastings	Squid	38 17 794	145 13 656
Western Port	Hastings	Squid	38 18 803	145 13 640
Western Port	Hastings	16 m. Snapper	38 19 188	145 14 030
Western Port	Hi 5.	Snapper, gummies	38 27 554	145 09 590
Western Port	Jarrod Day. Buoy 16	Snapper Aug–Oct, approx. 20 m	38 25 063	145 13 793
Western Port	Jarrod Day. Middle Spit	Whiting, any tide, approx. 2 m	38 17 834	145 15 503
Western Port	Joes Island 1	7–10 m. Snapper all round.	38 16 600	145 21 100
Western Port	Joes Island 2	Snapper	38 16 784	145 21 454
Western Port	Joes Island. East cardinal mark	Gummies winter months, approx. 17 m	38 16 632	145 21 121
Western Port	Joes Island. West cardinal mark		38 16 557	145 20 711
Western Port	Long reef	Snapper	38 16 673	145 15 558
Western Port	Low 11.	Gummies and snapper	38 26 587	145 11 945
Western Port	Lyalls Channel	Snapper	38 15 566	145 23 544
Western Port	Lysaght's	Snapper	38 17 350	145 14 900
Western Port	McHaffie's	Whiting	38 28 341	145 09 030

Locality	Description	Comments	Latitude	Latitude
Western Port	Michael Ketelaar. Merricks sand patch	Whiting, pike, gummies, snapper, squid	38 25 008	145 06 224
Western Port	Michael Ketelaar. Somers sand hole	Whiting and flathead	38 24 510	145 08 999
Western Port	Middle Channel	12 m. Snapper	38 19 216	145 16 352
Western Port	Middle Channel.	8 m snapper at end of tide	38 17 372	145 15 184
Western Port	Middle Spit 1	Whiting	38 20 773	145 14 911
Western Port	Middle Spit 2	Whiting	38 22 392	145 15 376
Western Port	Mouth of Bouchier Channel.		38 16 434	145 23 588
Western Port	Mouth of Boulton Channel.		38 16 580	145 24 072
Western Port	Mouth of Chainmans Creek.		38 15 251	145 19 076
Western Port	Mouth of Charing Cross Channel.		38 15 227	145 21 181
Western Port	Mouth of Hastings Channel.		38 19 533	145 13 277
Western Port	Mouth of Horseshoe Channel.	Snapper, gummy whaler, seven gill	38 17 014	145 23 606
Western Port	Mouth of Irish Jack Channel.		38 15 162	145 21 208
Western Port	Mouth of Lyall's Channel.		38 16 185	145 23 104
Western Port	Mouth of Tooradin Channel.		38 15 914	145 19 404
Western Port	Mouth of Warneet Channel.		38 15 595	145 18 486
Western Port	Mouth of Watson Inlet.		38 15 703	145 15 672
Western Port	Mud / Shell	Jewfish	38 27 529	145 22 784
Western Port	No name		38 17 091	145 21 121
Western Port	No name	Whiting	38 22 376	145 15 520
Western Port	No name	Whiting	38 23 495	145 14 090
Western Port	No name	Whiting	38 23 697	145 14 150
Western Port	No name		38 24 649	145 09 654
Western Port	No name		38 24 829	145 08 966
Western Port	No name		38 25 333	145 13 840
Western Port	No name		38 26 426	145 12 050
Western Port	No name	Elephant fish	38 26 625	145 21 129
Western Port	No name	Snapper, gummies	38 26 631	145 11 369
Western Port	No name	Elephant fish	38 27 593	145 18 952
Western Port	North End of Middle Spit.		38 16 416	145 16 963
Western Port	Patric Neidhart. Buoy 1	Snapper, pike, reef fish, sharks	38 30 206	145 06 818
Western Port	Patric Neidhart. Buoy 11	Snapper	38 27 086	145 10 803
Western Port	Patric Neidhart. Buoy 12	Gummies with squid on slack water	38 26 321	145 11 589

Locality	Description	Comments	Latitude	Latitude
Western Port	Patric Neidhart. Buoy 14	Gummies ebb tide	38 25 477	145 13 286
Western Port	Patric Neidhart. Buoy 2	Gummy, small snapper, seven gill	38 29 317	145 05 971
Western Port	Patric Neidhart. Buoy 29	Gummy, snapper	38 18 712	145 14 302
Western Port	Patric Neidhart. Buoy 5	Gummies	38 28 606	145 08 853
Western Port	Patric Neidhart. Fairway Buoy	Good snapper, flathead	38 29 973	145 06 056
Western Port	Patric Neidhart. Ventnor	Squid and whiting	38 27 432	145 11 018
Western Port	Peninsula and Western Port Charters. Lysaghts	Snapper, Oct–Nov, approx. 14.5 m	38 16 256	145 16 165
Western Port	Peninsula and Western Port Charters. Observation point	Snapper Nov–march	38 26 898	145 18 338
Western Port	Peninsula and Western Port Charters. Rhyll	Snapper, approx. 16 m, Nov–Dec.	38 27 128	145 19 146
Western Port	Peninsula and Western Port Charters. Sandy Point	Whiting and pinkies, Nov–March, approx. 14.5 m	38 24 346	145 14 333
Western Port	Peninsula and Western Port Charters. Tankerton	Whiting, Nov–March, approx. 7.5 m	38 21 850	145 16 041
Western Port	Peninsula and Western Port Charters. Tortoise Head	Whiting, Jan–march, approx. 3.5 m	38 25 438	145 16 737
Western Port	Peninsula and Western Port Fishing Charters. Crib Point	Whiting, April–May	38 20 459	145 13 655
Western Port	Peter Ferguson. Crawfish Rock	Snapper and school shark, Nov–Dec., approx. 21 m	38 15 931	145 18 242
Western Port	Peter Ferguson's Browns Reserve.	Gummies and snapper, Feb–March approx. 8 m, last two hours of ebb and first hour flood	38 16 091	145 19 703
Western Port	Quail Bank		38 15 417	145 16 958
Western Port	Reef Island 1	Gummy, Pinkies, Whiting	38 27 890	145 23 806
Western Port	Reef Island 2	Whiting	38 28 067	145 24 135
Western Port	Reel Adventure Charters. Eagle Rock	Snapper and pinkies, Oct–March, approx. 19 m	38 16 173	145 16 355
Western Port	Reel Adventure Charters. Quail bank whiting, dec.– feb., approx. 3 m		38 15 473	145 16 299
Western Port	Reel Time Charters. Balnarring	Gummies year round, full moon, plus whiting, wrasse	38 24 852	145 08 204
Western Port	Reel Time Charters. Buoy 14	Gummies year round	38 25 613	145 13 056
Western Port	Reel Time Charters. Buoy 18	Pinkies, snapper, small gummies	38 23 936	145 14 500
Western Port	Reel Time Charters. Buoy 7	Snapper, gummies	38 27 267	145 10 158
Western Port	Reel Time Charters. Cat bay	Gummies, pinkies, snapper, good year round best on ebb tide	38 29 062	145 08 125
Western Port	Reel Time Charters. Cowes	Gummies year round, snapper Sep–Dec, pinkies Dec–April	38 26 177	145 16 792

Locality	Description	Comments	Latitude	Latitude
Western Port	Reel Time Charters. Flinders	Squid, good early Sep To early Dec. Drift between	38 28 494	145 02 118
Western Port	Reel Time Charters. Flinders	Squid, good early Sep to early Dec. Drift between	38 28 601	145 02 157
Western Port	Reel Time Charters. Joes Island	Best On The First Two Hours Of The Ebb	38 16 807	145 20 850
Western Port	Reel Time Charters. Lysaghts	Snapper, early season Sept–Nov.	38 18 094	145 14 255
Western Port	Reel Time Charters. Lysaghts	Snapper, early season Sept–Nov.	38 18 712	145 14 255
Western Port	Reel Time Charters. Sandy Point	Gummy year round, snapper Sep–Dec. Whiting and pinkies Dec–April	38 24 509	145 14 303
Western Port	Reel Time Charters. Tortoise Head	Whiting, salmon	38 25 317	145 15 887
Western Port	Reel Time Fishing Charters. Buoy 5	Seven gill shark, snapper, gummies, salmon	38 28 594	145 08 309
Western Port	Rhyll	8 m. Reef patches	38 26 740	145 19 980
Western Port	Rhyll Ramp		38 27 953	145 18 620
Western Port	Road mark		38 26 397	145 12 070
Western Port	Sand Stone Island 1	Squid	38 19 572	145 13 258
Western Port	Sand Stone Island 2	Squid	38 20 219	145 13 208
Western Port	Sand Stone Island 3	Squid	38 20 482	145 13 228
Western Port	Scott Harper.	Gummy shark, approx. 22 m	38 15 811	145 17 489
Western Port	Silver leaves	12 m. Reef, snapper	38 26 070	145 18 230
Western Port	South End of Middle Spit.		38 22 480	145 15 396
Western Port	South End Spit		38 22 197	145 15 390
Western Port	Spit Point 1	Snapper	38 20 769	145 30 276
Western Port	Spit Point 2	Snapper	38 21 663	145 30 785
Western Port	Spit Point 3	Snapper	38 22 075	145 30 049
Western Port	Stony Point	Whiting	38 21 743	145 14 136
Western Port	Tankers.	Whiting	38 26 811	145 12 817
Western Port	Tankerton 1		38 22 776	145 16 250
Western Port	Tankerton 2	Whiting	38 22 994	145 15 675
Western Port	Tankerton 3		38 23 558	145 16 110
Western Port	Tankerton 4		38 23 946	145 16 006
Western Port	The Cut	Whiting	38 21 035	145 15 507
Western Port	Tortoise Head	Whiting	38 25 248	145 16 351
Western Port	Tortoise Head 1	19 m. Snapper	38 26 268	145 16 450
Western Port	Tortoise Head 2	16 m. Snapper	38 26 086	145 12 572
Western Port	Tyabb Bank		38 16 400	145 15 600

Locality	Description	Comments	Latitude	Latitude
Western Port	Tyabb Bank 1	Squid	38 15 966	145 14 842
Western Port	Tyabb Bank 2	Squid	38 16 406	145 14 366
Western Port	Tyabb Bank 3	Squid	38 16 630	145 14 066
Western Port	Tyabb Bank 4	Squid	38 16 845	145 13 868
Western Port	Tyabb Bank 5	Squid	38 16 996	145 13 943
Western Port	Ventnor 1	26 m. Snapper	38 26 388	145 12 650
Western Port	Ventnor 2	Squid	38 27 451	145 11 247
Western Port	West Entrance	20 m. Snapper	38 29 400	145 04 996
Western Port	West Entrance to The Cut.		38 19 960	145 15 126
Western Port	Western Entrance	Gummies	38 30 170	145 03 590
Western Port	Western Entrance	Good snapper	38 30 800	145 04 600
Western Port	Western Entrance.	Early/late season snapper, gummies	38 30 827	145 04 585
Western Port	Woolamai 5 Mile reef		38 38 730	145 22 220
Western Port	Yaringa	Whiting Pinkies Snapper	38 15 742	145 15 576
Western Port		Squid	38 08 511	144 33 647
Western Port		Whiting	38 09 212	144 30 376
Western Port		Squid	38 11 142	144 43 697
Western Port		Whiting	38 11 573	144 44 500
Western Port		Whiting	38 11 951	144 43 460
Western Port		Squid	38 14 184	144 42 071
Western Port		Gummy Shark	38 15 280	144 44 370
Western Port		Whiting	38 16 427	144 38 944
Western Port		Whiting	38 18 484	145 16 827
Western Port		Gummy	38 19 221	145 14 680
Western Port		Gummy Shark	38 19 855	144 31 041
Western Port		Snapper and Gummy	38 29 947	145 08 427

QUEENSLAND

MARKS

Locality	Description	Comments	Latitude	Latitude
Bowen	Banana wreck	Spanish Mackerel, Reds, Fingermark and Trout	19 55 775	148 16 395
Bowen	Black Reef	Fingermark and Grunter, best fished at Night	19 59 453	148 28 481
Bowen	Brady's Reef	Deep water reef, hosts Trevally and Cobia	20 03 982	148 24 982
Bowen	Cheynassa	Hosts Sweetlip and Coastal Trout	20 04 296	148 20 211
Bowen	Double Cone Island north		20 05 500	148 42 750
Bowen	Foul	Spanish Mackerel, Reds, Fingermark and Trout	19 55 825	148 16 326
Bowen	Gloucester Reef	40 m	19 58 100	148 27 650
Bowen	Holbourne Island northwest	50 m	19 43 000	148 20 900
Bowen	Inner Mackerel Patch	Spotted and Spanish Mackerel	19 55 558	148 14 350
Bowen	Northern edge	Deep water Grunter, black Jew and Nannygai	19 58 011	148 26 711
Bowen	Outer Mackerel Patch	Spotted and Spanish Mackerel	19 52 285	148 12 515
Bowen	Pakhoi Bank	20 m	19 26 000	147 53 000
Bowen	Phillips Reef	Mixed reef, bait and Predatory Species	19 52 117	148 05 450
Bowen	Second Mackerel Patch	Spotted and Spanish Mackerel	19 52 272	148 12 544
Bowen	Southern Cross 1	Mixed Reef Species	19 59 673	148 16 311
Bowen	Southern Cross 2	Mixed Reef Species	19 59 559	148 16 340
Bowen	Stony Bombie 1	Large coastal Trout	20 02 998	148 17 072
Bowen	Stony Bombie 2	Large coastal Trout	20 02 839	148 16 833
Bowen	The Glouster Passage	Hosts big fish, GT and Tusk Fish	20 03 223	148 28 140
Bowen	The Ledge	Mixed reef, bait and Predatory Species	19 54 625	148 05 777
Bowen	Wintershoal	Hosts Sweetlip and Coastal Trout	20 04 503	148 18 210
Bowen	Wreck	Spanish Mackerel, Reds, Fingermark and Trout	19 56 726	148 16 326
Brisbane and Moreton Bay	29's		27 19 500	153 33 000
Brisbane and Moreton Bay	Amber Jack		27 15 091	153 36 004
Brisbane and Moreton Bay	Artificial Reef	Water depth 5 m.	27 29 300	153 19 444
Brisbane and Moreton Bay	Boat Rock	Take care	27 25 108	153 33 266
Brisbane and Moreton Bay	Cathedral Reef	Pinnacle	27 29 640	153 36 220
Brisbane and Moreton Bay	Cathedrals		27 27 955	153 35 017
Brisbane and Moreton Bay	Cathedrals		27 30 000	153 36 200
Brisbane and Moreton Bay	Cathedrals		27 30 646	153 36 566

Locality	Description	Comments	Latitude	Latitude
Brisbane and Moreton Bay	Cathedrals		27 31 000	153 34 330
Brisbane and Moreton Bay	Cathedrals	Good pinnacle	27 34 700	153 35 750
Brisbane and Moreton Bay	Cathedrals—north of Sullies	36 m. snapper	27 31 750	153 34 200
Brisbane and Moreton Bay	Cleveland Point N		27 30 227	153 17 386
Brisbane and Moreton Bay	Drilling Track		27 30 250	153 37 200
Brisbane and Moreton Bay	Green Island	6 m. Winter snapper.	27 24 931	153 14 753
Brisbane and Moreton Bay	Harry Atkinson artificial reef	12 m snapper	27 24 428	153 18 680
Brisbane and Moreton Bay	Harry Atkinson artificial reef 1		27 23 998	153 18 374
Brisbane and Moreton Bay	Ledge		27 31 480	153 36 400
Brisbane and Moreton Bay	Middle Reef		27 24 244	153 32 071
Brisbane and Moreton Bay	Moreton Island Reef	8 fathoms. Shallow reef. Blue mackerel	27 16 100	153 25 370
Brisbane and Moreton Bay	Mud Island 1	5 m. Night snapper.	27 20 290	153 16 232
Brisbane and Moreton Bay	Mud Island 2	8 m. Summer snapper.	27 20 173	153 13 791
Brisbane and Moreton Bay	No name	Round Patch	27 10 208	153 33 201
Brisbane and Moreton Bay	No name	Round Patch	27 10 221	153 32 812
Brisbane and Moreton Bay	No name	Round Patch	27 10 302	153 33 600
Brisbane and Moreton Bay	No name	Round Patch	27 10 567	153 33 193
Brisbane and Moreton Bay	No name	Round Patch	27 10 786	153 33 661
Brisbane and Moreton Bay	No name	Round Patch	27 10 951	153 33 639
Brisbane and Moreton Bay	No name	Drop off	27 11 073	153 36 222
Brisbane and Moreton Bay	No name	Square Patch	27 13 866	153 36 784
Brisbane and Moreton Bay	No name	Square Patch	27 14 587	153 36 954

Locality	Description	Comments	Latitude	Latitude
Brisbane and Moreton Bay	No name	Square Patch	27 14 799	153 36 118
Brisbane and Moreton Bay	No name	29 Fathoms reef	27 18 058	153 32 769
Brisbane and Moreton Bay	No name	35 fathoms reef	27 18 544	153 34 296
Brisbane and Moreton Bay	No name	35 fathoms	27 18 823	153 34 957
Brisbane and Moreton Bay	No name	50 fathoms	27 27 500	153 40 000
Brisbane and Moreton Bay	No name	15 fathoms	27 29 641	153 35 216
Brisbane and Moreton Bay	No name	40 fathoms	27 32 500	153 41 000
Brisbane and Moreton Bay	No name	Snapper grounds	27 34 428	153 35 687
Brisbane and Moreton Bay	Pearlie Reef		27 19 795	153 36 689
Brisbane and Moreton Bay	Raby Bay	Snapper	27 30 360	153 16 530
Brisbane and Moreton Bay	Rufus King		27 22 706	153 27 895
Brisbane and Moreton Bay	Shag Rock		27 24 832	153 31 513
Brisbane and Moreton Bay	Spit Beacon		27 30 339	153 19 324
Brisbane and Moreton Bay	Stevens	Hump	27 22 800	153 33 800
Brisbane and Moreton Bay	The Mile		27 24 859	153 35 053
Brisbane and Moreton Bay	Turrum	30 fathoms	27 22 044	153 35 314
Brisbane and Moreton Bay	Wide ground		27 27 575	153 41 216
Brisbane and Moreton Bay	Wide ground		27 27 828	153 41 188
Brisbane and Moreton Bay	Wire Patch		27 22 988	153 37 580
Bundaberg	15 Mile Reef	Mainly Hosts Large reef Fish	24 38 290	152 37 850
Bundaberg	2 Mile Reef	Queenfish, Tuna, Trevally and Mackerel	24 48 100	152 28 100
Bundaberg	4 Mile Reef	Pelagics and mixed reef fish	24 59 470	152 33 600
Bundaberg	Althea	Trevally, Cod, Cobia and yellowfin	24 33 570	152 49 447

Locality	Description	Comments	Latitude	Latitude
Bundaberg	Barjon	Mackerel, Tuna, Trevally and possible Sailfish	24 40 468	152 34 513
Bundaberg	Cochrane Artificial Reef 1	Snapper and other Reef fish Possible Sharks	24 54 177	152 31 986
Bundaberg	Cochrane Artificial Reef 2	Snapper and other Reef fish Possible Sharks	24 54 130	152 32 139
Bundaberg	Elliot Artificial Reef	Pelagics and mixed reef fish	24 54 275	152 31 920
Bundaberg	Evans Patch	Tuna, Yellow tail king, black king and Barracuda	24 32 400	152 37 410
Bundaberg	Five Degree	Mixed Reef species, Spanish Mackerel and Tuna	24 29 067	152 30 486
Bundaberg	Kama	Schools of Trevally and Grunter	24 23 830	152 10 139
Bundaberg	Kolan Patch	15 metres Pelagics and mixed reef fish	24 32 270	152 18 950
Bundaberg	Nursery	Slate Bottom Mackerel and snapper during winter	24 39 270	152 20 000
Bundaberg	Plane	Pelagics and mixed reef fish	24 24 145	152 35 750
Bundaberg	Ryan's Reef	Mackerel	24 44 200	152 37 280
Bundaberg	Wide of Ryan's	Mac Tuna and Spotted Mackerel schools	24 43 194	152 28 183
Cairns	Arlington Reef SE		16 44 606	146 05 396
Cairns	Boat Wreck 1	Mixed Reef Species	16 45 322	145 40 583
Cairns	Channel Reef		16 56 130	146 26 738
Cairns	Coates Reef SE		17 12 342	146 22 017
Cairns	Double Island Wrecks 1	Best for small boats, abundant in Pelagics species	16 42 564	145 40 729
Cairns	Double Island Wrecks 2	Best for small boats, abundant in Pelagics species	16 40 631	145 42 499
Cairns	Double Island Wrecks 3	Best for small boats, abundant in Pelagics species	16 39 052	145 44 238
Cairns	Egret Reef	Cooktown. Reef fish, Pelagics. Reef gutter, reef bottom.	15 28 700	145 24 865
Cairns	Fitzroy Island Wreck	Wreck area, Trevally and other Pelagics	16 57 554	146 03 788
Cairns	Green island 1	Coral Trout and Nannygai	16 47 421	146 03 057
Cairns	Green island 2	Coral Trout and Nannygai	16 47 526	146 04 543
Cairns	Green Island East		16 47 565	146 03 415
Cairns	Innisfail	Mackerel. Reef species. Water depth 30 m. Rock bottom.	17 39 496	146 09 414
Cairns	Jenny Louise Shoals 1	continental shelf, Deep water Species	16 44 049	146 19 997
Cairns	Jenny Louise Shoals 2	continental shelf, Deep water Species	16 44 616	146 20 449
Cairns	Jones Patch		17 13 320	146 04 700
Cairns	Kings point 1	deep water trenches, Black Jew, Finger Mark, Trout	16 56 294	145 56 346
Cairns	Kings point 2	deep water trenches, Black Jew, Finger Mark, Trout	16 56 768	145 56 113
Cairns	Linden Banks	Red Emperor, Nannygai, Flame Tail Snapper	16 16 448	146 00 135
Cairns	Marlin Fingers	Back Marlin	16 51 899	146 04 742
Cairns	Off Hervey Shoals		17 03 776	146 22 451

Locality	Description	Comments	Latitude	Latitude
Cairns	Pellowe Reef		16 51 148	146 20 976
Cairns	Pixie/ Oyster Reef 1	Inshore reef area, good for Bottom and Pelagic fish	16 31 072	145 48 546
Cairns	Pixie/ Oyster Reef 2	Inshore reef area, good for Bottom and Pelagic fish	16 31 072	145 53 757
Cairns	Pratt Rock	Coral trout, reef fish. Water depth 12–30 m. Reef bottom.	16 09 015	145 37 526
Cairns	Round Island W		17 12 928	146 05 019
Cairns	Sandy bottom	18.5 m mackerel	16 40 658	145 42 458
Cairns	The Crane	Reef species	17 35 879	146 12 912
Cairns	The Pinnacle	Reef and pelagic species	17 33 991	146 09 507
Cairns	The Sisters		17 25 270	146 04 573
Cairns	The Twins		17 28 805	146 05 155
Cairns	Trinity Passage	Holds variety of Red fish	16 30 895	145 54 748
Cairns	Trinity Wreck	Trevally, small Nannygai and Cobia	16 30 079	145 40 465
Cairns	White Lady Bombie		17 39 600	146 09 830
Cairns	Wreck	21 m	16 39 051	145 44 428
Cairns	Wreck	12 m	16 40 660	145 42 515
Cairns	Wreck	Water depth 11.9 m.	16 42 508	145 40 655
Cairns	Wreck		16 45 367	145 41 668
Cairns	Wreck	33 m	16 46 480	145 56 945
Cairns	Wreck	12 m	16 57 579	146 03 821
Cairns	Wreck	50 m	17 09 497	146 23 091
Gladstone	1770 Bar		24 08 943	151 52 879
Gladstone	1770 Llewellyn Reef NW		23 40 020	152 08 000
Gladstone	18 Mile	33 m	24 07 220	152 12 800
Gladstone	18 Mile		24 07 630	152 12 790
Gladstone	Banana Gutter		24 06 880	152 11 100
Gladstone	Banana Gutter		24 07 240	152 09 420
Gladstone	Bombies Off Lamont		23 36 470	152 00 400
Gladstone	Boult Reef	30 m	23 44 840	152 15 135
Gladstone	Fitzroy Bombies	15 m	23 42 680	152 02 960
Gladstone	Lady Musgrave Island	50 m channel	23 53 300	152 27 720
Gladstone	Lady Musgrave Island		23 53 900	152 27 600
Gladstone	Lady Musgrave Island		23 54 876	152 22 088
Gladstone	Lady Musgrave Island WP		23 54 480	152 22 360

Locality	Description	Comments	Latitude	Latitude
Gladstone	Lamont Reef		23 36 490	152 00 970
Gladstone	One Tree	40 m	23 27 890	152 03 230
Gladstone	South of Heron Island		23 29 300	151 59 700
Gladstone	Western Warragoes	14 m	24 06 820	152 22 030
Gladstone	Western Warragoes	16 m	24 07 000	152 22 000
Gladstone	Western Warragoes	24 m	24 07 180	152 22 360
Gladstone	Wistari Reef		23 27 220	151 52 540
Gladstone	Wistari Reef		23 27 280	151 52 440
Gladstone	Wistari Reef		23 27 320	151 52 400
Gladstone	Wistari Reef		23 27 380	151 52 090
Gladstone	Wistari Reef west		23 28 440	151 50 390
Gold Coast	12 Fathom Reef		27 59 650	153 28 710
Gold Coast	60 Fathom SE		28 01 845	153 47 431
Gold Coast	Deep Southern		28 05 230	153 46 110
Gold Coast	Focus Reef	34 m. Snapper	27 59 640	153 28 910
Gold Coast	Gravel Patch		28 04 250	153 29 500
Gold Coast	Jew Reef	Jewfish	28 04 260	153 35 550
Gold Coast	Kirra		28 07 200	153 35 160
Gold Coast	Mermaid Reef		28 01 982	153 26 968
Gold Coast	Mermaid Reef		28 02 500	153 27 200
Gold Coast	Mud hole	Hump 24 m.	28 10 290	153 36 360
Gold Coast	Nine Mile Reef		28 11 904	153 38 040
Gold Coast	No name	24 fathoms	27 58 429	153 31 539
Gold Coast	No name	40 fathoms	27 58 845	153 40 639
Gold Coast	No name	22 fathoms	27 59 155	153 30 690
Gold Coast	No name	32 fathoms	27 59 300	153 36 540
Gold Coast	No name	20 fathoms	27 59 520	153 28 760
Gold Coast	No name	24 fathoms	27 59 600	153 30 290
Gold Coast	No name	36 fathoms	27 59 678	153 39 210
Gold Coast	No name	Traps	27 59 821	153 45 991
Gold Coast	No name	24 fathoms	28 00 400	153 31 528
Gold Coast	No name	36 fathoms	28 01 120	153 38 360
Gold Coast	No name	Traps, 46 fathoms	28 01 240	153 45 880
Gold Coast	No name	34 fathoms	28 01 600	153 39 390

Locality	Description	Comments	Latitude	Latitude
Gold Coast	No name	77 metres	28 01 680	153 45 000
Gold Coast	No name	79 metres	28 01 810	153 45 930
Gold Coast	No name	36 fathoms	28 01 890	153 38 770
Gold Coast	No name	48 fathoms	28 02 090	153 45 910
Gold Coast	No name	Traps	28 02 155	153 45 943
Gold Coast	No name	Traps	28 02 240	153 46 010
Gold Coast	No name	40 fathoms	28 05 000	153 45 900
Gold Coast	No name	Traps	28 05 690	153 46 230
Gold Coast	Palm Beach	Reef	28 06 370	153 28 700
Gold Coast	Palm Beach		28 06 385	153 28 810
Gold Coast	Palm Beach Reef		28 05 941	153 28 909
Gold Coast	Palm Beach Reef		28 06 280	153 28 660
Gold Coast	Tweed Canyons		28 12 767	153 52 362
Gold Coast	Tweed Canyons 2		28 13 983	153 53 027
Gold Coast	Tweed Nine Mile	Outer reef 5 m hump. Snapper	28 11 790	153 37 740
Great Sandy Strait	11 mile		25 49 970	153 23 240
Great Sandy Strait	11 mile		25 50 310	153 22 630
Great Sandy Strait	13 mile		25 49 220	153 24 180
Great Sandy Strait	16 mile		25 58 500	153 26 500
Great Sandy Strait	16 Mile Gutter		24 48 000	152 42 120
Great Sandy Strait	17 Mile		24 46 206	152 41 720
Great Sandy Strait	18 Mile		24 46 013	152 42 936
Great Sandy Strait	19 mile		25 45 970	153 27 780
Great Sandy Strait	2 Mile Bagara		24 47 360	152 30 120
Great Sandy Strait	3 Ships		25 16 530	152 58 096
Great Sandy Strait	5 mile		25 50 810	153 12 490
Great Sandy Strait	5 mile		25 51 130	153 12 780
Great Sandy Strait	6 mile	15 m broken coral–best in winter for snapper	25 05 280	152 59 310
Great Sandy Strait	8 mile		25 54 270	153 19 870
Great Sandy Strait	8 mile		25 54 600	153 19 030
Great Sandy Strait	8 Mile Reef	9 m	25 09 730	152 43 970
Great Sandy Strait	Arch Cliff	18 m	25 01 100	153 06 500
Great Sandy Strait	Arch Cliff	20 m	25 02 410	153 05 620
Great Sandy Strait	Arch Cliff North		25 03 900	153 04 580

Locality	Description	Comments	Latitude	Latitude
Great Sandy Strait	Arch Cliff Wide		25 05 350	152 59 310
Great Sandy Strait	Bogimbar Cars		25 17 526	153 01 743
Great Sandy Strait	Bogimbar Ledge		25 17 895	153 02 000
Great Sandy Strait	Bombie		25 29 518	153 42 662
Great Sandy Strait	Burrum Heads	8 Mile. 9 m	25 09 840	152 43 020
Great Sandy Strait	Cars		25 16 081	152 57 598
Great Sandy Strait	Coral Patch		24 45 737	153 04 469
Great Sandy Strait	Double Island Point east		25 45 650	153 28 070
Great Sandy Strait	Elliot Heads	4 mile	24 56 500	153 33 000
Great Sandy Strait	Fish Haven		25 16 030	153 00 448
Great Sandy Strait	Gardner Bank		24 53 500	153 29 000
Great Sandy Strait	Gardner Bank	38 m	24 56 962	153 28 371
Great Sandy Strait	Gardner Bank	38 m	24 57 308	153 28 061
Great Sandy Strait	Gardner Bank	27 m	24 57 873	153 25 512
Great Sandy Strait	Gardner Bank	36 m	24 58 090	153 27 814
Great Sandy Strait	Gardner Bank	32 m	24 58 238	153 28 325
Great Sandy Strait	Gardner Bank		24 58 486	153 27 974
Great Sandy Strait	Gardner Bank	27 m	24 59 226	153 27 573
Great Sandy Strait	Gardner Bank	27 m	25 00 400	153 31 500
Great Sandy Strait	Gardner Bank	38 m	25 03 262	153 27 764
Great Sandy Strait	Gardner Bank	20 m	25 03 574	153 31 818
Great Sandy Strait	Gardner Bank	42 m	25 06 546	153 31 818
Great Sandy Strait	Gardner Bank	60 m	25 55 000	153 28 500
Great Sandy Strait	Goori Wreck		25 17 016	152 58 235
Great Sandy Strait	Hall's Reef	Reef species Water depth 15–21 m Reef and rock bottom	26 20 377	153 05 101
Great Sandy Strait	Hards		26 14 850	153 40 850
Great Sandy Strait	Hards		26 17 280	153 38 530
Great Sandy Strait	Hards		26 18 700	153 36 670
Great Sandy Strait	Hards	Rise	26 20 390	153 35 920
Great Sandy Strait	Hards		26 21 700	153 35 030
Great Sandy Strait	Indian Head East		25 04 300	153 33 500
Great Sandy Strait	Indian Head Shelf		25 06 000	153 37 000
Great Sandy Strait	Jew Shoal	Take care. 9–19 m. Summer snapper.	26 21 630	153 07 120

Locality	Description	Comments	Latitude	Latitude
Great Sandy Strait	Jew Shoal Reef	Reef ground, 15 m deep, steep (Laguna Bay) pinnacles–good baitfish ground, mackerel.	26 21 950	153 06 880
Great Sandy Strait	Lasagari 1	Artificial reef	25 16 517	152 57 985
Great Sandy Strait	Little Hall Reef	Reef Species	26 21 280	153 05 610
Great Sandy Strait	Near Shallows		25 44 660	153 30 180
Great Sandy Strait	Nimbi Ledge		25 16 535	153 00 489
Great Sandy Strait	No name	15 Fathoms	24 54 300	152 47 180
Great Sandy Strait	No name	20 Fathoms	24 54 560	152 47 600
Great Sandy Strait	No name	10 Fathoms	24 54 700	152 49 720
Great Sandy Strait	No name	30 m hole	24 58 390	153 10 790
Great Sandy Strait	North Reef		26 16 480	153 10 420
Great Sandy Strait	North Reef		26 16 850	153 13 340
Great Sandy Strait	North Reef	Reef Ground, close to Noosa, Charter Boat stop, 35–45 m deep, coral and weed. Reef extends N and NNW for 1 km. Winter snapper.	26 18 550	153 10 130
Great Sandy Strait	North Shelf		25 36 000	153 40 000
Great Sandy Strait	Off Congal Creek	8 m	25 09 771	153 02 353
Great Sandy Strait	Off Rooney Point	30 m	24 47 500	153 04 010
Great Sandy Strait	Offshore Fraser Island	48 m	25 13 110	153 30 260
Great Sandy Strait	Offshore Fraser Island	53 m	25 17 850	153 30 100
Great Sandy Strait	Offshore Fraser Island	53 m	25 20 300	153 30 580
Great Sandy Strait	Offshore Fraser Island	50 m	25 22 590	153 30 100
Great Sandy Strait	Offshore Fraser Island	60 m	25 22 590	153 37 530
Great Sandy Strait	Offshore Fraser Island	58 m	25 25 200	153 30 100
Great Sandy Strait	Rooney Point		24 49 180	153 06 869
Great Sandy Strait	Rooney's 4 Mile		24 46 040	152 04 300
Great Sandy Strait	Rooney's 9 Mile		24 46 560	152 58 290
Great Sandy Strait	Rooney's 9 Mile		24 46 700	152 58 800
Great Sandy Strait	Sammy's	3 km deep	25 11 680	153 59 920
Great Sandy Strait	Shallows		25 45 660	153 28 480
Great Sandy Strait	Shallows		25 46 900	153 29 390
Great Sandy Strait	Shelf		25 33 450	153 43 950
Great Sandy Strait	Shelf		25 48 370	153 45 950
Great Sandy Strait	Shelf		25 52 320	153 47 290
Great Sandy Strait	Southern Gutter		24 45 730	152 48 113
Great Sandy Strait	Southern Gutter		24 45 930	152 48 020

Locality	Description	Comments	Latitude	Latitude
Great Sandy Strait	Southern Gutter	Tip	24 46 397	152 48 089
Great Sandy Strait	Southern Gutter		24 47 390	152 45 500
Great Sandy Strait	Southern Gutter		24 47 700	152 47 600
Great Sandy Strait	Station Hill area		24 52 720	153 05 230
Great Sandy Strait	The Pinnacles	Double Island Point NE of sanctuary zone. Mackerel, kingfish, reef fish. Water depth 25 m	25 54 175	153 12 690
Great Sandy Strait	Timber Barge		25 16 388	152 58 035
Great Sandy Strait	Trevally Alley	17 m	24 58 647	153 05 135
Great Sandy Strait	Washing Machine		24 55 385	153 13 044
Great Sandy Strait	Washing Machine		24 55 790	153 12 780
Great Sandy Strait	Wathumba	23 m	24 52 500	153 02 250
Great Sandy Strait	Wathumba	20 m hole	24 55 070	153 10 920
Great Sandy Strait	Wathumba		24 55 850	153 12 700
Great Sandy Strait	Wathumba One Mile	14 m reef. Snapper	24 57 600	153 11 730
Great Sandy Strait	Wathumba. 1 mile	14 m	24 58 774	153 04 903
Great Sandy Strait	Wreck		25 16 176	152 57 808
Great Sandy Strait	Wreck/Artificial Reef	Squire, snapper, Sweetlip, cod, assorted reef fish.	25 16 970	152 58 460
Hervey Bay	15 Mile Gutter	24 m	24 36 803	152 47 000
Hervey Bay	15 Mile Gutter		24 37 360	152 38 420
Hervey Bay	17 Mile	24 m	24 45 640	152 42 380
Hervey Bay	Big Cave		24 39 030	153 25 799
Hervey Bay	Drop off	110 m snapper	24 39 260	153 27 150
Hervey Bay	Drop off	100 m snapper	24 44 590	153 29 170
Hervey Bay	East Sandy Cape		24 39 600	153 26 435
Hervey Bay	Eastern Warragoes		24 30 120	152 29 000
Hervey Bay	Evans Patch	17 m	24 44 988	152 37 383
Hervey Bay	Evans Patch	17 m	24 45 056	152 37 322
Hervey Bay	Ferguson Spit	Coral Patch	24 45 618	153 04 397
Hervey Bay	Herald Patch		24 13 060	152 40 000
Hervey Bay	Kolan Patch	15 m	24 32 158	152 19 060
Hervey Bay	Kolan Patch	15 m	24 32 220	152 19 040
Hervey Bay	Kolan Patch	16 m	24 32 261	152 19 880
Hervey Bay	No name	15 Fathom	24 14 120	152 49 300
Hervey Bay	No name	23 Fathom	24 15 300	152 56 300
Hervey Bay	No name	56 m gutter	24 19 101	152 54 690

Locality	Description	Comments	Latitude	Latitude
Hervey Bay	No name	10 miles from S. Cape	24 38 804	153 26 750
Hervey Bay	Northern Gutter	40 m	24 35 000	152 49 350
Hervey Bay	Northern Gutter		24 37 000	152 49 000
Hervey Bay	Northern Gutter		24 39 730	152 47 990
Hervey Bay	Outside Breaksea Spit	East of Sandy Cape Shoal	24 35 830	153 23 620
Hervey Bay	Plane Wreck		24 45 145	152 35 750
Hervey Bay	Rooney Point		24 45 133	153 04 460
Hervey Bay	Rooney's	40 m hole	24 43 200	152 57 500
Hervey Bay	Rooney's	30 m	24 44 390	152 48 660
Hervey Bay	Rooney's coral patch	24 m reef	24 45 700	153 04 430
Hervey Bay	Shipwreck		24 29 520	152 37 450
Hervey Bay	Southern Gutter	35 m	24 22 700	152 46 980
Hervey Bay	Southern Gutter	36 m	24 41 540	152 50 420
Hervey Bay	Southern Gutter		24 44 316	152 46 456
Hervey Bay	Southern Gutter		24 45 042	152 48 307
Hervey Bay	Spur	36 m	24 32 480	152 46 120
Hervey Bay	Stepping Stones		24 41 890	152 43 880
Hervey Bay	Trawler	20 m	24 40 378	152 34 518
Hinchinbrook	Isolated Bombie	11m drop off to 45m, Coral Reef area	18 09 886	146 44 579
Hinchinbrook	Kennedy Shoal	Rubble area	18 03 837	146 27 664
Innisfail	Bramble Reef east	50 m	18 25 000	146 39 000
Innisfail	Eva Island	8 m	18 14 109	146 19 664
Innisfail	Fingers	Hinchinbrook Channel. Fingermark, barramundi, mangrove jack, estuary cod. Water depth 9 m. Sand and mud bottom.	18 24 585	146 10 826
Innisfail	Haycock Island south		18 28 547	146 13 105
Innisfail	Pelorus Island west	15 m	18 33 246	146 28 484
Mackay	East Three Rocks	Marlin, sailfish and a variety of reef fish	20 54 560	149 47 683
Mackay	Flag Pole	Cobia and Mackerel	20 46 704	149 35 112
Mackay	Four Mile Patch	Snapper during winter months	21 07 499	149 17 314
Mackay	Geranium Shoal	Grassy Sweetlip and coral trout	20 38 822	149 13 561
Mackay	Heskett Lump	Variety of reef fish	20 56 154	149 28 432
Mackay	Hyde Rock	Mackerel and Trevally, Trout and Snapper in winter	20 54 754	149 21 370
Mackay	Llewellyn Shoal	Sweetlip, Grunter, Mackerel and Tuna	20 59 876	149 18 564
Mackay	NE Calder	Marlin, sailfish and a variety of reef fish	20 44 200	149 40 300

Locality	Description	Comments	Latitude	Latitude
Mackay	Oom Shoal	Mackerel, Tuna and Grunter at night	21 03 143	149 18 209
Mackay	Overfall Rock	Variety of reef fish	21 16 025	149 37 773
Mackay	Reichelmann Reef	Cod, small trout, Mackerel and wolf herring	21 11 301	149 14 780
Mackay	Six Mile Patch	Snapper during winter months	21 04 851	149 19 220
Noosa	Barwon Banks		26 22 055	153 40 690
Noosa	Barwon Banks		26 23 840	153 35 640
Noosa	Barwon Banks		26 27 300	153 32 300
Noosa	Barwon Banks		26 27 425	153 35 920
Noosa	Barwon Banks		26 28 290	153 32 250
Noosa	Barwon Banks		26 32 240	153 31 590
Noosa	Chardon's Reef		26 24 250	153 15 770
Noosa	Chardon's Reef		26 25 180	153 13 670
Noosa	Chardon's Reef		26 26 520	153 14 390
Noosa	Masoud's Reef		26 22 550	153 10 010
Noosa	Misery Reef	Southern most point of reef (Sunshine Reef) ground, 31 m deep. Deep fishing for Pelagics such as mackerel, reef species.	26 23 680	153 09 240
Noosa	Sunshine Reef		26 23 100	153 04 150
Noosa	Sunshine Reef		26 23 300	153 08 330
Noosa	Sunshine reef	30 m. Strong current. Snapper	26 24 326	153 09 294
Noosa	Sunshine Reef	Reef species Reef bottom water depth 20–25 m	26 25 999	153 10 000
Seventeen Seventy	1.5 Mile	Big reef fish & coral trout	24 07 696	151 59 429
Seventeen Seventy	10 mile Banana Gutter	Assorted reefies and coral trout	24 06 949	152 03 811
Seventeen Seventy	8 Fathom	Mixed species	23 42 800	152 03 000
Seventeen Seventy	Boult Reef	Flat ground and rocky areas, good for small fish	23 50 065	152 07 064
Seventeen Seventy	Eastern Warrego's	Reds, hussar and Cods	23 06 800	152 07 300
Seventeen Seventy	Fitzroy Bombies	Good reef fish, as well as Predatory night fish	23 42 809	152 03 032
Seventeen Seventy	Inner Wides	Sweetlip, Hussar and Reds	23 50 700	151 59 500
Seventeen Seventy	Musgrave SW1	Good reef fish	24 01 000	152 16 458
Seventeen Seventy	Musgrave SW2	Flat country assorted reef fish incl red emperor	24 00 896	152 16 418
Seventeen Seventy	Outer Wides	Trout, Sweetlip and Cods	23 49 800	152 00 810
Seventeen Seventy	Outside boult 75M	Home to Trophy fish also red bass	23 41 837	152 21 793
Seventeen Seventy	Outside boult reef	Variety of reef fish incl, coral trout and red throat	23 44 878	152 20 491
Seventeen Seventy	Outside Fitzroy	NE of Fitzroy lagoon, good bait and good reds	23 35 289	152 11 684
Seventeen Seventy	South Bustard	Mixed species	23 55 000	152 03 800

Locality	Description	Comments	Latitude	Latitude
Seventeen Seventy	Wreck	Wreck sites, some reef fish incl trevally	24 00 671	151 59 969
Stradbroke Island	24 Fathom East		27 57 442	153 30 598
Stradbroke Island	Alan's reef		27 39 144	153 39 220
Stradbroke Island	Alf's reef Pinnacle	Off Jumpinpin Bar	27 44 220	153 33 270
Stradbroke Island	Black King Reef		27 39 960	153 42 570
Stradbroke Island	Bobs Reef	32 Fathoms	27 42 470	153 42 600
Stradbroke Island	Cathedral		27 35 220	153 36 680
Stradbroke Island	Cotton Reef		27 47 200	153 33 110
Stradbroke Island	Cotton Reef		27 47 474	153 36 532
Stradbroke Island	Cotton Reef		27 48 100	153 33 200
Stradbroke Island	East of J/Pin		27 41 940	153 33 510
Stradbroke Island	Fish Board Reef		27 42 326	153 33 559
Stradbroke Island	Hutchinson Shoal		27 56 600	153 29 230
Stradbroke Island	Jew Reef		27 43 340	153 35 501
Stradbroke Island	Lump		27 34 906	153 35 846
Stradbroke Island	No name	36 fathoms	27 39 300	153 36 750
Stradbroke Island	No name	40 fathoms	27 39 500	153 42 500
Stradbroke Island	No name	120 fathoms	27 39 680	153 52 740
Stradbroke Island	No name	40 fathoms	27 40 020	153 42 420
Stradbroke Island	No name	30 fathoms	27 42 240	153 43 010
Stradbroke Island	No name	40 fathoms	27 42 323	153 43 754
Stradbroke Island	No name	45 fathoms	27 42 510	153 43 790
Stradbroke Island	No name	50 fathoms	27 43 190	153 53 600
Stradbroke Island	No name	40 fathoms	27 43 440	153 43 600
Stradbroke Island	No name	40 fathoms	27 43 446	153 43 607
Stradbroke Island	No name	34 fathoms	27 48 473	153 36 476
Stradbroke Island	No name	36 fathoms	27 48 487	153 36 520
Stradbroke Island	No name	34 fathoms	27 48 610	153 36 456
Stradbroke Island	No name	36 fathoms	27 48 850	153 37 480
Stradbroke Island	No name	34 fathoms	27 49 197	153 36 484
Stradbroke Island	No name	34 fathoms	27 49 274	153 37 450
Stradbroke Island	No name	40 fathoms	27 51 100	153 44 600
Stradbroke Island	No name	25 fathoms	27 52 000	153 32 500
Stradbroke Island	No name	22 fathoms	27 52 645	153 30 640

Locality	Description	Comments	Latitude	Latitude
Stradbroke Island	No name	36 fathoms	27 53 155	153 37 925
Stradbroke Island	No name	26 fathoms	27 55 500	153 33 150
Stradbroke Island	No name	18 fathoms	27 55 626	153 28 921
Stradbroke Island	No name	36 fathoms	27 55 946	153 38 389
Stradbroke Island	No name	22 fathoms	27 56 139	153 31 341
Stradbroke Island	No name	20 Fathoms	27 56 253	153 30 887
Stradbroke Island	No name	10 fathoms	27 56 724	153 26 722
Stradbroke Island	No name	20 fathoms	27 56 750	153 29 510
Stradbroke Island	No name	10 fathoms	27 57 000	153 26 570
Stradbroke Island	No name	40 fathoms	27 57 000	153 43 000
Stradbroke Island	No name	26 fathoms	27 57 100	153 32 510
Stradbroke Island	Off Jumpinpin		27 42 280	153 33 550
Stradbroke Island	One Mile		27 57 055	153 26 983
Stradbroke Island	Pin Reef–North East	50 m	27 37 241	153 36 624
Stradbroke Island	Pinnacle	30 fathoms	27 39 220	153 36 551
Stradbroke Island	Reef off Pin Bar	21 fathoms	27 43 160	153 32 852
Stradbroke Island	Scottish Prince		27 57 600	153 26 150
Stradbroke Island	Scottish Prince	Wreck	27 57 700	153 26 120
Stradbroke Island	Southport Seaway		27 56 124	153 25 900
Stradbroke Island	Sullie's mark		27 38 540	153 36 580
Stradbroke Island	Sullies Reef	50 m. snapper	27 41 470	153 33 550
Sunshine Coast / Maroochydore	36 Fathom East		26 56 015	153 38 139
Sunshine Coast / Maroochydore	Arkwright Point		26 32 690	153 07 840
Sunshine Coast / Maroochydore	Arkwright Shoals	Fishes best at night	26 33 200	153 10 000
Sunshine Coast / Maroochydore	Barwon Banks		26 29 145	153 34 92
Sunshine Coast / Maroochydore	Barwon Banks		26 32 000	153 31 500
Sunshine Coast / Maroochydore	Barwon Banks		26 32 090	153 31 813
Sunshine Coast / Maroochydore	Barwon Banks		26 36 500	153 30 500
Sunshine Coast / Maroochydore	Barwon Banks		26 36 800	153 30 000

Locality	Description	Comments	Latitude	Latitude
Sunshine Coast / Maroochydore	Bowling Green		26 30 000	153 25 000
Sunshine Coast / Maroochydore	Bowling Green East		26 32 300	153 29 000
Sunshine Coast / Maroochydore	Brennan Shoal	Take care	27 01 210	153 29 140
Sunshine Coast / Maroochydore	Caloundra 12 Mile		26 48 250	153 18 000
Sunshine Coast / Maroochydore	Caloundra 12 Mile		26 48 410	153 17 000
Sunshine Coast / Maroochydore	Caloundra 12 Mile		26 49 520	153 16 710
Sunshine Coast / Maroochydore	Caloundra Patches		26 46 400	153 11 910
Sunshine Coast / Maroochydore	Caloundra South		26 55 300	153 17 100
Sunshine Coast / Maroochydore	Caloundra Wide		26 46 000	153 26 100
Sunshine Coast / Maroochydore	Caloundra Wide		26 47 800	153 25 200
Sunshine Coast / Maroochydore	Caloundra Wide		26 48 500	153 18 550
Sunshine Coast / Maroochydore	Caloundra Wide		26 50 500	153 26 400
Sunshine Coast / Maroochydore	Caloundra Wide 2	Snapper	26 50 580	154 31 620
Sunshine Coast / Maroochydore	Caloundra Wide SE		26 50 000	153 19 250
Sunshine Coast / Maroochydore	Caloundra Wide SW		26 49 300	153 18 000
Sunshine Coast / Maroochydore	Coolum		26 32 720	153 07 750
Sunshine Coast / Maroochydore	Coolum	Best at night, close in. Hole.	26 34 250	153 15 300
Sunshine Coast / Maroochydore	Currimundi	18 m	26 44 900	153 10 511
Sunshine Coast / Maroochydore	Currimundi North		26 44 000	153 10 300
Sunshine Coast / Maroochydore	Currimundi South		26 45 250	153 10 550
Sunshine Coast / Maroochydore	Curtain Artificial Reef	14 m. Winter snapper.	27 06 600	153 21 750
Sunshine Coast / Maroochydore	Deep Tempest		27 07 064	153 33 140

Locality	Description	Comments	Latitude	Latitude
Sunshine Coast / Maroochydore	Deep Tempest		27 07 071	153 34 310
Sunshine Coast / Maroochydore	Deep Tempest		27 07 434	153 34 773
Sunshine Coast / Maroochydore	Deep Tempest		27 07 971	153 34 310
Sunshine Coast / Maroochydore	Deep Tempest		27 08 828	153 34 014
Sunshine Coast / Maroochydore	Franks Reef		27 06 668	153 28 803
Sunshine Coast / Maroochydore	Gneerings Shoals		26 38 610	153 10 250
Sunshine Coast / Maroochydore	Hamilton Patches		26 50 700	153 09 800
Sunshine Coast / Maroochydore	Hamilton Patches North		26 47 250	153 12 550
Sunshine Coast / Maroochydore	Hamilton Patches South	24 m	26 50 300	153 13 250
Sunshine Coast / Maroochydore	Hancock Shoal		26 30 400	153 06 500
Sunshine Coast / Maroochydore	Kingfish Reef		26 40 070	153 42 470
Sunshine Coast / Maroochydore	Leach Shoal		26 39 300	153 12 300
Sunshine Coast / Maroochydore	Lump		26 46 887	153 27 209
Sunshine Coast / Maroochydore	Murphy's North	Reef	26 41 000	153 15 300
Sunshine Coast / Maroochydore	Murphy's Reef		26 40 050	153 14 310
Sunshine Coast / Maroochydore	Murphy's Reef		26 43 620	153 16 950
Sunshine Coast / Maroochydore	No name	60 m	26 50 390	153 27 170
Sunshine Coast / Maroochydore	North Moreton Trench	Marlin, sailfish	26 56 300	153 23 400
Sunshine Coast / Maroochydore	Raper Shoal		26 45 300	153 09 200
Sunshine Coast / Maroochydore	Shallow Tempest		27 05 400	153 28 750
Sunshine Coast / Maroochydore	Smith Rock W	Sweetlip, snapper.	27 00 290	153 28 050
Sunshine Coast / Maroochydore	The Rock at Tempest		27 07 726	153 34 810

Locality	Description	Comments	Latitude	Latitude
Sunshine Coast / Maroochydore	Twelve Mile	50 m	26 43 000	153 21 000
Sunshine Coast / Maroochydore	Twelve Mile		26 43 000	153 28 000
Townsville	Merinda Shoals		19 09 000	147 38 160
Townsville	10 mile shoal - Alva beach	Mixed Species	19 20 109	147 37 257
Townsville	8 mile shoal - Alva beach	Mixed Species	19 22 997	147 34 334
Townsville	Albino Rock	Mixed Species	18 46 476	146 43 199
Townsville	Balgal creek	Mixed Species	19 00 146	146 24 917
Townsville	Bels Bomber	Cobia and other Reef species	18 55 030	147 09 240
Townsville	Bohle River	Mixed Species	19 06 930	147 15 840
Townsville	Bomber	Mixed Species	18 56 000	147 10 130
Townsville	Chilcott Rock	Mixed Species	18 47 421	146 42 989
Townsville	Discovery Wreck	Mackerel, Cobia, Nannygai	18 45 000	147 28 050
Townsville	Hidden Reef	Coral Trout, Mackerel, Sweetlip and Red emperor	18 56 604	146 42 147
Townsville	Merinda Shoals	Red Emperor and other reef species	19 11 250	147 37 800
Townsville	Molongle Creek	Mixed Species	19 49 560	147 42 140
Townsville	Old Reef	Cape Upstart, Coral Trout and Red Emperor	19 22 000	148 03 000
Townsville	Sally	Mixed Species	19 10 780	147 03 700
Townsville	Sea Hound - Cordelia	Mixed Species	19 00 110	146 43 530
Townsville	Sea Hound - Lucinda	Mixed Species	18 24 439	146 25 752
Townsville	Wreck of Trawler	Nannygai, Trevally and Sweet lips	19 19 800	147 37 500
Townsville	Yongala	Mixed Species	18 55 965	147 10 198
Weipa	9 Mile Reef	Reef and Rubble Patches, Mackerel and Tuna	12 57 504	141 26 625
Weipa	Bones	Gun Mackerel	12 57 490	141 26 609
Weipa	Cats Eyes	Shallow Reef, Black Spot Tusk fish	12 27 416	141 35 774
Weipa	Mangrove Island	Cod, Fingermark, Jacks and Barramundi	12 35 194	141 47 721
Weipa	Mission River Bridge	Barramundi	12 36 061	141 53 667
Weipa	Weipa Billfish Club FAD1	Dolphin Fish, Marlin and Sailfish	12 49 762	141 32 658
Weipa	Westminster Reef	Reef and Rubble, Queenfish, Mackerel and Tuna	12 43 281	141 44 003
Yepoon	27 Mile	Mixed Species	23 08 010	151 29 200
Yepoon	40 acre	Sweet lip, Coral Trout, Mackerel, Cobia	23 08 985	250 53 314
Yepoon	Baron Ground	Mixed Species	23 08 600	151 20 200
Yepoon	Baron Wreck	Reef Species	23 09 700	151 15 700
Yepoon	Corio HD Barge	Mixed Species	22 57 540	150 49 350

Locality	Description	Comments	Latitude	Latitude
Yepoon	Corio HD Barge 2	Mixed Species	22 58 000	150 50 000
Yepoon	Fam'Brch	Mixed Species	23 03 690	150 46 880
Yepoon	Finlay's Reef 1	Variety of Reef Species	23 00 200	150 49 800
Yepoon	Finlay's Reef 2	Variety of Reef Species	23 00 100	150 49 720
Yepoon	Finlay's Reef 3	Variety of Reef Species	23 00 100	150 49 660
Yepoon	Flat Island	Coral Trout, Nannygai, Sweetlip	22 44 137	151 00 110
Yepoon	Greasy Alley	Nannygai, Mackerel, Cobia and Marlin	23 02 869	150 59 327
Yepoon	Hannah's Rock	Mixed Species	23 11 970	150 00 180
Yepoon	Hannah's Rock 2	Mixed Species	23 12 970	150 59 327
Yepoon	Hannah's Rock 3	Mixed Species	23 12 200	150 00 180
Yepoon	Hummocy Bombie	Mixed Species	23 08 100	151 23 600
Yepoon	Liza Jane Shoal	Mackerel, Coral Trout, Sweetlip	23 18 341	151 04 877
Yepoon	Nth greasy Alley	Nannygai, Mackerel, Cobia and Marlin	23 03 000	150 59 100
Yepoon	Nth Man and Wife	Mixed Species	23 05 900	150 59 500
Yepoon	Outer Rock	Mixed Species	23 02 863	150 59 331
Yepoon	Patch off Conical	Mixed Species	23 02 060	150 52 300
Yepoon	Patch off Conical 2	Mixed Species	23 02 900	150 52 590
Yepoon	Perforated Island	Produces great Reef and Pelagic action	22 39 336	150 56 876
Yepoon	Pinnacles	Grunter, Black Jew, Fingermark, Mackerel, Trevally	22 50 422	150 56 600
Yepoon	Ross Reef	Sweet lip, Coral Trout, Mackerel, Cobia	23 06 315	150 53 121
Yepoon	Wide Grounds 1	Mixed Species	22 51 700	151 12 700
Yepoon	Wide Grounds 2	Mixed Species	22 52 220	151 12 350
Yepoon	Wide Grounds 3	Mixed Species	22 52 700	151 15 600
Yepoon	Wide Grounds 4	Mixed Species	22 53 380	151 15 050

NEW SOUTH WALES

Locality	Description	Comments	Latitude	Latitude
Ballina	Ballina	32 fathoms South	28 59 613	153 39 825
Ballina	Ballina 42 fathoms South		28 55 327	153 46 283
Ballina	Ballina 42 fathoms South		28 56 945	153 46 345
Ballina	Black Head		28 51 670	153 36 570
Ballina	Lennox Head	32 fathoms	28 49 620	153 41 940
Ballina	No name	32 fathoms	28 54 965	153 40 825
Ballina	No name	Mackerel grounds, 20 m	28 56 700	153 32 820
Ballina	North Riordans	Mackerel	28 58 260	153 31 487
Ballina	South Riordans	Mackerel	29 00 400	153 30 152
Batemans Bay	Charter Boat Reef	Reef Ground	35 48 200	150 19 146
Batemans Bay	Charter Boat Reef 2	Reef Ground. Deep	35 51 600	150 23 150
Batemans Bay	Malua Bay SE	40 m. Snapper, reef species.	35 49 311	150 14 984
Batemans Bay	No name	Yellowfin	35 49 520	150 31 525
Batemans Bay	Redfin Reef	Morwong, snapper, parrot fish reef species. Reef/gravel bottom. Water depth 45 m.	35 47 892	150 17 138
Batemans Bay	Redfin Reef #2	Morwong, snapper, parrot fish, reef species. Reef/gravel bottom. Water depth 45 m	35 48 019	150 17 170
Batemans Bay	The Chimney	Cod, sergeant baker, wrasse, groper. Water depth 9–27 m. Sandy with broken reef bottom.	35 46 550	150 14 450
Batemans Bay	Tom's mark	40 m. Morwong, snapper, reef species.	35 48 808	150 15 334
Bateman's Bay	Moruyan Canyon	Various Species	35 54 950	150 32 780
Bateman's Bay	Tennent Reef	Snapper,Trevally	35 45 537	150 15 400
Bateman's Bay	Tollgate Island	Various Reef Species	35 45 000	150 55 400
Bermagui	100 fathoms		36 25 120	150 18 240
Bermagui	1000 fathoms		36 25 120	150 24 420
Bermagui	12 Mile Reef	Tuna, shark, marlin.	36 29 240	150 15 000
Bermagui	12 Mile Reef – bottom		36 31 622	150 15 000
Bermagui	12 Mile Reef Central		36 30 000	150 15 000
Bermagui	12 Mile Reef E		36 30 000	150 16 000
Bermagui	12 Mile Reef NE		36 27 000	150 16 000
Bermagui	12 Mile Reef NW	Mixed reef fish	36 27 000	150 14 200
Bermagui	12 Mile Reef S	Mixed Reef Fish	36 32 800	150 15 000
Bermagui	12 Mile Reef SE		36 32 800	150 16 000
Bermagui	12 Mile Reef South	Reef	36 27 100	150 15 000
Bermagui	12 Mile Reef South	Reef	36 32 400	150 14 200
Bermagui	12 Mile Reef SW	Mixed reef fish	36 32 800	150 14 000

Locality	Description	Comments	Latitude	Latitude
Bermagui	12 Mile Reef W		36 30 000	150 14 000
Bermagui	4 Mile Reef		36 24 570	150 08 990
Bermagui	4 Mile Reef Centre	Tuna, shark, morwong, snapper	36 24 000	150 08 400
Bermagui	4 Mile Reef North		36 22 400	150 09 050
Bermagui	4 Mile Reef North	Reef	36 25 090	150 08 990
Bermagui	4 Mile Reef South		36 25 000	150 00 800
Bermagui	6 Mile		36 26 440	150 10 000
Bermagui	6 Mile Reef Centre	Tuna, shark, marlin	36 24 440	150 10 000
Bermagui	6 Mile Reef NE		36 25 500	150 10 500
Bermagui	6 Mile Reef North	Reef	36 25 300	150 09 350
Bermagui	6 Mile Reef NW	Flathead, morwong	36 25 020	150 09 160
Bermagui	6 Mile Reef SE		36 28 300	150 09 000
Bermagui	6 Mile Reef South	Reef	36 28 100	150 08 300
Bermagui	7 Mile Reef	Reef ground, 105 m deep	36 30 150	150 10 160
Bermagui	Bait ground		36 25 368	150 04 509
Bermagui	Bait Hole		36 29 000	150 17 000
Bermagui	Bermagui canyon n		36 20 750	150 20 450
Bermagui	Bermagui Harbour	Navigation point at ramp	36 25 490	150 04 380
Bermagui	Bermagui Lobster 1	Lobster reef–yellowtail kingfish, morwong, snapper	36 30 490	150 06 380
Bermagui	Bermagui Lobster 2	Reef–yellowtail	36 29 850	150 06 440
Bermagui	Bermagui Water Tank	100 fathom line east of.	36 25 807	150 18 200
Bermagui	Bermi Canyon	South west	36 24 450	150 22 100
Bermagui	Bermi Canyon	South east	36 24 500	150 24 300
Bermagui	Bunga		36 32 698	150 06 460
Bermagui	Bunga Head	Navigation point	36 34 590	150 03 200
Bermagui	Bunga Head Shelf	100 fathom mark	36 34 900	150 17 400
Bermagui	Camel Rock	Flathead and reef fish.	36 23 005	150 05 142
Bermagui	Cemetary	Flathead	36 20 830	150 07 200
Bermagui	Coral Reef – centre of		36 38 000	150 05 000
Bermagui	Cuttagee Lake Entrance	Navigation point	36 29 400	150 03 200
Bermagui	Entrance Yachta Patch		36 25 250	150 05 070
Bermagui	Fish Trap		36 29 452	150 06 914
Bermagui	Four Mile–Bermagui	47 m	36 24 000	150 08 300
Bermagui	Gaolen Head	Broken reef	36 34 000	150 04 200

Locality	Description	Comments	Latitude	Latitude
Bermagui	Gaolen Wide Reef	Shale	36 33 900	150 05 800
Bermagui	Goelen Shelter	Good shelter in w–flathead	36 32 390	150 06 060
Bermagui	Light at entrance to Harbour		36 25 400	150 04 600
Bermagui	Montague gravel		36 20 665	150 16 099
Bermagui	No name	Albacore	36 21 027	150 21 270
Bermagui	No name	Tuna	36 21 980	150 22 562
Bermagui	No name	Flathead	36 22 407	150 06 460
Bermagui	No name		36 24 421	150 04 851
Bermagui	No name		36 24 451	150 04 798
Bermagui	No name		36 24 646	150 04 665
Bermagui	No name		36 25 471	150 08 979
Bermagui	No name		36 25 873	150 08 716
Bermagui	No name	Morwong	36 29 318	150 06 401
Bermagui	No name	Tuna	36 30 730	150 21 512
Bermagui	No name		36 32 348	150 04 572
Bermagui	North Bunga		36 34 060	150 19 060
Bermagui	SE Bermi	1000 fathoms	36 34 040	150 22 260
Bermagui	Six Mile	75 m	36 26 300	150 09 600
Bermagui	Six Mile north	60 m	36 25 100	150 10 100
Bermagui	South Bermagui – bottom fishing		36 28 000	150 04 600
Bermagui	South Reef	Ground–pelagics and bottom fish in calm waters	36 30 620	150 15 760
Bermagui	The Foulhouse	Reef	36 25 125	150 12 846
Bermagui	Tuna YF drift	Yellowfin tuna	36 21 710	150 18 440
Botany Bay	59 m peak		33 58 700	151 21 570
Botany Bay	Bare Island Bommie	Botany Bay. Snapper, mulloway. Water depth 7.5 m. Reef bottom.	33 59 771	151 13 833
Botany Bay	Boat Harbour	35–40 m. Snapper, morwong, flathead, kingfish, leatherjackets	34 02 990	151 12 270
Botany Bay	Boomerang Reef	Reef fish, snapper, mulloway, kingfish, leatherjacket, flathead, bream. Water depth 60 m. Rock bottom.	34 04 500	151 12 600
Botany Bay	Botany Bay Heads		34 00 257	151 14 265
Botany Bay	Botany Heads Wide		34 02 460	151 15 300
Botany Bay	Botany Heads Wide		34 03 000	151 27 000
Botany Bay	Browns Mountain		34 02 130	151 39 400
Botany Bay	Browns Mountain 2	Water depth 220 fathoms. Rocky bottom.	34 02 061	151 39 227

Locality	Description	Comments	Latitude	Latitude
Botany Bay	Browns Mountain 3	Groper, hapuka, yellowfin, mako shark, marlin	34 01 541	151 38 803
Botany Bay	Browns Mountain 4	Marlin, tuna, shark, reef fish.	34 02 040	151 39 500
Botany Bay	Cronella Flathead Grounds	Sandy. Drift for tiger and sand flathead.	34 03 830	151 11 890
Botany Bay	Cronulla Offshore	Flathead	34 03 828	151 11 890
Botany Bay	Fish Trap	Water depth 300 fathoms.	34 03 053	151 37 502
Botany Bay	Fish Traps	Reef bottom. Water depth 120 m.	33 58 608	151 23 013
Botany Bay	Flathead	Sand bottom. Water depth 24 m.	34 04 118	151 10 803
Botany Bay	Flathead Drift	Flathead	34 07 055	151 09 050
Botany Bay	Hot Water	Sand bottom. Water depth 3m.	34 00 243	151 12 566
Botany Bay	Jew Nose	Botany Bay. Flathead, blue swimmer crab. Sand and weed bottom.	34 00 026	151 13 823
Botany Bay	Jibbon Bombora	Breaking water–danger.	34 04 850	151 10 550
Botany Bay	Jibbon Bombora W		34 04 900	151 10 450
Botany Bay	Jibbon Wide	Reef and gravel bottom. Water depth 126 m.	34 05 666	151 17 627
Botany Bay	Kurnell Car Park	Reef edge. 7–24 m. Be careful in a southerly. Snapper, morwong, kingfish, leatherjackets	34 01 320	151 14 300
Botany Bay	Last Ditch	Reef bottom.	34 01 768	151 13 861
Botany Bay	Lighthouse	Reef. Snapper, morwong, leatherjackets	34 02 200	151 14 000
Botany Bay	Long Reef Wide 3	Pelagics.	33 58 199	151 18 558
Botany Bay	Maroubra Peak	Drop Off. Snapper, morwong, kingfish.	33 58 580	151 21 780
Botany Bay	Mountains Reef	Marlin, yellowfin tuna.	34 01 550	151 25 610
Botany Bay	MV Mallabar	Wreck. Mulloway, tiger shark, kingfish. Water depth 9–13 m.	33 58 130	151 15 430
Botany Bay	No name	Water depth 65–100 m.	33 58 540	151 21 570
Botany Bay	No name	Water depth 65 m.	33 58 749	151 21 634
Botany Bay	No name	Reef bottom.	33 58 750	151 22 610
Botany Bay	No name	Reef bottom. Water depth 65 m.	33 58 800	151 21 500
Botany Bay	Osborn Shoal	12–24 m. Locate fish in area. Snapper, bream, mulloway, morwong, trevally, kingfish, flathead.	34 03 150	151 11 350
Botany Bay	Osborne Shoal	12–24 m. Locate fish in area. Snapper, bream, mulloway, morwong, trevally, kingfish, flathead.	34 03 520	151 11 240
Botany Bay	Osbourne Shoal 1	Tailor, redfish, kingfish. Reef bottom. Water depth 9 m. Dangerous in heavy swell.	34 03 580	151 10 770
Botany Bay	Osbourne Shoal 2	Reef bottom. Water depth 10 m.	34 03 592	151 11 211
Botany Bay	Osbourne Shoal 3	Kingfish, trevally, bream, yellowtail, sweep, snapper. Water depth 12–15 m. Reef bottom.	34 03 634	151 11 197
Botany Bay	Party Boat	Reef bottom. Water depth 80 m.	33 57 984	151 18 735

Locality	Description	Comments	Latitude	Latitude
Botany Bay	Peak	Anchor or troll. Marlin, tuna, sharks, albacore, dolphin fish, wahoo, kingfish other reef species.	33 58 680	151 21 570
Botany Bay	Peak No.1	Kingfish, snapper, mulloway, morwong, surface pelagics. Water depth 65 m. Reef bottom.	33 58 582	151 21 703
Botany Bay	Port Hacking		34 07 160	151 08 070
Botany Bay	Southeast Reef	Reef bottom. Water depth 64 m.	33 58 169	151 20 775
Botany Bay	Tancred	Wreck at 450 m	34 07 000	151 16 060
Botany Bay	Tank	1 km off Coogee Beach. Teraglin, mulloway. Reef bottom. Water depth 75m.	33 57 610	151 17 780
Botany Bay	Tank 1	Snapper. Reef bottom. Water depth 71 m.	33 57 660	151 17 660
Botany Bay	The Grave	Snapper, pigfish, morwong, flathead. Gravel bottom.	33 58 200	151 27 530
Botany Bay	The Peak	Tuna, marlin, shark, pelagic,	33 58 760	151 21 650
Botany Bay	The Plonk Hole		34 00 160	151 26 280
Botany Bay	The Wave Buoy	Kingfish, bonito, dolphin fish, tailor, salmon.	34 02 570	151 15 160
Botany Bay	Third Runway	Snapper, bream, flathead, tailor. Water depth 15 m. Sand bottom.	33 58 376	151 11 784
Botany Bay	Watts Reef		34 00 080	151 11 300
Botany Bay	Watts Reef 2	Reef bottom. Water depth 5 m.	34 00 023	151 13 021
Botany Bay	Waynes Spot	Sydney Heads. Morwong.	33 58 700	151 21 370
Broken Bay	2 Buoys	Snapper, kingfish, bonito, morwong. Water depth 36 m. Sand and gravel bottom.	33 46 730	151 20 372
Broken Bay	3 Buoys	Snapper, kingfish, bonito, morwong. Water depth 51 m. Sand and gravel bottom.	33 48 095	151 20 832
Broken Bay	3 Buoys North	Snapper, kingfish, bonito, morwong. Water depth 50 m. Sand and gravel bottom.	33 47 449	151 20 987
Broken Bay	30-36 M Ground		33 32 400	151 24 900
Broken Bay	4th point		33 31 770	151 29 140
Broken Bay	Avalon Gutter	35 m reef. Snapper, trevally, morwong, leatherjackets.	33 38 120	151 21 400
Broken Bay	Avoca Wide		33 30 050	151 32 300
Broken Bay	Bangalley Head	32 m. reef	33 37 172	151 21 714
Broken Bay	Barrenjoey	20 m Wreck	33 34 838	151 20 694
Broken Bay	Barrenjoey	Fix is eastern shore, Small reef extends SE for 500 m. Tideline shows from fix across reef on runout, small peak at 9 m drops to sand at 15 m. Fish drop-off into 15 m from bombora on nth side.	33 34 900	151 20 100
Broken Bay	Barrenjoey NE		33 34 750	151 20 050
Broken Bay	Barrenjoey Wide	36 fathoms. Reef species on pilchards, prawns and squid.	33 34 990	151 31 650

Locality	Description	Comments	Latitude	Latitude
Broken Bay	Big Red		33 32 117	151 25 043
Broken Bay	Birchgrove Wreck	Snapper, trevally, morwong, leatherjackets. Try pilchards, prawns and squid.	33 38 270	151 22 400
Broken Bay	Birchgrove wreck		33 38 440	151 22 570
Broken Bay	Blue Metal Grounds		33 44 490	151 49 888
Broken Bay	Bluefish Point	18–30 m. Yellowtail close in. Snapper, kingfish, trevally, bream, morwong.	33 48 430	151 18 450
Broken Bay	Bobs Spot	Morwong, snapper.	33 46 960	151 57 470
Broken Bay	Boltons Reef	Bonito. Snapper, morwong, flathead. Water depth 28–35 m. Gravel, sand, reef bottom.	33 36 471	151 22 399
Broken Bay	Boltons Reef 2	Snapper, flathead, reef fish. Water depth 62 m. Sand patches.	33 36 600	151 22 255
Broken Bay	Boltons Reef 3	Kingfish, yellowfin tuna.	33 36 632	151 22 106
Broken Bay	Boltons Reef 4	Snapper. reef species. Reef bottom.	33 36 396	151 22 145
Broken Bay	Boltons Reef 6		33 36 649	151 22 229
Broken Bay	Bombora		33 32 090	151 23 600
Broken Bay	Boultons	40 m. reef	33 36 550	151 22 416
Broken Bay	Boultons Reef	40–44 m	33 36 000	151 22 260
Broken Bay	Box head		33 32 970	151 20 710
Broken Bay	Box head		33 33 200	151 20 600
Broken Bay	Broken Bay	Flathead	33 34 000	151 22 000
Broken Bay	Broken bay inner		33 34 780	151 30 430
Broken Bay	Broken Bay Offshore		33 32 290	151 24 430
Broken Bay	Broken bay shelf		33 36 810	151 52 800
Broken Bay	Broken Bay Traps	Pelagics.	33 36 018	151 31 499
Broken Bay	Broken Bay Wide	63 fathoms.Reef species.	33 34 622	151 36 997
Broken Bay	Broken bay wide		33 35 050	151 31 810
Broken Bay	Broken Bay Wide	Reef species	33 36 287	151 25 306
Broken Bay	Bungan Head	Water depth 50 m.	33 40 320	151 21 850
Broken Bay	Bungan Wide	Snapper, mulloway. Water depth 32–40 m. Hard reef on mud bottom.	33 40 510	151 20 711
Broken Bay	Close In Snapper	Snapper	33 40 527	151 20 821
Broken Bay	Daniels Mark	Snapper, mulloway, shark, morwong. Water depth 80 m.	33 38 835	151 31 769
Broken Bay	Dave's Reef	Snapper, mulloway, reef species. Water depth 30 fathoms.	33 40 900	151 20 250
Broken Bay	Dee Why Headland	Snapper, jew, morwong, flathead 40–50 m, Sandy bottom, between reef	33 46 240	151 21 300

Locality	Description	Comments	Latitude	Latitude
Broken Bay	Dee Why Wide	54–58 m. Snapper, mulloway, morwong, kingfish, leatherjackets flathead, bonito, teraglin.	33 45 710	151 22 280
Broken Bay	Dee Why Wide	Marlin, shark, pelagic, snapper morwong, bream.	33 46 590	151 21 000
Broken Bay	East reef		33 33 010	151 24 420
Broken Bay	East Reef	22 m. reef	33 33 020	151 23 839
Broken Bay	East Reef Close	Snapper, yellowtail kingfish, bonito, tailor, reef fish. Water depth 21–30 m. Rock reef.	33 32 809	151 24 094
Broken Bay	East Reef North	Snapper, morwong, trevally, kingfish. Reef bottom.	33 33 650	151 24 060
Broken Bay	East reef wide		33 33 080	151 24 380
Broken Bay	East reef wide		33 33 560	151 24 030
Broken Bay	Esmeralda Close		33 39 640	151 24 604
Broken Bay	Esmeralda Reef	Snapper, morwong, trevally, kingfish. Reef bottom.	33 39 528	151 25 643
Broken Bay	Esmeralda Reef 2	Snapper, morwong, teraglin,	33 39 670	151 25 180
Broken Bay	Esmeralda Reef 3	Leatherjacket. Water depth 67 m. Broken reef, sand, gravel bottom. Snapper, reef species.	33 39 451	151 25 234
Broken Bay	Esmeralda Wide	Shark, marlin, snapper, kingfish, dolphinfish, striped tuna. Water depth 50 fathoms. Reef bottom.	33 39 765	151 25 958
Broken Bay	Esmerelda 1	65 m. reef Pelagic and reef species.	33 39 584	151 25 381
Broken Bay	Flathead Grounds1	Flathead.	33 34 164	151 26 744
Broken Bay	Flathead Grounds 2	Flathead.	33 35 100	151 26 000
Broken Bay	Flint and Steel		33 34 294	151 17 124
Broken Bay	Forresters wide		33 26 140	151 29 140
Broken Bay	Foul Grounds	Snapper, leatherjacket, kingfish, traglin.	33 46 930	151 21 025
Broken Bay	Freshwater Wide	44–50 m reef. Trevally, morwong, kingfish, leatherjackets, flathead.	33 46 500	151 21 800
Broken Bay	Glasshouse	Shark, snapper, mulloway.	33 39 020	151 21 100
Broken Bay	Glasshouse 2	Mako shark, kingfish. Water depth 50 m. Sand and broken bottom.	33 39 270	151 23 400
Broken Bay	Good Property	55 m. Snapper, bream, mulloway, morwong, trevally, kingfish, flathead, leatherjackets	33 44 510	151 21 980
Broken Bay	Halfway		33 31 891	151 25 726
Broken Bay	Hans Spot	Mulloway. Reef bottom.	33 33 000	151 21 000
Broken Bay	Iggy's Spot	Snapper, morwong. Water depth 25 m. Reef bottom.	33 46 110	151 19 410
Broken Bay	Jewhole	Shark, mulloway, teraglin, bream	33 41 570	151 20 150
Broken Bay	Kilcare bommie		33 33 273	151 23 882
Broken Bay	Little Head		33 36 500	151 20 800

Locality	Description	Comments	Latitude	Latitude
Broken Bay	Lobster ground		33 26 713	151 44 723
Broken Bay	Long Reef	Snapper, mulloway	33 43 680	151 21 410
Broken Bay	Long Reef	Snapper, yellowtail kingfish, mulloway.	33 47 500	151 26 000
Broken Bay	Long Reef Close	Snapper, kingfish. Water depth 21 m. Reef bottom.	33 44 409	151 19 677
Broken Bay	Long Reef Wall	26–8 m. Take care. Snapper, bream, trevally, kingfish. Dangerous.	33 44 370	151 19 500
Broken Bay	Long Reef Wide	56 m. Snapper, morwong, flathead and other reef species	33 44 450	151 22 250
Broken Bay	Long Reef Wide 2		33 45 560	151 22 220
Broken Bay	Long Reef Wreck	Wreck. Water depth 42 m.	33 43 086	151 20 943
Broken Bay	Lousy		33 34 892	151 21 741
Broken Bay	Maitland bay bommie		33 32 240	151 23 760
Broken Bay	Maitland Bay East Reef		33 32 126	151 23 743
Broken Bay	Manly/North Steyne Reef	13–7 m. Reef. Snapper, bream, mulloway, morwong, trevally, kingfish, flathead.	33 47 469	151 17 400
Broken Bay	Mc Masters		33 30 070	151 26 720
Broken Bay	Midway Reef	Hawkesbury River	33 32 700	151 23 200
Broken Bay	Mugs	30 m. reef	33 47 477	151 19 324
Broken Bay	Murphy's	50–40 m reef. Snapper, morwong, trevally, leatherjackets	33 47 495	151 22 045
Broken Bay	Murphy's 1	Morwong, trevally, yellowtail	33 47 600	151 22 100
Broken Bay	Narrabeen Wreck	Snapper, mulloway, morwong, kingfish, leatherjackets, sharks, teraglin.	33 43 112	151 19 444
Broken Bay	Newport Reef	Snapper, trevally, morwong, kingfish, leatherjackets	33 39 598	151 20 234
Broken Bay	No name	Bonito, tailor. Water depth 19 m rising from 28m. Reef bottom.	33 32 920	151 23 990
Broken Bay	No name		33 33 197	151 24 373
Broken Bay	No name	Juno Point	33 34 167	151 15 643
Broken Bay	No name	Dolphinfish, tuna, kingfish. Water depth 80 m. Broken reef bottom.	33 34 737	151 32 178
Broken Bay	No name	Wide fishtrap snapper, morwong, trevally, kingfish. Reef bottom.	33 34 855	151 31 773
Broken Bay	No name	Whale Beach	33 36 367	151 20 381
Broken Bay	No name	Cottage Point hairtail spot	33 36 603	151 12 317
Broken Bay	No name	Boultons Reef	33 36 610	151 22 246
Broken Bay	No name	Reggies	33 38 126	151 21 409
Broken Bay	No name	Snapper, morwong.	33 38 256	151 21 948

Locality	Description	Comments	Latitude	Latitude
Broken Bay	North Head Bommie	7–8 m. Be careful for breakers. Snapper, bonito, taylor, salmon.	33 48 990	151 18 290
Broken Bay	North of Broken Bay.	Leatherjacket, bream, tarwhine, jewfish. Water depth 40 m. Gravel bottom.	33 31 962	151 25 690
Broken Bay	Old Dee Why	Snapper, bream, shark.	33 46 590	151 19 400
Broken Bay	Old FAD	Tuna, dolphin fish. flat bottom. Water depth 60 fathoms.	33 34 442	151 36 101
Broken Bay	Pips		33 27 870	151 28 680
Broken Bay	Queenscliff Reef		33 47 575	151 17 725
Broken Bay	Reddie Run	Snapper. Gravel bottom.	33 39 500	151 21 000
Broken Bay	Reds		33 47 151	151 18 631
Broken Bay	Reggies	47 m	33 37 954	151 22 221
Broken Bay	Reggies Snapper	Snapper	33 38 501	151 21 752
Broken Bay	Reggies Snapper II	Snapper	33 38 656	151 21 330
Broken Bay	Snapper	Snapper. Water depth 50 fathoms. Reef bottom.	33 32 121	151 24 890
Broken Bay	Terrigal		33 26 460	151 29 290
Broken Bay	Terrigal		33 26 750	151 28 110
Broken Bay	Terrigal		33 27 170	151 27 570
Broken Bay	Terrigal		33 27 400	151 29 330
Broken Bay	Terrigal		33 27 450	151 28 000
Broken Bay	Terrigal		33 27 520	151 27 880
Broken Bay	Terrigal		33 27 620	151 30 730
Broken Bay	Terrigal		33 28 240	151 27 200
Broken Bay	Terrigal		33 28 460	151 33 010
Broken Bay	Terrigal		33 28 470	151 27 310
Broken Bay	Terrigal		33 28 730	151 27 080
Broken Bay	Terrigal 2.5 nm e		33 26 500	151 30 030
Broken Bay	Terrigal Wide		33 29 250	151 32 200
Broken Bay	Terrigal wide		33 29 520	151 32 750
Broken Bay	Terrigal wide		33 29 840	151 32 570
Broken Bay	Terrigal wide inner		33 27 880	151 33 930
Broken Bay	Terrigal wide north		33 28 560	151 32 990
Broken Bay	Terrigal wide nth		33 29 720	151 32 950
Broken Bay	The Colours		33 34 600	151 19 450
Broken Bay	The Flathouse	Flathead	33 33 690	151 28 690

Locality	Description	Comments	Latitude	Latitude
Broken Bay	The wreck		33 27 669	151 30 700
Broken Bay	Third Point		33 31 300	151 26 500
Broken Bay	Trap N	60 m	33 47 530	151 22 700
Broken Bay	Trap S	60 m	33 48 150	151 21 780
Broken Bay	Trawleys	Snapper, trevally, morwong, mulloway. Broken reef with sand. Water depth 28–30 m.	33 35 590	151 20 761
Broken Bay	Trawleys 2	Reef species. Reef bottom.	33 36 026	151 21 025
Broken Bay	Trawleys 3		33 36 222	151 20 977
Broken Bay	Trawleys 5	Mixed reef.	33 36 184	151 21 014
Broken Bay	Trawleys 6		33 36 593	151 20 760
Broken Bay	Trawleys 7		33 35 059	151 20 076
Broken Bay	Trawleys Reef 2	Kingfish, reef species.	33 35 618	151 21 182
Broken Bay	Trawleys Reef 3	Mulloway, yellowtail kingfish, snapper. Water depth 28–30 m.	33 35 951	151 21 091
Broken Bay	Tripod		33 46 910	151 22 600
Broken Bay	Tuna Hole		33 39 560	152 01 650
Broken Bay	Two Lights	Reef bottom. Water depth 80 m.	33 46 550	151 24 140
Broken Bay	Valiant Wreck 4		33 34 742	151 20 750
Broken Bay	Valiant Wreck 5		33 34 840	151 20 700
Broken Bay	Valiant Wreck 1	Sand bottom. Pelagics and reef species.	33 34 701	151 20 711
Broken Bay	Valiant Wreck 2	Kingfish, Snapper.	33 34 713	151 20 725
Broken Bay	Valiant Wreck 3	Kingfish, Reef species, snapper, morwong. Water depth 6 m gravel bottom.	33 34 793	151 20 657
Broken Bay	Wave Rider Buoy		33 46 100	151 25 045
Broken Bay	Wave Rider Buoys	Marlin, salmon, dolphin fish, wahoo, kingfish, trevally	33 46 302	151 25 045
Broken Bay	Wave Ryda		33 46 380	151 24 970
Broken Bay	Waverider Buoy		33 46 140	151 24 560
Broken Bay	West Reef	Snapper, tailor, bream.	33 32 221	151 22 114
Broken Bay	West Reef 1	Blue Groper and Wrasse	33 32 850	151 23 900
Broken Bay	West Reef 2	25 m. reef	33 33 330	151 22 099
Broken Bay	West Reef 3	Snapper and mulloway	33 33 442	151 22 196
Broken Bay	West Reef S		33 32 492	151 22 386
Broken Bay	West Reef SW		33 33 289	151 22 344
Broken Bay	Whale		33 47 070	151 22 480
Broken Bay	Whale 2	Tuna, marlin, shark, mulloway, teraglin, snapper.	33 47 000	151 22 550

Locality	Description	Comments	Latitude	Latitude
Broken Bay	Whale Beach		33 36 800	151 21 350
Broken Bay	Whale Beach 42m	Water depth 42 m.	33 36 800	151 22 300
Broken Bay	Wide 2	Dolphin fish.	33 35 005	151 31 081
Broken Bay	Wide E	Dropoff. Snapper, morwong, kingfish, mulloway, teraglin.	33 35 162	151 31 810
Broken Bay	Wide Main		33 35 018	151 31 633
Broken Bay	Wide Reef		33 31 420	151 25 070
Broken Bay	Winnie bay		33 29 240	151 27 360
Broken Bay	Wreck		33 32 616	151 25 447
Broken Bay	Wreck		33 45 715	151 21 828
Brunswick Heads	No name	19 fathoms	28 24 475	153 37 300
Brunswick Heads	No name	28 fathoms	28 31 550	153 41 275
Brunswick Heads	Norries Reef	42 m	28 20 610	153 38 285
Brunswick Heads	North Windarra Banks		28 25 950	153 42 000
Brunswick Heads	Windarra Banks		28 27 390	153 41 498
Byron Bay	FAD		28 35 002	153 38 005
Byron Bay	No name	32 fathoms	28 37 498	153 42 691
Byron Bay	No name	32 fathoms	28 37 957	153 42 764
Coffs Harbour	Coffs Canyon N	Inside drop off	30 17 380	153 26 600
Coffs Harbour	Coffs Canyon N	Outside drop off	30 17 900	153 27 100
Coffs Harbour	Coffs Canyon S	Inside drop off	30 18 200	153 26 000
Coffs Harbour	Coffs Canyon S	Outside drop off	30 19 000	153 27 630
Coffs Harbour	Jeffreys Shoal	32 m	30 19 600	153 11 700
Coffs Harbour	Mackerel Alley	Mackerel 15 m	30 04 020	153 13 330
Coffs Harbour	North coast		29 59 025	153 35 300
Coffs Harbour	North Rock	Snapper, mackerel, surface fish	29 58 600	153 16 200
Coffs Harbour	North Rock 1	Rough bottom snapper, pearl perch	30 15 660	153 16 240
Coffs Harbour	North Rock 10	Rough bottom snapper, pearl perch 60 m	30 07 370	153 18 990
Coffs Harbour	North Rock 11	Rough bottom snapper, pearl perch 60 m	30 24 360	153 15 610
Coffs Harbour	North Rock 12	Rough bottom snapper, pearl perch	30 25 720	153 15 510
Coffs Harbour	North Rock 13	Rough bottom snapper, pearl perch	30 26 500	153 13 570
Coffs Harbour	North Rock 14	Rough bottom snapper, pearl perch	30 27 630	153 14 170
Coffs Harbour	North Rock 15	Rough bottom snapper, pearl perch 60 m	30 05 890	153 22 060
Coffs Harbour	North Rock 16	Rough bottom snapper, pearl perch 40 m	30 04 900	153 16 590
Coffs Harbour	North Rock 17	Rough bottom snapper, pearl perch	30 03 420	153 23 120

Locality	Description	Comments	Latitude	Latitude
Coffs Harbour	North Rock 2	Rough bottom snapper, pearl perch	30 16 130	153 16 120
Coffs Harbour	North Rock 3	Rough bottom snapper, pearl perch 49 m	30 15 62	153 15 480
Coffs Harbour	North Rock 4	Rough bottom snapper, pearl perch 50 m	30 16 010	153 15 350
Coffs Harbour	North Rock 6	Rough bottom snapper, pearl perch	30 09 330	153 18 120
Coffs Harbour	North Rock 7	Rough bottom snapper, pearl perch	30 08 170	153 18 720
Coffs Harbour	North Rock 8	Rough bottom snapper, pearl perch	30 10 400	153 20 060
Coffs Harbour	North Rock 9	Rough bottom snapper, pearl perch	30 08 990	153 18 000
Coffs Harbour	Red rock		29 58 730	153 14 190
Coffs Harbour	Red Rock Canyon N	300 m	29 59 030	153 35 300
Coffs Harbour	Red Rock Canyon S		30 00 820	153 39 180
Coffs Harbour	Sawtell	Canyon	30 25 875	153 24 800
Coffs Harbour	Sawtell Canyon N		30 25 830	153 24 80
Coffs Harbour	Sawtell Canyon S		30 34 600	153 22 800
Coffs Harbour	Sawtell Shoal	Fishes well to the NE	30 22 100	153 07 900
Coffs Harbour	Solitary Canon N	300 m	29 51 400	153 43 000
Coffs Harbour	Solitary Canon N	300 m	29 52 025	153 44 900
Coffs Harbour	Solitary Canyon S	300 m	29 56 030	153 41 000
Coffs Harbour	Sth Coffs Canyon N		30 21 000	153 28 220
Coffs Harbour	Sth Coffs Canyon N		30 21 575	153 28 000
Coffs Harbour	Sth Coffs Canyon S		30 23 800	153 25 600
Coffs Harbour	Sth Coffs Canyon S		30 24 175	153 27 175
Coffs Harbour	The Drift	Snapper flathead	30 02 470	153 16 720
Coffs Harbour	The Patch	35 m	30 27 000	153 11 600
Coffs Harbour	The Trap	Snapper 15 m	30 04 740	153 12 990
Coffs Harbour	Whitmore Shoal		30 20 965	153 08 173
Coffs Harbour	Yamba canyon	Far north coast	29 29 100	153 47 600
Coffs Harbour	Yamba canyon	Far north coast	29 29 425	153 49 025
Eden	Bittangabee	Out from sheltered bay	37 12 880	150 02 710
Eden	Boydes Tower	Snapper	37 06 026	149 56 962
Eden	Boyde's Tower 2	Snapper	37 06 030	149 57 000
Eden	Boyds Tower	Snapper	37 06 030	149 56 960
Eden	Green Cape	Deep water	37 15 700	150 03 680
Eden	Green Cape Canyon	West	37 17 100	150 23 300
Eden	Green Cape Canyon	East	37 17 100	150 29 500

Locality	Description	Comments	Latitude	Latitude
Eden	Haycock	40 m. Shale	36 56 950	149 57 750
Eden	Horseshoe Reef	40 m	36 58 300	149 58 510
Eden	Hunter Rocks Reef. Merim-bula.	Snapper.	36 56 390	149 57 030
Eden	Lenards Island	Broken reef	37 01 810	149 58 510
Eden	Mowarry Point	32 m	37 08 650	150 01 280
Eden	North Head	43 m	37 03 770	149 57 130
Eden	Pambula River Mouth	Bait grounds.	36 56 270	149 55 310
Eden	Shallow Hunter	10 m	36 56 350	149 56 760
Eden	South Head	5 m	37 06 060	149 57 130
Eden	Twofold Bay Canyon	West	37 09 400	150 23 000
Eden	Twofold Bay Canyon	East	37 09 400	150 27 500
Forster	2EE's		32 07 250	152 39 540
Forster	5 Mile Reef 1		32 05 400	152 40 070
Forster	5 Mile Reef 2		32 05 150	152 40 670
Forster	Bait ground		32 10 757	152 31 313
Forster	Black Rock		32 05 820	152 33 500
Forster	Cape Hawk	Canyon	32 14 650	153 03 480
Forster	Cape Hawk	Canyon	32 15 350	153 05 850
Forster	Chinook string #6		32 05 380	152 38 970
Forster	Cliffys ground		32 06 950	152 38 600
Forster	DJ 1		32 06 240	152 39 150
Forster	DJ 2		32 07 670	152 39 500
Forster	Ellsies ground		32 05 275	152 40 190
Forster	Forster Barge	Reef Fish 27 m	32 09 230	152 32 360
Forster	Forster entrance		32 10 494	152 30 688
Forster	Forster Triangle		32 06 510	152 37 000
Forster	Hogan's Hole		32 07 420	152 35 600
Forster	Meagan's Hole		32 06 420	152 36 770
Forster	Ross's Ground		32 05 270	152 38 200
Forster	Tabs #2		32 06 242	152 39 153
Forster	Tabs #3		32 07 675	152 39 500
Forster	Tonys reef		32 10 927	152 38 433
Forster	Tony's Reef 2		32 10 920	152 38 480
Hat Head	Cooks Knob	Reef	31 00 274	153 06 709

Locality	Description	Comments	Latitude	Latitude
Hat Head	Dew Hole	25–28 fathoms. Good drifting	31 03 800	153 05 050
Hat Head	Fish Rock	Reef	30 56 435	153 06 076
Hat Head	Flathead Ground	Reef	31 03 072	153 04 865
Hat Head	Hat Head	Canyon	31 05 760	153 18 500
Hat Head	Inner Reef	34 fathoms (runs south)	31 03 250	153 05 240
Hat Head	No name	Canyon	31 06 170	153 19 680
Hat Head	North Reef	37 fathoms. (Flat running south)	31 01 480	153 06 310
Hat Head	SE Reef	37 fathoms	31 02 240	153 05 910
Hat Head	Second Reef	Reef	31 03 276	153 06 172
Hat Head	Snapper Hole	Reef	31 04 251	153 05 715
Hat Head	Third Reef	Reef	31 02 285	153 07 892
Hat Head	Trag Hole	Reef	31 04 024	153 05 665
Jervis Bay	Arch	Depth 25m	35 04 983	150 49 270
Jervis Bay	Aztec Reef	Depth 18m	35 06 723	150 46 033
Jervis Bay	Brooks Reef	Snapper and Reef Species	35 14 160	150 36 020
Jervis Bay	Drum Drumstick		35 02 320	151 04 460
Jervis Bay	Fairey Firefly	Depth 12m	35 00 905	150 44 313
Jervis Bay	JB Canyon NE	Canyon	35 13 000	151 06 600
Jervis Bay	JB Canyon NW	Canyon	35 13 000	150 51 600
Jervis Bay	JB Canyon SE	Canyon	35 16 160	151 00 400
Jervis Bay	JB Canyon SW	Canyon	35 16 600	151 00 400
Jervis Bay	Jervis Bay Canyon Mid	Canyon	35 11 200	151 03 450
Jervis Bay	Jervis Bay Canyon N	Canyon	35 08 150	151 02 250
Jervis Bay	Jervis Bay Canyon N	Canyon	35 10 650	151 00 600
Jervis Bay	Jervis Bay Canyon Sth	Canyon	35 12 200	151 59 050
Jervis Bay	Jervis Bay Canyon Sth	Canyon	35 12 620	151 02 000
Jervis Bay	Jervis canyons		35 08 650	151 05 000
Jervis Bay	Merimbula Wreck	Depth 0m	35 00 173	150 49 770
Jervis Bay	Mid Grounds	Mixed species	35 06 090	150 46 190
Jervis Bay	Northern Deep Reef	Depth 45m	35 05 609	150 47 908
Jervis Bay	Pyramid Cave	Mixed species	35 05 463	150 47 985
Jervis Bay	Smugglers Cave	Mixed species	35 04 628	150 49 691
Jervis Bay	Spider Cave	Mixed species	35 08 223	150 45 870
Jervis Bay	St George Canyon N	Canyon	35 13 600	150 57 800

Locality	Description	Comments	Latitude	Latitude
Jervis Bay	St George Canyon S	Canyon	35 15 600	151 00 200
Jervis Bay	St George Canyon S	Canyon	35 15 620	150 56 400
Jervis Bay	Wandra Wreck	Depth 20m	35 02 707	150 50 353
Jervis Bay	Waypoint 20	Reef fish, 100 m	35 05 920	150 50 880
Jervis Bay	Whorehouse	Depth 30m	35 05 151	150 49 037
Moruya	1st Reef 4 mile	40 m	35 55 181	150 12 729
Moruya	2nd Reef 5 mile	44 m	35 55 642	150 13 076
Moruya	40 m Reef		35 55 656	150 12 030
Moruya	50 m Reef		35 56 458	150 14 006
Moruya	Andy's spot	42 m. Reef fish	35 56 041	150 13 068
Moruya	Batemans Bay Canyon		35 53 000	150 36 015
Moruya	Batemans Bay Plateau		35 53 020	150 36 035
Moruya	Beyond 2nd Reef	42 m Snapper, trevally	35 56 169	150 13 356
Moruya	Broulee close	Drop off. Reef species	35 52 172	150 13 490
Moruya	Broulee Is S	22 m.	35 52 649	150 11 534
Moruya	Broulee Is SE	Reef. 40 m. Reef species	35 52 637	150 13 192
Moruya	Canyon		35 56 020	150 32 990
Moruya	Kingfish 1		35 53 931	150 10 775
Moruya	Kingfish 2		35 54 017	150 10 747
Moruya	Moruya Bar	Snapper	35 54 215	150 10 353
Moruya	Mossy Pt East	40 m. Flathead	35 52 008	150 13 490
Moruya	No name	Stripy tuna	35 53 432	150 28 213
Moruya	No name	Shelf	35 53 471	150 30 140
Moruya	No name	22 m.	35 55 329	150 11 106
Moruya	No name	Marlin	35 58 867	150 22 878
Moruya	Red Reef	Snapper, Trevally.	35 51 610	150 26 150
Moruya	Reef	44 m Kingfish, big snapper.	35 55 750	150 13 040
Moruya	Toragy Pt		35 54 557	150 10 605
Moruya	Toragy Pt		35 54 920	150 10 385
Moruya	Two Mile Reef	Drop 18 to 25 m.	35 53 922	150 10 858
Nambucca Head	Live Bait Grounds	3 fathoms. Very dangerous area	30 37 726	153 01 638
Nambucca Head	Nambucca	Canyon	30 41 450	153 18 650
Nambucca Head	Nambucca Canyon	300 m	30 42 400	153 20 650
Nambucca Head	No name	20 fathoms	30 36 390	153 04 600

Locality	Description	Comments	Latitude	Latitude
Nambucca Head	No name	23 fathoms	30 36 430	153 06 380
Nambucca Head	No name	20 fathoms	30 36 460	153 05 000
Nambucca Head	No name	28 fathoms. Very Flat	30 36 510	153 08 810
Nambucca Head	No name	22 fathoms	30 36 760	153 06 290
Nambucca Head	Nursery	16 fathoms	30 37 030	153 03 540
Nambucca Head	Sambo City	8 fathoms	30 36 670	153 01 950
Nambucca Head	Rowans Peak	Bluefin and Mackerel	30 36 880	153 01 850
Narooma	Aughinish Rock		36 16 400	150 12 800
Narooma	Aughinish Rocks Sth	Game fish tuna, shark, marlin, dolphin fish	36 17 200	150 13 000
Narooma	Auginsh Reef	Kingfish and Striped Tuna	36 16 438	150 12 880
Narooma	Bermi Canyon	North West	36 17 180	150 24 150
Narooma	Broken Reef		36 16 150	150 16 180
Narooma	Broken reef ne		36 10 000	150 19 000
Narooma	Broken reef se		36 18 500	150 17 000
Narooma	Craigs Spot.	Striped mackerel, mako shark	36 14 380	150 13 550
Narooma	Flathead ground		36 16 470	150 10 960
Narooma	Flathead ground		36 17 810	150 10 580
Narooma	Flathead ground		36 18 847	150 11 710
Narooma	Island light	Navigation point	36 15 200	150 13 600
Narooma	Montague broken		36 15 630	150 16 340
Narooma	Montague Canyon		36 15 054	150 21 067
Narooma	Montague Canyon		36 17 175	150 24 450
Narooma	Montague East	Marlin,Yellowfin and Tuna	36 16 460	150 21 420
Narooma	Montague Seamount N		36 10 000	150 37 000
Narooma	Montague Seamount S		36 19 000	150 35 000
Narooma	Montague South	Navigation point	36 16 073	150 13 092
Narooma	Mount Dromedary	Navigation point	36 18 500	150 01 700
Narooma	Narooma Entrance		36 12 660	150 08 010
Narooma	NE Canyon	West	36 17 180	150 24 450
Narooma	NE Canyon	East	36 17 200	150 20 600
Narooma	No name	Flathead	36 14 286	150 12 817
Narooma	No name		36 18 000	150 14 000
Narooma	No name		36 19 200	150 19 500
Narooma	No name		36 19 541	150 11 925

Locality	Description	Comments	Latitude	Latitude
Narooma	North end of Kink		36 17 120	150 19 450
Narooma	Presto	Yellowfin Tuna	36 19 480	150 21 020
Narooma	South end of Kink		36 18 480	150 19 100
Narooma	South Kink	Tuna	36 18 050	150 19 000
Narooma	The Kink		36 18 100	150 19 050
Newcastle	Birrusi Wide	Mixed species	32 50 320	152 04 040
Newcastle	Harvey Inner	Mixed species	32 50 160	152 00 240
Newcastle	Harveys outer		32 50 820	152 00 000
Newcastle	Jewhole	Mixed species	33 00 500	151 44 850
Newcastle	Lake Macquire Tyre Reef	Reef Species	33 03 840	151 37 610
Newcastle	Moon Island Wreck	Reef Species	33 05 530	151 43 450
Newcastle	Motor Mouth		32 52 480	151 56 090
Newcastle	Mudhole Reef		32 52 660	151 50 580
Newcastle	Newcastle Entrance		32 54 390	151 50 120
Newcastle	North Reef		32 54 000	151 50 820
Newcastle	Osprey		32 55 970	151 52 600
Newcastle	Pogonoski 1	Mixed species	32 58 680	151 45 580
Newcastle	Pogonoski 2	Mixed species	32 58 360	151 45 090
Newcastle	Pogonoski 3	Mixed species	32 58 810	151 50 310
Newcastle	Red buoy Newcastle		32 54 914	151 48 293
Newcastle	Surf Club Gravel 2	Mixed species	33 02 090	151 43 310
Newcastle	Sygna wreck		32 51 740	151 50 750
Newcastle	The bubbles	75 m	32 51 005	152 04 812
Newcastle	The Pines		32 55 260	151 50 120
Newcastle	The Steps	Take care	32 57 520	151 45 580
Newcastle	The Stones		32 51 000	152 04 810
Newcastle	The Tank		32 52 350	151 54 950
Newcastle	Top of the shot		32 54 150	152 06 500
Newcastle	Uralla	Mixed species	32 49 290	152 03 640
Newcastle	Uralla Wide 1		32 50 440	152 03 530
Newcastle	Uralla Wide 2		32 50 620	152 00 430
Newcastle	Valentines Ramp	Mixed species	33 00 640	151 37 770
Newcastle	Wave rider		32 54 954	151 48 456
Newcastle	Yarra Yarra		32 54 290	151 48 030

Locality	Description	Comments	Latitude	Latitude
Norah Head	Crackneck		33 23 790	151 32 630
Norah Head	Drum ground		33 24 160	151 38 920
Norah Head	Drummer		33 24 200	151 38 899
Norah Head	Faulkins		33 17 220	151 46 440
Norah Head	Faulklin plateau 1		33 17 980	151 43 970
Norah Head	Faulklin plateau 2		33 18 030	151 43 950
Norah Head	Foggy cave		33 24 150	151 32 210
Norah Head	Forresters tank		33 25 720	151 28 610
Norah Head	Grumpy		33 17 490	151 43 930
Norah Head	Harolds texas		33 22 707	151 40 870
Norah Head	Mollyhawk		33 24 000	151 32 550
Norah Head	Norah hd canyon mid		33 19 200	152 13 000
Norah Head	Norah Hd canyon n		33 17 100	152 19 000
Norah Head	Norah Hd canyon st		33 21 707	152 08 034
Norah Head	Norah Head		33 17 000	151 35 400
Norah Head	Norah Head Canyon Sth		33 24 500	152 10 100
Norah Head	Norah perch ground		33 23 830	151 45 800
Norah Head	Norah wide no.1		33 20 030	151 39 460
Norah Head	Norah wide no.2		33 20 370	151 39 010
Norah Head	Norah wide no.3		33 20 240	151 39 190
Norah Head	Shallow patch		33 23 951	151 32 095
Norah Head	South Faulklins, 3		33 17 160	151 45 260
Norah Head	Spot x		33 24 520	151 31 950
Norah Head	Sse foggy cave		33 24 300	151 32 190
Norah Head	Terrigal		33 24 120	151 32 330
Norah Head	Terrigal		33 24 280	151 31 870
Norah Head	Terrigal		33 24 303	151 38 974
Norah Head	Terrigal		33 24 340	151 32 010
Norah Head	Terrigal		33 24 370	151 31 840
Norah Head	Terrigal		33 24 500	151 31 060
Norah Head	Terrigal		33 25 280	151 30 360
Norah Head	Terrigal		33 25 320	151 30 760
Norah Head	Terrigal		33 25 350	151 30 250
Norah Head	Terrigal		33 25 480	151 29 560

Locality	Description	Comments	Latitude	Latitude
Norah Head	Terrigal		33 25 500	151 30 000
Norah Head	Terrigal		33 25 790	151 29 650
Norah Head	The banks		33 19 995	151 39 268
Norah Head	The drum ground		33 22 476	151 38 597
Norah Head	Toowoon bay bommie		33 21 610	151 32 490
Norah Head	Wamberal point		33 25 280	151 30 200
Norah Head	Wide 4		33 21 020	151 45 960
Nowra	3 Mile Reef	Snapper, morwong. Water depth 36–40 m. Reef bottom.	34 53 378	150 48 461
Nowra	Blue Eye Cod Gnd		34 47 900	151 10 760
Nowra	Broken Bay Wide		34 46 000	151 39 000
Nowra	Crookhaven Entrance	Navigation mark just outside Crookhaven River.	34 53 567	150 46 285
Nowra	First Reef		34 53 300	150 48 630
Nowra	Kiama Canyon		34 48 338	151 10 339
Nowra	Kiama Canyon N/E	Winter–gemfish, blueye trevalla summer–shark, marlin, yellowfin tuna. Water depth 260–380 m. Broken bottom reef and pinnacles, edge of shelf.	34 47 590	151 10 590
Nowra	Middle Ground		34 53 600	150 49 600
Nowra	Nowra Hill		34 53 200	150 48 400
Old Bar	Black Head Reef	29 m	32 04 350	152 35 390
Old Bar	Chini 3		32 04 740	152 39 680
Old Bar	Chinook string 1		31 58 576	152 40 548
Old Bar	Chinook string 2		32 01 215	152 39 817
Old Bar	Chinook string 3		32 01 743	152 39 682
Old Bar	Chinook string 4		32 02 364	152 39 516
Old Bar	Chinook string 5		32 04 110	152 39 209
Old Bar	Crowdy head canyon		31 58 700	153 05 750
Old Bar	Crowdy head canyon		32 00 300	153 08 000
Old Bar	Frank's Flathead Ground	50 m	32 04 670	152 38 380
Old Bar	King Ground North	39 m	32 04 300	152 39 650
Old Bar	Schnapper Rock	Snapper 20 m	32 01 660	152 36 138
Port Hacking	Artificial Reef North	SE Fromg Barrens Hut	34 05 660	151 10 658
Port Hacking	Artificial Reef south	SE Fromg Barrens Hut	34 05 936	151 10 438
Port Hacking	Balcony	South of Barrens Hut	34 05 957	151 09 820
Port Hacking	Barrens Hut	Depth 27m	34 05 388	151 10 452
Port Hacking	Lilli Pilli	Depth 13m	34 04 292	151 06 648

Locality	Description	Comments	Latitude	Latitude
Port Hacking	Marley Point	Depth 20m	34 06 960	151 09 111
Port Hacking	Marley Sponge Garden	Depth 22m	34 06 867	151 09 305
Port Hacking	Middle ground	Bate Bay, Depth 30m	34 04 348	151 11 457
Port Hacking	Oak Park	Cronulla Point, Depth 7m	34 04 208	151 09 441
Port Hacking	Osborne Shoals	Bate Bay, Depth 25m	34 03 496	151 11 291
Port Hacking	Red Rooster Reef	Bate Bay, depth 25m	34 04 673	151 10 937
Port Hacking	Shiprock	Port Hacking, Depth 15m	34 04 147	151 07 789
Port Hacking	Six Fathom Reef	Bate Bay, Depth 24m	34 04 207	151 10 287
Port Hacking	Six Fathom Reef East	Bate Bay, Depth 18m	34 04 219	151 10 360
Port Hacking	Voodoo	Depth 28m	34 02 983	151 12 033
Port Hacking	Windy point	Depth 11	34 04 004	151 09 503
Port Hacking	Xanadu Reef	North Cronulla, Depth 28m	34 02 957	151 12 187
Port Jackson	12 Mile		33 55 510	151 28 340
Port Jackson	12 Mile		33 55 510	151 28 650
Port Jackson	12 Mile		33 56 400	151 28 410
Port Jackson	12 Mile Reef		33 55 100	151 26 800
Port Jackson	Annie Millar	Wreck–nannygai, yellowtail	33 52 000	151 17 360
Port Jackson	BH_9M	Morwong, snapper, flathead Water depth 115 m. Gravel and sand bottom.	33 51 764	151 26 689
Port Jackson	Big Red		33 55 360	151 24 760
Port Jackson	Big Steve's Spot	Yellowtail kingfish, trevally, yellowfin tuna, snapper, marlin. Reef bottom.	33 56 760	151 21 650
Port Jackson	Bobby's Head Reef		33 55 320	151 16 080
Port Jackson	Gladesville Bridge	Paramatta River. Mulloway. Sand and rock bottom. Water depth 19–23 m.	33 50 515	151 08 750
Port Jackson	Middle Head	Bream, kingfish, mulloway, trevally, tailor, flathead and squid	33 49 600	151 16 200
Port Jackson	No name	Kingfish, snapper, mulloway.	33 55 000	151 21 150
Port Jackson	Nods		33 49 930	151 19 290
Port Jackson	Obelisk	Tuna, marlin, shark, bream, snapper, pelagics.	33 50 480	151 19 220
Port Jackson	Pines #2	Snapper, morwong, trevally.	33 53 735	151 20 053
Port Jackson	Reef	Kingfish, perch, trevally. Reef bottom. Water depth 124 m.	33 55 300	151 28 550
Port Jackson	South Head Wreck	Flathead, snapper, bream, trevally. Water depth 25 m. Wreck and sand bottom.	33 50 215	151 17 238
Port Jackson	Sydney Heads	43 m. Snapper, sweep, morwong, gurnard, trevally, flathead and the occasional mulloway.	33 50 000	151 18 000

Locality	Description	Comments	Latitude	Latitude
Port Jackson	Taylor's Bay north of channel	Bream, trevally, john dory, tailor and small kingfish	33 50 320	151 16 100
Port Jackson	The 12 miler	Marlin, tuna, sharks,albacore, dolphin fish, wahoo, kingfish	33 55 660	151 28 510
Port Jackson	The Colours		33 49 600	151 19 450
Port Jackson	The Colours		33 50 300	151 17 200
Port Jackson	The Colours	Bream, kingfish, mulloway, trevally, tailor, flathead.	33 50 930	151 17 650
Port Jackson	The Gap	Bream, Sea perch, old wife. Water depth 25–40 m.	33 50 790	151 17 200
Port Jackson	The Leads	Snapper, Reef species.	33 50 780	151 19 910
Port Jackson	The wreck	Yellowtail and snapper	33 52 070	151 17 860
Port Jackson	Thommos		33 51 802	151 20 462
Port Jackson	Top of Shot		33 53 927	153 04 555
Port Jackson	Trag Grounds	25–30 m. Snapper, morwong, kingfish, leatherjackets flathead.	33 56 070	151 16 240
Port Jackson	Wedding Cake Island	Can get live bait here. Snapper, kingfish, leatherjackets, bream.	33 55 544	151 15 900
Port Jackson	Wedding Cake Island East	Yellowtail Kingfish, baitfish.	33 55 544	151 16 082
Port Jackson	Wreck	Wreck–snapper, nannygai. Depth 75 m. Sand bottom.	33 54 770	151 19 640
Port Macquarie	Camden haven canyon		31 38 900	153 08 800
Port Macquarie	Camden haven canyon		31 39 350	153 10 350
Port Macquarie	First Reef	Reef	31 32 500	153 05 240
Port Macquarie	Port Macquarie canyon n		31 26 350	153 15 355
Port Macquarie	Port Macquarie canyon s		31 29 350	153 15 500
Port Macquarie	Port Macquarie peak		31 26 300	153 14 350
Port Macquarie	Pt. Plummer canyon		31 16 700	153 16 550
Port Macquarie	Pt. Plummer peak		31 20 700	153 13 650
Port Stephens	Air Force Reef		32 39 410	152 19 130
Port Stephens	Bait Wreck		32 43 350	152 11 580
Port Stephens	Big Gibber		32 29 830	152 24 470
Port Stephens	Big gibber reef		32 33 289	152 26 037
Port Stephens	Big sand hill		32 48 631	152 01 315
Port Stephens	Big Tommy		32 45 080	152 12 560
Port Stephens	Birrubi Wide		32 50 310	152 04 040
Port Stephens	Black marlin marina		32 43 154	152 08 831
Port Stephens	Blue Mud Gravel		32 43 130	152 18 490
Port Stephens	Bobs gravel		32 49 701	152 01 050

Locality	Description	Comments	Latitude	Latitude
Port Stephens	Broughton Pinnacle		32 38 840	152 17 350
Port Stephens	East head		32 37 540	152 20 220
Port Stephens	Edith Break Inner		32 29 110	152 30 050
Port Stephens	Esmeralda bay ent.		32 37 880	152 19 030
Port Stephens	Esmerelda 2		32 37 110	152 18 950
Port Stephens	Gibber gravel		32 32 850	152 22 650
Port Stephens	Gibber Inner		32 32 610	152 25 500
Port Stephens	Gibber Shoals		32 32 350	152 21 200
Port Stephens	Inner gibber		32 32 660	152 25 400
Port Stephens	Inner gibber north		32 32 600	152 25 490
Port Stephens	Inner light	Mark only	32 42 601	152 09 662
Port Stephens	Inner mungo (richo)		32 33 550	152 20 160
Port Stephens	Inner pinnacle		32 43 840	152 13 040
Port Stephens	Inner Vee		32 39 750	152 17 640
Port Stephens	Little island west		32 42 200	152 14 350
Port Stephens	Little rocky		32 46 200	152 09 400
Port Stephens	Marlin Reef 1		32 35 080	152 27 210
Port Stephens	Marlin Reef 2		32 35 151	152 27 281
Port Stephens	Marlin Reef 3		32 35 266	152 27 846
Port Stephens	Marlin Reef 4		32 35 270	152 27 350
Port Stephens	McLeay Wreck		32 42 340	152 14 710
Port Stephens	North island		32 36 130	152 19 420
Port Stephens	OJ's Reef	Mixed Species	32 40 850	152 18 550
Port Stephens	Outer "21"		32 40 130	152 19 520
Port Stephens	Outer Boulders		32 47 140	152 11 050
Port Stephens	Outer Edith		32 29 500	152 30 700
Port Stephens	Outer Gibber		32 33 250	152 26 190
Port Stephens	Outer light east		32 45 100	152 12 300
Port Stephens	Pinnacle	15 m	32 43 820	152 13 260
Port Stephens	Pinnacles		32 40 000	152 35 960
Port Stephens	Port Stephens ent		32 42 736	152 11 336
Port Stephens	Port Stephens Ent.		32 44 680	152 12 800
Port Stephens	Sea eagle		32 41 262	152 14 914
Port Stephens	Seal Rock Canyons	Canyon	32 33 100	153 57 800

Locality	Description	Comments	Latitude	Latitude
Port Stephens	Shark island		32 44 670	152 12 600
Port Stephens	Sisters		32 36 700	152 17 300
Port Stephens	South Sisters		32 36 910	152 17 020
Port Stephens	Springers reef		32 34 440	152 29 920
Port Stephens	The Big M		32 39 650	152 19 570
Port Stephens	The Oaklands		32 48 800	152 14 010
Port Stephens	Three Mile 1		32 35 380	152 23 260
Port Stephens	Three Mile 2		32 35 880	152 23 260
Port Stephens	Tomaree Head		32 42 760	152 11 480
Port Stephens	Traps		32 43 570	152 42 450
Port Stephens	Vee Pinnacle	Mixed Species	32 38 940	152 17 350
Seal Rocks	7 Mile Reef		32 16 840	152 36 230
Seal Rocks	7 Mile Reef 1		32 16 080	152 34 570
Seal Rocks	Middle 7 Mile		32 16 150	152 35 270
Seal Rocks	Seal Rock Canyons	Canyon	32 23 600	153 01 100
Seal Rocks	Sugar Loaf Point	Mixed Species	32 26 600	152 32 420
Seal Rocks	Werner's	20 m	32 25 057	152 33 640
Shoalhaven	Ajax		34 57 790	150 54 730
Shoalhaven	Banks East		34 57 120	150 56 460
Shoalhaven	Banks East	Tuna, marlin, kingfish, Bottom species.	34 58 300	150 54 100
Shoalhaven	Banks North	Tuna, marlin, kingfish, bottom species.	34 56 640	150 56 410
Shoalhaven	Berry On Steps	Water depth 100 fathoms	34 57 860	151 05 170
Shoalhaven	Bills		34 57 100	150 48 480
Shoalhaven	Block and Cheese	Snapper, morwong, kingfish. Water depth 90 m.	34 58 200	150 58 380
Shoalhaven	Block and Cheese		34 58 442	150 59 158
Shoalhaven	Burkett's Reef	Snapper, morwong, kingfish. Water depth 30 m.	34 54 465	150 48 123
Shoalhaven	Crookhaven Heads		34 54 490	150 49 680
Shoalhaven	Culburra Banks 1		34 56 320	150 54 140
Shoalhaven	Culburra Banks 2		34 56 470	150 55 380
Shoalhaven	Culburra Bombora		34 55 673	150 47 047
Shoalhaven	East Reef		34 59 560	150 50 050
Shoalhaven	Inside Reef		34 54 498	150 55 797
Shoalhaven	Kill	Kiama	35 01 580	151 05 150
Shoalhaven	No name	Snapper, morwong. Reef bottom.	34 57 264	150 54 693

Locality	Description	Comments	Latitude	Latitude
Shoalhaven	Rods Red		34 57 730	150 53 870
Shoalhaven	Sir John Young Banks		34 58 650	150 52 880
Shoalhaven	Sir Joseph Young Banks		34 56 940	150 55 660
Shoalhaven	Steps		34 56 254	150 54 341
Shoalhaven	The Banks	Reef species and pelagic species. Water depth 23 m. Reef bottom.	34 56 945	150 55 664
Shoalhaven	The Mud		34 56 400	150 54 920
South West Rocks	1st Reef	11 fathoms	30 44 700	153 00 400
South West Rocks	Andies 1	37–40 fathoms	30 44 880	153 09 380
South West Rocks	Andies 2	29 fathoms	30 44 890	153 07 400
South West Rocks	Bait reef		30 52 630	153 03 130
South West Rocks	Boulders	Live Bait Grounds	30 52 910	153 02 560
South West Rocks	Breakwall	Navigation Point	30 52 354	153 01 714
South West Rocks	Buoy	Bait ground	30 52 650	153 03 080
South West Rocks	Fish rock north		30 55 930	153 06 850
South West Rocks	Fish rock s.w.		30 55 020	153 06 860
South West Rocks	Goal Peak	Snapper (19 fathoms)	30 51 790	153 04 720
South West Rocks	Grassy hd bait grnd	10 m	30 47 320	153 00 320
South West Rocks	Grassy main reef #2		30 47 910	153 00 740
South West Rocks	Grassy main reef #3	Snook	30 47 510	153 00 730
South West Rocks	Grassy se mark #2		30 48 500	153 01 940
South West Rocks	Grassy se mark #3		30 47 780	153 01 940
South West Rocks	Grassy se mark #4	27 m	30 47 080	153 02 290
South West Rocks	Grassy wide #1	30 m	30 46 290	153 03 440
South West Rocks	Grassy wide #2	30 m	30 46 270	153 03 400
South West Rocks	J.h.t	65 m.	30 45 320	153 07 860
South West Rocks	Jew hole		30 51 180	153 05 380
South West Rocks	Kimi	25 m	30 46 870	153 01 540
South West Rocks	Light house wide		30 54 330	153 18 430
South West Rocks	Mid Snook	8 fathoms	30 47 590	153 00 810
South West Rocks	No name	60 m.	30 45 060	153 07 960
South West Rocks	River bar		30 52 350	153 01 600
South West Rocks	Rocks in line #2		30 55 550	153 08 310
South West Rocks	Rocks in line #3		30 55 910	153 07 000
South West Rocks	Scott's hd reef #2		30 47 240	153 02 810

Locality	Description	Comments	Latitude	Latitude
South West Rocks	Scott's hd reef #3		30 47 630	153 01 480
South West Rocks	Scott's Head	Canyon	30 48 150	153 18 800
South West Rocks	Scott's Head	Canyon	30 48 600	153 20 600
South West Rocks	Tadpole 1	37–39 fathoms	30 43 350	153 09 110
South West Rocks	Tadpole 2	21–19 fathoms	30 44 060	153 03 360
South West Rocks	Tadpole 3	21–19 fathoms	30 44 090	153 02 990
South West Rocks	Tadpole 4	10 fathoms	30 44 520	153 00 380
South West Rocks	The Dot		30 51 380	153 06 870
South West Rocks	The Dot	38 fathoms. Flat, good drifting	30 51 390	153 07 540
South West Rocks	The dot west		30 51 370	153 07 630
South West Rocks	The gap		30 53 240	153 05 900
South West Rocks	The Wreck	5F Bait, Cobia and kingies	30 48 470	153 00 240
South West Rocks	Trap #1		30 46 110	153 08 110
South West Rocks	Trap #2		30 45 570	153 07 840
South West Rocks	Trev's Reef	28 fathoms. Look north for more	30 46 220	153 06 700
South West Rocks	Trial Bay	Canyon	30 51 400	153 19 800
South West Rocks	Trial bay canyon		30 50 800	153 17 800
South West Rocks	Wide Snook	20 fathoms	30 46 730	153 03 170
South West Rocks	Yellowfin drift		30 46 940	153 18 430
South West Rocks	Yellowfin drift		30 49 500	153 18 800
Stanwell Park	Burning Palms	12 m. Flathead drifting.	34 12 530	151 04 660
Stanwell Park	Fin Mark	Albacore, Yellowfin tuna, baitfish. Water depth 140 m.	34 08 370	151 22 230
Stanwell Park	Garie Beach Wide		34 10 600	151 06 880
Stanwell Park	Hacking Wreck	Rise. Snapper, mulloway, kingfish–live bait.	34 08 330	151 09 050
Stanwell Park	Humps		34 14 410	151 04 410
Stanwell Park	No name	Snapper, Reef fish, Pelagic. Reef bottom.	34 13 783	151 04 600
Stanwell Park	Restaurant Alley	Snapper, mulloway, morwong, leatherjackets and other reef species.	34 14 200	151 00 200
Stanwell Park	SS Undola Wreck	Garie Beach. Snapper, Kingfish, leatherjacket. Water depth 43m.	34 10 510	151 05 330
Stanwell Park	SS Undola Wreck	43 m. Snapper, kingfish, morwong, leatherjackets.	34 10 890	151 05 610
Stanwell Park	The Hump		34 13 850	151 04 460
Stanwell Park	The Humps	Snapper, mulloway, morwong, trevally, kingfish, leatherjackets, nannygai, surface fish. and other reef species.	34 13 667	151 07 145
Swansea	48 metre mark		32 58 610	151 50 310

Locality	Description	Comments	Latitude	Latitude
Swansea	48 metre mark		32 58 680	151 50 240
Swansea	Advance wreck		33 10 836	151 42 197
Swansea	Belmont barge		33 02 780	151 38 000
Swansea	Bird island east		33 13 920	151 36 280
Swansea	Blacksmith's Bait Reef 1		33 04 910	151 39 590
Swansea	Blacksmith's Bait Reef 2		33 04 910	151 39 687
Swansea	C.h.bay farm #1		33 10 665	151 49 519
Swansea	C.h.bay farm #2		33 10 695	151 49 519
Swansea	Cabel hook-up		32 58 144	151 51 357
Swansea	Catherine Hill Bay	13 fathoms	33 09 130	151 39 300
Swansea	Catherine hill bay		33 09 900	151 38 200
Swansea	Catherine Hill Bay	Wreck, 48 m. Baitfish	33 09 963	151 42 546
Swansea	Caves Beach	8 fathoms	33 06 720	151 39 700
Swansea	Caves beach reef		33 01 720	151 37 740
Swansea	Ch.bay farm #4		33 11 885	151 49 327
Swansea	Dudley north		32 58 700	151 43 730
Swansea	Finchies		33 13 800	151 48 693
Swansea	Hales Bluff		33 09 630	151 38 200
Swansea	Inner farm		33 09 019	151 46 922
Swansea	Inner farm north		33 08 632	151 47 174
Swansea	Jetty mark c/h/b		33 09 635	151 39 230
Swansea	Laverty's rise		32 57 897	151 52 151
Swansea	Macquarie's Reef		33 03 820	151 37 160
Swansea	Moon Island w		33 05 600	151 40 460
Swansea	Moonie boulders		33 10 840	151 38 430
Swansea	NCLE	Canyon inner	33 06 000	152 25 200
Swansea	NCLE	Canyon outer	33 08 000	152 28 700
Swansea	Neaders knob		33 05 550	151 43 420
Swansea	No name		32 57 620	151 52 100
Swansea	No name		33 09 038	151 49 128
Swansea	Norah Canyon	North West	33 14 400	152 15 000
Swansea	Norah Canyon	North East	33 15 600	152 17 200
Swansea	North east farm		33 07 550	151 49 080
Swansea	Pro Grounds	60 fathoms	33 15 710	151 48 560

Locality	Description	Comments	Latitude	Latitude
Swansea	Redhead Pinnacle	13 fathoms	33 02 120	151 43 590
Swansea	Redhead wide		33 02 130	151 43 840
Swansea	Shark Fin Reef		33 10 960	151 45 360
Swansea	Stinky Point		33 07 350	151 39 370
Swansea	Surf Club Gravel 1		33 02 086	151 43 908
Swansea	Swansea bombies		33 05 686	151 40 133
Swansea	Swansea entrance		33 05 160	151 39 800
Swansea	Swansea Gravel		33 05 570	151 43 380
Swansea	Teds hook-up #3		32 57 620	151 52 190
Swansea	The doctors		33 12 180	151 38 400
Swansea	The Fad		33 10 005	151 48 976
Swansea	The farm #1		33 09 043	151 49 101
Swansea	The farm #3		33 10 559	151 49 383
Swansea	The farm #4		33 09 065	151 49 153
Swansea	The farm 2	50 fathoms	33 10 560	151 49 380
Swansea	The Farm CHB3	50 fathoms	33 11 390	151 49 330
Swansea	Toms 30 metre mark		32 59 686	151 45 225
Swansea	Wybung Head		33 11 950	151 37 500
Sydney Harbour	Centennial Wreck	Depth 13m	33 50 873	151 15 003
Sydney Harbour	Centurion Wreck	Depth 25m	33 49 048	151 16 863
Sydney Harbour	Currajong Wreck	Depth 20m	33 51 307	151 14 937
Sydney Harbour	Royal Sheppard Wreck	Depth 25m	33 50 138	151 17 270
Tathra	Baronda Head		36 40 510	150 00 320
Tathra	Broken Reef – centre of		36 40 000	150 05 000
Tathra	Long Point	Gutters and drop-offs	36 54 240	149 57 640
Tathra	North Tip Canyons		36 44 020	150 21 020
Tathra	Pinnacle Reef	25 m. Shale	36 40 170	150 01 030
Tathra	Ross's 2		36 50 610	150 21 400
Tathra	Ross's 3		36 44 780	150 19 720
Tathra	Ross's 4		36 48 570	150 20 840
Tathra	Tathra Canyon	North West	36 44 500	150 19 700
Tathra	Tathra Canyon	South East	36 54 200	150 25 700
Tathra	Tathra Canyon	South West	36 54 250	150 21 300
Tathra	Tathra Canyon North		36 44 800	150 25 000

Locality	Description	Comments	Latitude	Latitude
Tathra	Tathra Head	Navigation point at entrance. Kingfish, morwong, snapper	36 43 400	149 59 600
Tathra	The Shelf	100 fathom mark east.	36 43 400	150 17 700
Tathra	Tuna YF	Tathra Nth yellowfin tuna	36 45 550	150 17 710
Tathra	Turingal Point	45 m	36 47 900	150 00 300
Tathra	White Rock	40 m. Broken reef	36 45 600	150 00 000
Tuross Heads	BB Canyon–SE		36 09 100	150 25 000
Tuross Heads	BB Canyon–SW		36 09 100	150 29 350
Tuross Heads	Lake reef		36 08 368	150 09 730
Tuross Heads	Moruya Plateau		35 55 750	150 33 200
Tuross Heads	No name	40 m	36 03 730	150 09 920
Tuross Heads	Potato Point Reef	Snapper, morwong, shark, leatherjacket. Water depth 20–30 m.	36 06 100	150 09 000
Tuross Heads	Reef	50 m	36 04 538	150 10 414
Tuross Heads	Tuross Canyons	North East	36 04 800	150 29 200
Tuross Heads	Tuross Canyons	North West	36 04 880	150 27 200
Tuross Heads	Tuross canyons		36 07 000	150 24 540
Tuross Heads	Tuross Canyons	South East	36 08 350	150 25 850
Tuross Heads	Tuross Canyons	South West	36 08 350	150 29 350
Tweed Heads	36F	Snapper, cobia, v-tusk	28 05 830	153 40 510
Tweed Heads	9 Mile		28 11 376	153 36 743
Tweed Heads	9 Mile	Take care	28 11 627	153 37 820
Tweed Heads	9 Mile peak		28 11 744	153 37 785
Tweed Heads	Cudgen hd. Canyon		28 20 550	153 56 375
Tweed Heads	Danger pt. Canyon		28 10 800	153 55 850
Tweed Heads	Harry's Rock	Snapper	28 12 400	153 35 360
Tweed Heads	Kev's	Trag, squire, reef fish, 44 m	28 08 350	153 37 090
Tweed Heads	Lead Mine	50 fathoms, perch, snapper	28 01 030	153 45 960
Tweed Heads	Morley's	Trag, snapper, v-tusk	28 07 350	153 34 950
Tweed Heads	No name	36 fathoms	28 08 318	153 40 510
Tweed Heads	No name	40 fathoms	28 08 513	153 46 095
Tweed Heads	No name	32–38 fathoms	28 08 559	153 40 505
Tweed Heads	No name	36 fathoms	28 09 918	153 41 488
Tweed Heads	No name	14 fathoms	28 10 350	153 36 657
Tweed Heads	No name	Traps south	28 10 840	153 46 750

Locality	Description	Comments	Latitude	Latitude
Tweed Heads	No name	18 fathoms	28 10 912	153 35 579
Tweed Heads	No name	28 fathoms, strong ripples	28 11 455	153 41 965
Tweed Heads	No name	1 mile south of 9 mile	28 12 292	153 37 960
Tweed Heads	No name	12 fathoms	28 12 700	153 37 627
Tweed Heads	North East of Cook Is		28 11 580	153 34 770
Tweed Heads	NW of Cook Island		28 11 431	153 34 569
Tweed Heads	Reefs	12 fathoms	28 12 440	153 37 400
Tweed Heads	SE 9 Mile		28 11 905	153 38 040
Tweed Heads	Taz's 61m	Snapper, cobia, p-perch	28 05 640	153 39 390
Ulladulla	Canberra Ave	Popular local spot	35 24 370	150 30 900
Ulladulla	Drum Drumstick		35 23 320	150 51 010
Ulladulla	Snapper Grounds	Snapper	35 29 140	150 29 140
Ulladulla	Ulladulla Canyon		35 20 100	150 55 660
Ulladulla	Ulladulla Canyon		35 23 200	150 49 800
Ulladulla	Ulladulla Harbour	Navigation point	35 21 340	150 28 750
Ulladulla	Ulladulla Traps	Yellowtail Kingfish, reef species	35 22 680	150 32 240
Wollongong	Annie Powell Wreck	Depth 30m	34 24 683	150 57 200
Wollongong	Arch	Near Shell Habour	34 35 978	150 54 120
Wollongong	Bass Islet	Depth 18m	34 27 815	150 56 756
Wollongong	Bass Point	Snapper, trevally.	34 35 141	150 55 491
Wollongong	Bass Point	Flathead, shark. Water depth 40 m. Weed bottom.	34 35 317	150 55 327
Wollongong	Bulli Bandit Reef	Snapper, Leatherjacket, Reef species. Water depth 40–50 m. Reef bottom.	34 19 730	150 59 010
Wollongong	Bulli Sands	Water depth 40–50 m. Sand bottom	34 20 150	151 02 030
Wollongong	Flagstaff Point	Snapper, winter and spring.	34 26 156	150 56 497
Wollongong	Hump	Near Shell Habour	34 35 138	150 54 770
Wollongong	Hump 2	Near Shell Habour	34 35 069	150 54 719
Wollongong	Illawarra Mark	Snapper, morwong, nannygai. Water depth 32 fathoms. Reef bottom.	34 41 830	150 54 090
Wollongong	Lou's Rock North	Near Shell Habour	34 35 755	150 54 437
Wollongong	Lou's Rock South	Near Shell Habour	34 35 860	150 54 398
Wollongong	Marks Bump 20	Snapper. Reef bottom.	34 18 633	151 00 795
Wollongong	Marks Spot 1	Flathead. Water depth 12–15 m.	34 26 286	150 56 266
Wollongong	Marks Spot 2	Morwong, snapper, flathead.	34 26 435	150 56 144
Wollongong	Martin Islet	Port Kembla, Depth 18m	34 29 338	150 55 857

Locality	Description	Comments	Latitude	Latitude
Wollongong	Martin islet Seals	Port Kembla, Depth 8m	34 29 676	150 56 176
Wollongong	Martins Wall NE	Port Kembla, Depth 28m	34 29 618	150 56 440
Wollongong	Martins Wall SW	Port Kembla, Depth 28m	34 29 732	150 56 307
Wollongong	No name	Reef. Snapper, morwong, sweep, groper, yellowtail kingfish.	34 18 040	151 02 050
Wollongong	No name	Snapper, Reef fish, pelagic. Reef bottom. Water depth 30–52 m.	34 18 210	151 02 443
Wollongong	No name	Morwong, snapper, leatherjacket, sergeant baker, Reef species. Reef bottom.	34 21 457	151 01 982
Wollongong	No name	Morwong, yellowtail kingfish, snapper, reef fish. Reef bottom.	34 26 190	150 59 170
Wollongong	Shellharbour	Safe exit navigation from Harbour. Yellowtail, slimy mackerel. Water depth 6 m.	34 34 653	150 52 720
Wollongong	Slipper Reef	Near Shell Habour	34 35 480	150 54 423
Wollongong	Snapper 2	Reef and gravel. Snapper. Water depth 24–27 m.	34 23 072	150 57 787
Wollongong	The Bombo	Kingfish, jewfish, snapper.	34 26 640	150 55 570
Wollongong	The Snapper Hole	Snapper, mulloway, morwong, leatherjackets and other reef species.	34 18 400	151 02 400
Wollongong	Toothbrush island	Port Kembla, Depth 18m	34 27 271	150 55 806
Wollongong	Toothbrush island south	Port Kembla	34 27 512	150 55 638
Wollongong	Trap Reef	Dolphinfish, marlin.	34 28 770	151 03 730
Wollongong	Wollongong Reef	Trevally, snapper, reef fish.	34 26 080	150 55 570
Wonboyn	Saltwater Creek	Snapper	37 16 681	150 00 280

SOUTH AUSTRALIA

Locality	Description	Comments	Latitude	Latitude
Adelaide	Bag Ground	Broken bottom. Whiting	34 56 445	138 28 605
Adelaide	Ballast Ground	Scattered lumps. Whiting, rugger, snapper	34 50 540	138 19 270
Adelaide	Banks	Whiting, garfish	34 58 849	138 28 780
Adelaide	Barge	Sunken barge. Whiting, snapper	34 58 719	138 26 351
Adelaide	Bent Tree	Lump. Whiting, flathead	34 58 643	138 26 381
Adelaide	Blackbird		35 03 840	138 28 565
Adelaide	Bower Road	Whiting, garfish	34 50 385	138 27 685
Adelaide	Brighton Jetty	Broken bottom and sand patches. Whiting	35 00 455	138 30 130
Adelaide	Brighton Reef 1	Mixed reef fish	35 01 120	138 29 400
Adelaide	Brighton Reef 2	Kink in reef. Whiting	35 01 122	138 29 132
Adelaide	Brighton Reef 3	Mixed reef fish	35 01 920	138 28 100
Adelaide	Caves		35 04 210	138 29 400
Adelaide	Concrete Reef	Reef. Whiting	34 58 406	138 30 494
Adelaide	Coral Patch 1	Coral bottom. Whiting, garfish	34 50 456	138 19 362
Adelaide	Coral Patch 2	Outer Harbour	34 50 520	138 19 200
Adelaide	Dickson's	Glenelg	34 55 260	138 25 900
Adelaide	Dredge	Least reduced depth over wreck is 11. 4 m. Artificial reef	34 58 803	138 26 359
Adelaide	Fred's		34 59 400	138 24 000
Adelaide	Gawler Ground 3	Sandy Patches. Whiting	34 49 452	138 24 457
Adelaide	Grange Tyre Reef	90m Foul ground. Average reduced depth is 18. 3 m. Snapper	34 55 000	138 24 000
Adelaide	Hopper Barge	Least reduced depth over wreck is 12 m. Artificial Reef	34 58 817	138 26 384
Adelaide	John Rob Wreck	13 m. Snapper	34 49 399	138 20 429
Adelaide	Kemps 1	Garfish, whiting, tommies	34 57 794	138 29 582
Adelaide	Kemps 2	Garfish, whiting	34 58 590	138 28 780
Adelaide	Mack's		34 58 640	138 27 000
Adelaide	Middle Ground		34 54 590	138 25 090
Adelaide	Middle Reef	Reef. Whiting	34 55 280	138 23 992
Adelaide	Milkys	Garfish, tommies, squid	34 59 178	138 27 276
Adelaide	Minda Ground	Whiting	35 00 620	138 28 729
Adelaide	Mud Patch	Flat Bottom. Whiting	35 00 822	138 28 982
Adelaide	No name	Outer Harbour ballast	34 50 457	138 19 346
Adelaide	No name	Whiting–in afternoon –good when the water is dirty.	34 53 648	138 27 450

Locality	Description	Comments	Latitude	Latitude
Adelaide	No name	Bag ground	34 57 408	138 27 638
Adelaide	No name	Whiting	34 57 785	138 28 801
Adelaide	No name	Whiting in afternoon and at night.	34 58 721	138 27 791
Adelaide	No name	Milky's	34 59 024	138 26 368
Adelaide	No name	Whiting in afternoon and at night.	34 59 120	138 27 777
Adelaide	Norma Wreck		34 49 400	138 25 000
Adelaide	North Ledge		34 58 910	138 26 200
Adelaide	Northern Ground	Snook, whiting	34 58 792	138 27 272
Adelaide	Northern Outer	Sand/broken bottom. Whiting	34 58 829	138 26 334
Adelaide	O'Sullivan's Beach	Ramp	35 07 150	138 28 000
Adelaide	O'Sullivans Beach 1	Barge1 in 20 m. Snapper	35 06 862	138 24 732
Adelaide	O'Sullivans Beach 2	Barge 2 in 20 m. Snapper	35 06 912	138 24 615
Adelaide	Outlet Ground 1	Outer	34 56 520	138 26 800
Adelaide	Outlet Ground 2	Inner	34 56 600	138 28 400
Adelaide	Red roof		34 57 436	138 26 770
Adelaide	Rock Patch	Broken bottom. Whiting	34 58 174	138 28 807
Adelaide	Seacliff Reef	Whiting	35 02 264	138 29 440
Adelaide	Seacliff Reef	Whiting	35 02 335	138 29 503
Adelaide	Sellick	Sand and weed. Whiting, garfish	35 01 509	138 25 722
Adelaide	Semaphore Reef Lower		34 51 660	138 26 930
Adelaide	Semaphore Reef Upper		34 50 770	138 26 660
Adelaide	Shag Patch	Lump. Garfish, whiting	34 58 204	138 28 768
Adelaide	Somerton	Reef. Whiting, red mullet	34 59 184	138 29 266
Adelaide	South West Ground		34 52 460	138 22 520
Adelaide	Spines 1	Whiting, garfish, tommies	35 01 127	138 29 420
Adelaide	Spines 2	Broken bottom. Whiting	35 01 265	138 28 982
Adelaide	State Bank	Snook, whiting	34 49 974	138 26 130
Adelaide	The Ledge	Mixed reef fish	35 02 190	138 29 300
Adelaide	The Patch	Whiting, garfish	34 55 860	138 26 500
Adelaide	Tower's	Garfish, whiting	34 58 431	138 26 691
Adelaide	Towers ground		34 59 930	138 26 790
Adelaide	Tyre Reef	Artificial reef. Whiting, snapper	34 59 000	138 26 600
Adelaide	Uni Ground	Sand patches. Whiting	34 58 237	138 27 515
Adelaide	Via	Large lumps. Whiting	34 58 899	137 29 950

Locality	Description	Comments	Latitude	Latitude
Adelaide	Wonga Shoal		34 50 000	138 27 330
Adelaide	Wreck		34 49 414	138 20 420
Adelaide	Wreck		34 49 497	138 25 176
Aldinga	Aldinga	Drop off. Snapper, whiting	35 18 352	138 19 917
Aldinga	Aldinga II	Broken bottom/drop off. Snapper	35 19 242	138 19 120
Aldinga	Aldinga III	Snapper, sharks	35 08 192	138 11 429
Aldinga	Gull Rock	Ledge. Whiting, leatherjackets	35 14 670	138 27 499
Aldinga	Moana Inner	Broken bottom. Squid, whiting	35 13 780	138 28 200
Aldinga	Moana Outer	Broken bottom. Whiting	35 12 999	138 26 345
Aldinga	Pt Willunga	Lumps and bumps. Snapper, whiting	35 15 393	138 13 418
Aldinga	Pt Willunga II	Lumps and bumps. Snapper, whiting	35 16 502	138 13 111
Aldinga	Sellicks Point	Huge lump. Whiting	35 18 509	138 26 322
Aldinga	Silver Sands	Sand and weed. Garfish, squid	35 17 700	138 26 620
Balgowan	Central	Broken bottom. Whiting, snook, squid	34 23 733	137 24 236
Balgowan	Jim's	Slight lumps. Whiting	34 14 992	137 03 157
Balgowan	Jim's Inner	Rock. Snapper	34 16 745	137 07 627
Balgowan	No name	Whiting, garfish , broken bottom	34 25 600	137 58 400
Balgowan	Pt. Victoria North	Reef. Snapper, whiting	34 24 802	137 20 117
Balgowan	Pt. Victoria Reef	Reef. Rugger snapper, whiting	34 24 472	137 19 238
Balgowan	Reef Point	Kink on ledge. Whiting	34 24 108	137 22 807
Balgowan	The Ranges	Drop off and broken bottom. Whiting	34 21 836	137 26 131
Balgowan	The Shack	Broken bottom and ledge. Whiting, squid	34 16 992	137 23 700
Balgowan	Trace's Ground	Broken bottom and ledges. Whiting	34 13 519	137 26 131
Edithburgh	Coldasack	Kink in reef. Whiting, snapper	35 06 600	137 56 651
Edithburgh	Ernie's Drop	Large lumps. Whiting, snapper	35 07 123	137 52 860
Edithburgh	Grumpies	Lumps and ledges. Whiting, snapper	35 05 184	137 55 248
Edithburgh	Grumpies II	Ledge. Whiting, rugger snapper	35 05 998	137 56 210
Edithburgh	Limits	Broken bottom. Whiting	35 04 342	137 55 449
Edithburgh	Marion Reef Light	Navigation mark	35 09 420	137 49 180
Edithburgh	Second Drop	Whiting	35 07 488	137 55 449
Edithburgh	Shoal II	Ledge. Whiting, snapper	35 07 466	137 53 755
Edithburgh	Snapper Head	Reef. Whiting, snapper	35 06 195	137 56 700
Edithburgh	Sultana Passage		35 06 070	137 45 390
Edithburgh	Sultana Passage (South Marker)	Navigation mark	35 07 877	137 45 661

Locality	Description	Comments	Latitude	Latitude
Edithburgh	Sultana Passage (North end pole)	Navigation mark	35 09 907	137 45 486
Edithburgh	Sultana Passage(Sth)		35 07 510	137 45 360
Edithburgh	Tapley Shoal 1	Reef ledge. Whiting, snapper	35 06 966	137 55 729
Edithburgh	Tapley Shoal 2		35 07 800	137 53 300
Edithburgh	The Caves	Kink in shoal. Snapper	35 06 301	137 52 200
Edithburgh	The Ledge	Large ledge. Whiting, snapper	35 06 600	137 56 553
Edithburgh	Whiting Hole	Ledge. Whiting, snapper	35 04 689	137 57 168
Elliston	No name	Flathead	33 39 408	134 51 766
Elliston	No name	Snapper	33 40 782	134 51 780
Gulf St Vincent	Ardrossan Barge	Artificial reef.	34 31 900	138 03 700
Gulf St Vincent	Tyre Modules		35 02 800	137 47 400
Gulf St Vincent	Zanoni	Spherical Bay	34 30 790	138 03 700
Kangaroo Island	Bay of Shoals	Snapper, whiting	35 36 355	137 42 430
Kangaroo Island	Borda	Large ledges–big boat fishing. Snapper	35 37 200	136 36 571
Kangaroo Island	Cape Dutton	Large reef. Snapper, trevally, nannygai	35 37 683	137 07 681
Kangaroo Island	Cape Forbin	Large rise. Whiting, snapper	35 33 270	136 45 491
Kangaroo Island	Cape Hart	Reef. Whiting, snapper, nannygai	35 54 992	138 02 493
Kangaroo Island	Cape Willoughby	Troll lures–kingfish	35 50 332	138 08 370
Kangaroo Island	East Cove	Lumps and bumps. Whiting, snapper	35 43 854	137 51 216
Kangaroo Island	East Cove II	Broken bottom. Whiting, trevally	35 44 673	137 50 891
Kangaroo Island	Hardstaff	Edge of shoal. Trevally, whiting	35 37 992	136 54 605
Kangaroo Island	Hardstaff II	Kink. Trevally	35 38 193	136 54 610
Kangaroo Island	Kingscote	Lumps and ledges. Trevally, whiting	35 35 983	137 45 317
Kangaroo Island	Kingscote Reef. Tyre modules	Reefy bottom. Whiting	35 41 200	137 40 200
Kangaroo Island	Landing Shoal	Drop off. Snapper, whiting	35 36 221	136 57 246
Kangaroo Island	Marsden Point	Broken reef. Whiting	35 35 742	137 42 767
Kangaroo Island	Morrison	Drop off. Snapper, whiting	35 37 968	136 55 311
Kangaroo Island	Morrison II	Drop off / ledge. Trevally, snapper	35 36 325	136 57 468
Kangaroo Island	Pro's Drop	Large lump–big boat fishing. Snapper	35 20 792	137 28 897
Kangaroo Island	Shoals II	Shallow water. Trevally, whiting	35 36 831	137 43 522
Kangaroo Island	Smiths	Broken bottom, Lumps and ledges. Snapper, whiting	35 34 117	137 23 530
Kangaroo Island	Smith's Bay	Broken bottom. Whiting, snapper	35 34 693	137 24 696
Kangaroo Island	Snug North	Broken bottom. Snapper, whiting	35 34 414	136 46 873

Locality	Description	Comments	Latitude	Latitude
Kangaroo Island	West Outer	Broken bottom. Whiting	35 36 388	137 43 639
Kangaroo Island	Western River	Broken bottom. Whiting	35 36 207	137 57 248
Kangaroo Island	Young Rocks	Rocky outcrop bluefin tuna–big boat fishing	36 22 122	137 14 907
Marion Bay	Clan Ranald	Wreck. Snapper	35 09 816	137 24 340
Marion Bay	Foul Bay	Broken bottom. Huge whiting	35 13 281	137 14 851
Marion Bay	Hillocks	Shallow and sandy. Whiting, garfish	35 15 260	137 05 308
Marion Bay	Hillocks/East	Broken bottom. Whiting	35 14 398	137 06 340
Marion Bay	Hillocks/East II	Broken bottom. Whiting	35 14 633	137 05 669
Marion Bay	Marion Reef	Reef. Whiting, rugger snapper	35 14 454	137 05 951
Marion Bay	Marion Reef II	Reef. Whiting, rugger snapper	35 09 480	137 49 330
Marion Bay	Orcades	Large drop off. Whiting, snapper	35 23 536	137 07 290
Marion Bay	Steelies	Broken bottom. Whiting	35 13 352	137 14 220
Marion Bay	Sturt Bay	Reefy bottom. Whiting	35 07 155	137 27 311
Marion Bay	The Drop	Drop Off (7 m). Whiting	35 15 280	137 03 702
Marion Bay	Yorke's Point	Broken bottom. Whiting	35 10 320	137 37 165
Noarlunga		Deep water. sharks	35 06 829	138 07 156
Outer Harbour	Buckets	Lumps. Whiting, garfish	34 46 388	138 25 314
Outer Harbour	Cabbage Patch	Bump. Whiting	34 46 832	138 23 843
Outer Harbour	Coral Patch		34 47 480	138 24 470
Outer Harbour	Coral Patch (North)	Whiting, Garfish–7 m sand bottom	34 47 230	138 24 470
Outer Harbour	Fairway Beacon	Channel. Snapper	34 47 220	138 24 594
Outer Harbour	Fairway Hole	Ledge. Squid, Whiting, Snapper	34 45 258	138 24 300
Outer Harbour	North/West	Large rock. Whiting	34 46 305	138 22 666
Outer Harbour	Outer Silt	Broken bottom. Whiting, snapper	34 46 382	138 25 348
Outer Harbour	Silt Ground	Broken bottom. Whiting, snapper	34 46 356	138 25 294
Outer Harbour	Snapper Rock	Large rock. Whiting, snapper	34 47 174	138 17 999
Outer Harbour	Wave Recorder	Broken bottom. Whiting, garfish	34 45 716	138 25 509
Point Giles	Mac's Ground	Broken bottom. Whiting	35 03 220	137 46 277
Point Giles	Marker	Lumps and ledges. Whiting, squid	35 03 808	137 55 367
Point Giles	The Ledge	Ledges and drop off. Whiting	35 03 785	137 55 360
Point Giles	Tyre Reef	Whiting, rugger, snapper	35 02 719	137 47 485
Point Turton	Bay	Sand and broken bottom. Whiting	34 53 720	137 25 155
Point Turton	Broken Rock	Broken bottom. Whiting, snapper	34 55 219	137 23 385
Point Turton	Fish Point	Whiting , broken bottom	34 54 273	137 22 548

Locality	Description	Comments	Latitude	Latitude
Point Turton	Fish Point II	Broken bottom. Whiting	34 54 600	137 20 391
Point Turton	Grange Ground		34 53 190	138 26 950
Point Turton	Inches	Slow drop. Whiting	34 49 358	137 21 969
Point Turton	Minlacowie	Shallow weedy bottom. Whiting, squid	34 51 367	137 25 390
Point Turton	No name	Whiting , broken bottom	34 53 072	137 25 155
Point Turton	Shoal	Ledge. Snapper	34 42 283	137 16 400
Point Turton	Sphinx	Reef. Whiting, rugger snapper	34 51 282	137 19 232
Point Turton	The Spit	Sand and reef. Whiting, garfish	34 50 850	137 13 706
Point Turton	Wayside	Large bump. Whiting	34 48 808	137 22 226
Port Augusta	Flinders	Channel. Snapper	32 42 710	137 47 295
Port Augusta	Flinders Channel	Drop off. Snapper	32 40 110	137 46 873
Port Augusta	Pat's	Hole. Whiting	32 38 209	137 47 583
Port Augusta	Power Station	Lumps and Bumps. Snapper, Kingfish	32 32 237	137 46 408
Port Augusta	Redcliffs	Drop off. Snapper	32 42 672	137 49 810
Port Augusta	Seagate's	Drop off. Rugger snapper	32 34 313	137 46 567
Port Augusta	Snapper Point	Channel / ledge. Snapper	32 35 280	137 46 776
Port Augusta	The Point	Channel. squid, Garfish	32 32 303	137 46 408
Port Augusta	Tyre Modules	Artificial reef.	32 40 000	137 45 800
Port Augusta	Tyre Reef	Artificial reef. Whiting, snapper	32 39 898	137 45 923
Port Broughton	Aggros	Lumps and bumps. Whiting, garfish	33 31 600	137 47 300
Port Broughton	Broughton Cars	Snapper	33 34 970	137 50 700
Port Broughton	Car Bodies 1	Artificial reef. Snapper	33 33 003	137 51 296
Port Broughton	Car Bodies 2	Artificial reef. Snapper	33 32 973	137 51 386
Port Broughton	Car Bodies 3	Artificial reef. Snapper	33 33 100	137 51 359
Port Broughton	Car Bodies II	Lumps. Snapper	33 34 980	137 33 241
Port Broughton	Council	Lumps and bumps. Snapper, whiting	33 35 122	137 51 277
Port Broughton	Dion		33 34 720	137 49 300
Port Broughton	Dunstan's	Whiting, squid	33 32 748	137 50 334
Port Broughton	Hump Point	Lumps. Whiting	33 29 926	137 50 699
Port Broughton	Illusion	Wreck (big boat water). Snapper	33 28 856	137 32 624
Port Broughton	Illusion II	Wreck. Snapper	33 29 614	137 32 743
Port Broughton	In Front	Drop off. Whiting	33 32 581	137 49 632
Port Broughton	No name	Snapper	33 32 580	137 49 630
Port Broughton	No name	Snapper	33 34 990	137 50 850

Locality	Description	Comments	Latitude	Latitude
Port Broughton	Plank Shoal		33 29 940	137 28 470
Port Broughton	Snowy's	KG whiting	33 34 200	137 50 740
Port Broughton	Webling Point	Whiting, squid	33 33 241	137 47 878
Port Broughton	Webling Point II	Broken bottom. Whiting	33 34 258	137 50 850
Port Broughton	Webling Point III	Weed line. Whiting, garfish	33 35 930	137 50 601
Port Broughton	West Drop	Broken bottom. Snapper, whiting	33 32 891	137 52 480
Port Broughton	Woodies	Shallow. Whiting, garfish	33 22 984	137 50 126
Port Gawler	Bastard Pole	Sand/lumps. Whiting	34 44 855	138 26 670
Port Gawler	Black Pole		34 44 091	138 27 897
Port Gawler	Boat Ramp		34 44 620	138 32 080
Port Gawler	Chapman Creek	Weed patches, broken bottom. Whiting	34 41 635	138 25 998
Port Gawler	Cockle Patch	Broken bottom. Whiting	34 37 567	138 18 386
Port Gawler	Gawler Ground 1	Sandy with small lumps. Whiting, garfish	34 39 175	138 22 450
Port Gawler	Gawler Ground 2		34 40 252	138 23 657
Port Gawler	Gawler Ground Sth		34 40 320	138 22 070
Port Gawler	Goannas		34 39 188	138 20 630
Port Gawler	Goannas 3		34 39 020	138 20 630
Port Gawler	Goannas Rock	10–16 m. Snapper	34 37 111	138 18 602
Port Gawler	Hardwick Inner	Broken bottom. Whiting	34 37 372	137 16 877
Port Gawler	Hardwick Reef	Reef. Snapper, whiting	34 39 221	137 20 050
Port Gawler	Middle Beach Ramp		34 36 650	138 24 790
Port Gawler	No name	Goannas 1	34 38 430	138 20 620
Port Gawler	No name	Goannas 2	34 38 750	138 20 370
Port Gawler	No name	Inner St Kilda	34 43 210	138 26 220
Port Gawler	No name	Silt ground marker	34 44 410	138 26 340
Port Gawler	Outer Goannas	Snapper	34 37 353	138 17 748
Port Gawler	Oyster Point	Shallow bottom. Whiting, garfish	34 40 370	137 55 897
Port Gawler	Port Gawler	Sandy patches. Crabs, whiting	34 41 355	138 25 726
Port Gawler	Snapper Rock	Large rock. Whiting, snapper	34 37 174	138 17 999
Port Gawler	St. Kilda	Sand and weed patches. Garfish, snook	34 42 409	138 27 190
Port Gawler	The Shed 1	Sandy patches. crabs, whiting, garfish	34 40 555	138 23 203
Port Gawler	The Shed 2		34 42 430	138 25 190
Port Hughes	Bay II	Sand. Whiting, garfish	34 06 495	137 30 810
Port Hughes	Cape Elizabeth	Broken bottom. Whiting	34 11 808	137 26 607

Locality	Description	Comments	Latitude	Latitude
Port Hughes	Cape Elizabeth, Port Hughes	Whiting ground	34 07 400	137 25 500
Port Hughes	Cape Outer	Reef. Snapper, whiting	34 06 788	137 23 339
Port Hughes	Gordon's Rock	Reef. Whiting	34 09 741	137 24 990
Port Hughes	Hughes Bay	Sand. Garfish, whiting	34 06 495	137 30 496
Port Hughes	Northern	Drop off. Whiting	34 06 144	137 15 413
Port Hughes	Nth/East Hole	Drop off. Snapper	34 02 573	137 24 724
Port Hughes	PH Point	Broken bottom. Garfish, squid	34 04 510	137 32 742
Port Hughes	Steamer	Channel drop off. Whiting, snapper	34 03 492	137 14 440
Port Hughes	Steamer II	Channel drop off. Whiting, snapper	34 04 405	137 12 619
Port Hughes	Sth/East Grnd	Lumps. Whiting	34 04 598	137 20 375
Port Hughes	The Cape	Reef. Whiting	34 07 155	137 27 311
Port Hughes	The Channel	Shipping channel. Snapper, whiting	34 03 662	137 14 442
Port Hughes	Tippara II	Reef. Squid	34 03 554	137 20 829
Port Hughes	Tippara Outer	Reef. Squid, whiting	34 02 681	137 21 826
Port Hughes	West Light	Whiting	34 03 672	137 21 415
Port Hughes	Whiting Hole	Lumps. Whiting, snook	34 03 743	137 29 617
Port Lincoln	Boston Island 1	Reef and broken bottom. Whiting	34 40 732	135 55 210
Port Lincoln	Boston Island 2	Rocky. Whiting	34 40 898	135 52 487
Port Lincoln	Buffalo Reef	Reef. Morwong, snapper	34 43 480	136 28 817
Port Lincoln	Buffalo Reef II	Reef. Morwong, snapper	34 43 183	136 28 938
Port Lincoln	Buffalo Reef South	Reef. Whiting, nannygai, morwong	34 43 547	136 26 960
Port Lincoln	Inner Gawler		34 40 620	138 24 520
Port Lincoln	No name	Snapper, whiting , big ledge	35 06 006	135 56 553
Port Lincoln	Reef Inner	Broken bottom. Whiting, snapper	34 43 651	136 26 962
Port Lincoln	Silt ground		34 45 518	138 26 738
Port Lincoln	Spilsby Inner	Broken bottom. Snapper	34 43 782	136 26 125
Port Lincoln	Spilsby Outer	Lump. Whiting, snapper	34 43 294	136 28 788
Port Lincoln	Stickney Point	Huge lumps. Whiting, snapper	34 43 554	136 27 979
Port Lincoln	Sunken Vessel	Snapper	34 41 000	135 52 400
Port Neill	Sunken Vessel		34 06 700	136 22 600
Port Noarlunga	Tyre Modules	Artificial reef	35 08 900	138 26 500
Port Victoria	Gawler Outer	Holes and bumps. Whiting	34 32 252	137 23 340
Port Victoria	West Wardang Island 1	Lumps and bumps. Whiting	34 31 754	137 19 303
Spencer Gulf south	All's Reef	Reef. Snapper	35 20 719	136 53 574

Locality	Description	Comments	Latitude	Latitude
Spencer Gulf south	Ally's Ground	Large lump. Nannygai	35 21 280	136 41 688
Spencer Gulf south	Althorpe II	Broken bottom. Whiting	35 21 520	136 50 150
Spencer Gulf south	Althorpe III	Large bumps. Whiting, snapper	35 22 231	136 44 812
Spencer Gulf south	Althorpe South	Rocky bottom. Whiting	35 24 191	136 51 937
Spencer Gulf south	Cray Is.	Broken bottom. whiting	35 17 380	136 51 391
Spencer Gulf south	Dirty Water	Broken bottom. Whiting	35 21 521	136 50 300
Spencer Gulf south	Haystack	Lumps and ledges. Whiting, snapper	35 19 400	136 54 339
Spencer Gulf south	Ken's	Drop off. Whiting	35 21 241	136 41 769
Spencer Gulf south	Lake Macquarie Bank	Edge of shoal. Whiting, snapper	35 18 847	136 38 315
Spencer Gulf south	Lake Macquarie Bank II	Edge of shoal. Whiting, snapper	35 20 127	136 38 482
Spencer Gulf south	Lake Macquarie Bank III	Steep incline. Snapper	35 19 680	136 38 949
Spencer Gulf south	Macquarie	Lump. Whiting, nannygai	35 21 253	136 41 807
Spencer Gulf south	Mt. Neptune	Pinnacle. Morwong, nannygai	35 25 169	136 30 192
Spencer Gulf south	Outer Lump	Steep incline. Whiting, snapper	35 25 388	136 30 527
Spencer Gulf south	Reef Head	Large Bombie. Whiting	35 17 209	136 45 509
Spencer Gulf south	Rosalind Shoal	Pinnacle (20 m). Whiting, morwong	34 47 612	136 33 129
Spencer Gulf south	S/W Rocks	Shallow reef. Whiting, snapper	35 20 328	136 48 481
Spencer Gulf south	Seal Island	Lumps and ledges. Whiting	35 20 914	136 55 336
Spencer Gulf south	Shoals East	Bumps. Whiting	35 21 160	136 41 896
Spencer Gulf south	Spencer's Rise	Huge lumps. Whiting, nannygai	35 24 048	136 51 752
Spencer Gulf south	Stenie	Large pinnacle. Whiting, snapper	35 20 466	136 54 662
Spencer Gulf south	Sth/Wst Rocks	Large rocks. Sweep, morwong, whiting	35 22 326	136 45 359

Locality	Description	Comments	Latitude	Latitude
Spencer Gulf south	Suzanne II	Large rise. Snapper	35 14 228	136 32 153
Spencer Gulf south	Suzanne Shoal 1	Reefy bottom. Whiting, snapper	35 14 879	136 33 683
Spencer Gulf south	Suzanne Shoal 2	Large rise. Whiting, snapper	35 15 153	136 33 934
Spencer Gulf south	Suzanne Shoal E	Edge of shoal. Snapper	35 15 214	136 37 324
Spencer Gulf south	The Shoals	Broken Bottom. Snapper	35 20 143	136 38 410
Spencer Gulf south	West Cape	Lumps and bumps. Whiting	35 16 200	136 46 699
Spencer Gulf south	West Lump	Ledge. Snapper	35 20 773	136 52 796
Stansbury	Bay	Sand and weed. Whiting, garfish	34 55 766	137 49 904
Stansbury	Beach Point	Weed bottom. Whiting, squid	34 50 710	137 51 509
Stansbury	Cliff	Lumps and bumps. Whiting	34 52 702	137 49 959
Stansbury	Couta's	Drop off. Whiting	34 54 613	137 56 246
Stansbury	No name	Snapper, whiting , drop off	34 40 183	138 02 558
Stansbury	Orentes	Sand and rock. Whiting	34 52 953	137 56 170
Stansbury	Oyster Point II	Whiting, garfish, squid	34 55 351	137 49 819
Stansbury	Sam's Reef	Reef, drop off (7 m). Snapper	34 53 628	137 56 500
Stansbury	The Drop	Sand/weed and rock. Whiting	34 55 242	137 58 703
Stansbury	The Hump	Large lump. Whiting, snapper	34 53 590	137 51 200
Stansbury	Vincent's Ground	Rocky bottom. Whiting	34 48 269	137 52 539
Streaky Bay	Blanche Point Stick Marker	Narrow channel. Big snapper, squid	32 46 360	134 13 418
Streaky Bay	Blanche Point Target Point	Deep hole. Snapper	32 46 674	134 13 213
Streaky Bay	Cannan Reef	Reef. Whiting, snapper	32 41 755	133 17 270
Streaky Bay	Dashwood Rock	Large lumps and ledges. Whiting, morwong	32 37 259	134 03 679
Streaky Bay	Frank Outer	Lump. Snapper	32 25 525	133 21 442
Streaky Bay	Franklin Isl.	Reefy broken bottom. Snapper	32 27 776	133 33 637
Streaky Bay	Gliddon Reef	Reef. Whiting, snapper	32 21 839	133 33 522
Streaky Bay	Jetty	Sandy patch. Whiting, squid, tommies	32 47 503	134 12 877
Streaky Bay	Near Goalen Rocks	Rocky bottom. Whiting	32 24 761	133 40 640
Streaky Bay	North Bank	Rocks and broken bottom. Whiting	32 33 280	134 08 832
Streaky Bay	Olive Island	Large lumps. Snapper	32 43 424	133 57 898
Streaky Bay	Smoky Bay	Broken bottom. Large whiting	32 22 270	133 46 868

Locality	Description	Comments	Latitude	Latitude
Streaky Bay	Tyre reef	9 m. Snapper	32 44 010	134 14 730
Victor Harbor	7 Mile (Outer)	Reef. Trevally, snapper	35 40 880	138 35 152
Victor Harbor	Encounter Ledge	Ledges. Trevally, snook, shark	35 40 116	138 36 292
Victor Harbor	Five Mile Reef		35 40 220	138 36 100
Victor Harbor	Mouth	Reef. Shark, rugger snapper	35 37 934	138 52 539
Victor Harbor	Mouth II	Lump. Mulloway, snapper	35 37 785	138 52 525
Victor Harbor	Newlands	Snook, mackerel	35 40 219	138 36 187
Victor Harbor	Outer	Reef. Sharks	35 38 171	138 52 406
Victor Harbor	Pinnacles II	Lump. Snapper, whiting	35 40 426	138 35 810
Victor Harbor	Rosetta	Broken bottom. Snook, mackerel	35 32 743	138 38 484
Victor Harbor	Seven Mile Reef		35 40 120	138 36 200
Victor Harbor	The Pinnacles	Large rise. Snapper, trevally	35 41 442	138 33 879
Wallaroo	Bird Reef	Broken bottom and lumps. Snapper, whiting	33 57 150	137 26 640
Wallaroo	Brian's Ledge	Drop off. Whiting	33 48 660	137 37 338
Wallaroo	Clinker	Broken bottom/sand. Whiting	33 54 654	137 37 57
Wallaroo	Cork Weed Ground	Broken bottom. Snapper, whiting	33 53 657	137 36 299
Wallaroo	High Ground	Broken bottom/lumps. snapper, whiting	33 51 855	137 33 222
Wallaroo	Magazine	Large deep hole. Snook, whiting	33 55 852	137 35 827
Wallaroo	Middle Bank Rocks	16 m. Snapper	33 41 730	137 33 645
Wallaroo	My Spot	Sand and weed. Garfish, squid	33 49 563	137 37 338
Wallaroo	No name		33 45 459	137 02 160
Wallaroo	Record III	Structure. Whiting	33 49 871	137 35 856
Wallaroo	Riley Shoal	Shoal. Whiting	33 54 280	137 32 685
Wallaroo	Tyre Modules		33 51 500	137 34 300
Wallaroo	Tyre Reef	12 m. Artificial reef. Snapper, whiting	33 52 345	137 33 992
Wallaroo	Wave Recorder	Structure. Whiting	33 50 463	137 33 222
Wallaroo	Whiting Drop	Whiting	33 55 520	137 36 640
Wardang Island	Barrons	Lumps and ledges. Whiting	34 28 572	137 18 665
Wardang Island	Bea Rock	Rock. Whiting	34 26 451	137 25 598
Wardang Island	Flat Rock	Large lmp. Whiting	34 32 190	137 20 477
Wardang Island	Innes	Weed line. Whiting	34 28 701	137 23 792
Wardang Island	Jetty Patch	Shallow water. Whiting, garfish	34 27 985	137 22 778
Wardang Island	Moorara	Wreck. Snapper, whiting	34 28 674	137 25 322
Wardang Island	No name	Reefy bottom. Whiting	34 32 964	137 22 645

Locality	Description	Comments	Latitude	Latitude
Wardang Island	North Goose	Whiting	34 26 921	137 22 270
Wardang Island	Outer	Lumps and bumps. Snapper	34 26 520	137 13 506
Wardang Island	Sim's Ground	Change in bottom. Whiting	34 30 843	137 25 318
Wardang Island	Snapper Hole	Ledge. Snapper	34 26 268	137 16 887
Wardang Island	Snook Patch	Troll, anchor or berley. Snook	34 32 173	137 22 500
Wardang Island	Songvar	Wreck. Snapper	34 27 626	137 23 226
Wardang Island	South Goose	Broken reefy bottom. Whiting, snapper	34 29 752	137 20 101
Wardang Island	South Wardang Island	Ledge. Snapper, whiting	34 32 565	137 20 464
Wardang Island	South Wardang Island 2	Whiting, mackerel, snapper	34 32 701	137 20 478
Wardang Island	Wardang Jetty Patch.	NE Coast Wardang Island. Depth 4 m. King George Whiting.	34 27 990	137 22 780
Wardang Island	Wardang South	Broken bottom. Whiting	34 32 602	137 20 821
Wardang Island	West Wardang Island 2	Reef. Whiting, snapper	34 30 422	137 19 106
Wardang Island	West Wardang Island 3	Reefy bottom. Whiting	34 31 160	137 25 377
Whyalla	8 km Bombie		33 06 158	137 37 149
Whyalla	Blast Furnace		33 01 960	137 40 460
Whyalla	Bus drop		32 57 316	137 46 314
Whyalla	Cars	Snapper, trumpeter	33 00 820	137 40 390
Whyalla	Community	Reef and scattered lumps. Snapper	33 05 314	137 41 123
Whyalla	Community Wreck		33 05 090	137 54 430
Whyalla	Deep Hole		33 09 490	137 45 610
Whyalla	Divers Reef	20 m. Weedy bottom	32 59 749	137 47 317
Whyalla	Eastern Shoal 1	Large drop off/ledge. Snapper	33 07 368	137 42 811
Whyalla	Eastern Shoal 2	10 m. Snapper	33 07 900	137 36 534
Whyalla	Eastern Shoal 3		33 09 940	137 43 570
Whyalla	Entrance	Structure. Snapper, whiting	33 09 742	137 38 437
Whyalla	Fairway 1	7 m. Snapper	33 04 950	137 41 855
Whyalla	Fairway 2	7 m. Snapper	33 04 971	137 41 648
Whyalla	Fairway Bank 1		33 04 440	137 44 300
Whyalla	Fairway Bank 2		33 05 023	137 42 203
Whyalla	Fairway Bank drop		33 05 109	137 34 946
Whyalla	Fairway Bank West		33 04 440	137 38 180
Whyalla	Fairway Banks	Large slope on ledge. Snapper	33 05 210	137 41 900
Whyalla	Haulies 1	Artificial reef. Snapper	33 01 938	137 40 474
Whyalla	Haulies 2		33 01 940	137 40 480

Locality	Description	Comments	Latitude	Latitude
Whyalla	Havelburgs	Lumps and bumps. Whiting, snapper	33 05 441	137 39 632
Whyalla	Jetty Patch	Shallow. Squid, garfish	33 03 488	137 36 280
Whyalla	Joe 18 km	7 m. Snapper	33 10 770	137 28 652
Whyalla	Joe's special		33 14 214	137 32 137
Whyalla	Leeton Tug	Snapper, trumpeter	33 09 780	137 38 490
Whyalla	Leighton Tug	Snapper, trumpeter	33 09 638	137 38 552
Whyalla	Leighton Tug 2	Sunken tug. Whiting, snapper	33 14 430	137 32 390
Whyalla	Marek's Reef	Snapper, trumpeter	33 05 690	137 36 390
Whyalla	McIntosh Bank		33 08 740	137 59 900
Whyalla	Mud Bank 1	Snapper, trumpeter	33 00 670	137 39 890
Whyalla	Mud Bank 2	Snapper, Trumpeter	33 00 960	137 40 220
Whyalla	Mud Banks	Silt ground. Snapper	33 01 360	137 40 132
Whyalla	Mudbanks	Snapper	33 00 798	137 39 761
Whyalla	Mystery	Shallow. Snapper	33 03 184	137 34 941
Whyalla	No name		32 56 036	137 46 084
Whyalla	No name	Big snapper	33 05 168	137 41 801
Whyalla	No name		33 05 300	137 44 300
Whyalla	No name		33 05 709	137 38 618
Whyalla	North Havelburg	Snapper, trumpeter	33 05 540	137 40 320
Whyalla	North Havelburgh	11 m. Snapper	33 01 539	137 40 319
Whyalla	Pedro's		33 08 344	137 34 691
Whyalla	Perry's	Lumps. Snapper	33 05 441	137 37 100
Whyalla	Pittman's		33 06 763	137 36 380
Whyalla	Pittman's Drop		33 02 680	137 35 550
Whyalla	Port	Ledge. Whiting	33 02 920	137 37 740
Whyalla	Port Germain Pipes		33 03 700	137 59 800
Whyalla	Port Germain Wreck	Community wreck	33 03 270	137 59 800
Whyalla	Pt Lowly Tyre Reef	Snapper	32 58 270	137 46 740
Whyalla	Pt Lowly Tyre Reef	Snapper	32 58 630	137 47 090
Whyalla	Rundall	13 m. Snapper	33 05 415	137 39 615
Whyalla	Shotgun		33 16 348	137 32 201
Whyalla	South Havelburg	Snapper, trumpeter	33 05 440	137 39 630
Whyalla	Spoil	Broken bottom. Snapper	33 01 406	137 38 794
Whyalla	Stanley's		33 01 740	137 40 460

Locality	Description	Comments	Latitude	Latitude
Whyalla	Terry's Last Stand	4 m, weed bottom, snapper and whiting	33 11 428	137 30 447
Whyalla	The Entrance		33 03 250	137 57 900
Whyalla	Tony's		33 04 461	137 39 180
Whyalla	Tree Reef 1	10 m. Snapper	33 00 719	137 39 761
Whyalla	Tree Reef 2	10 m. Snapper	33 00 720	137 39 753
Whyalla	Tyre Module 1	2 km north Point Lowly Lighthouse	32 58 100	137 46 900
Whyalla	Tyre Module 2	Point Lowly Lighthouse. Snapper. Strong rips	32 59 700	137 47 100
Whyalla	Tyre Module 3	7.3 km from Whyalla boat ramp bearing 162 deg, snapper, trumpeter.	33 07 772	137 36 349
Whyalla	Tyre reef 1	Snapper	33 05 200	137 54 300
Whyalla	Tyre reef 2	Snapper	33 06 300	137 36 300
Whyalla	Weeroona Sands		33 05 170	137 48 100
Whyalla	West pole		33 22 306	137 40 390
Whyalla	Western Shoal		33 09 620	137 30 580
Whyalla	Yacht		33 02 092	137 37 790

NORTHERN TERRITORY GPS MARKS

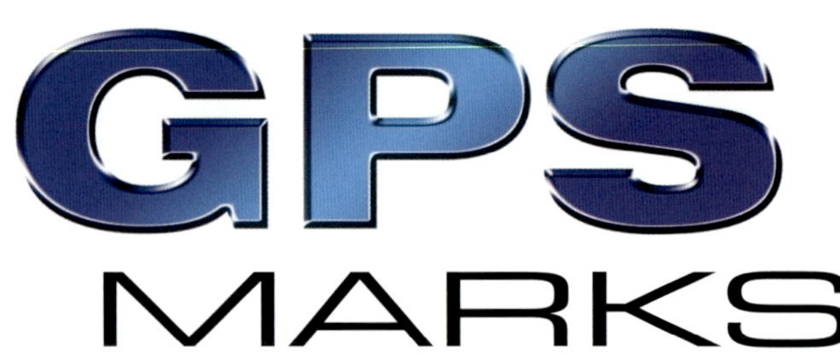

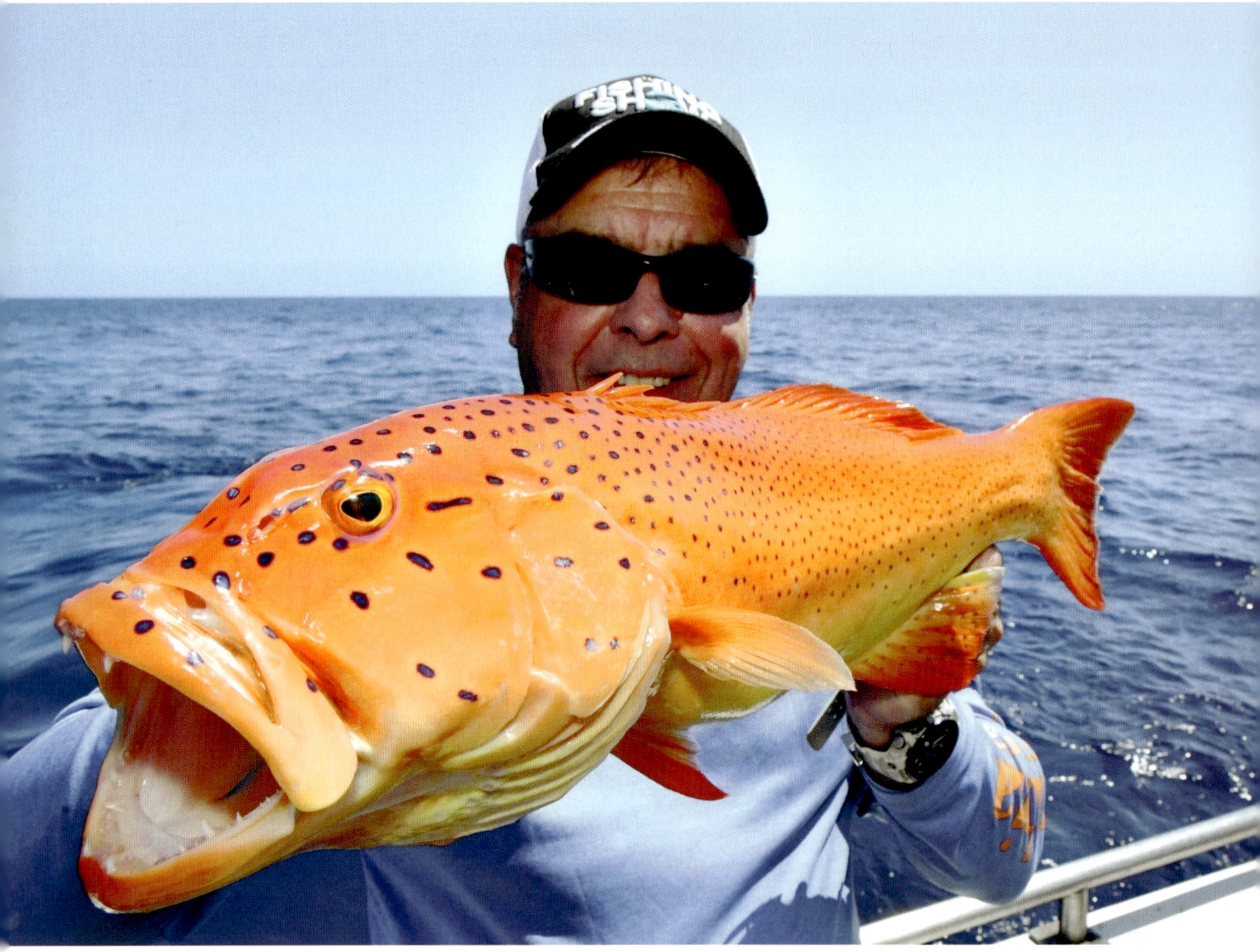

Locality	Description	Comments	Latitude	Latitude
Darwin Harbour	Angler Reef		12 19 060	130 52 150
Darwin Harbour	Bellbird	Fish haven	12 10 300	130 41 500
Darwin Harbour	Bellbird		12 28 136	130 50 090
Darwin Harbour	Boat Club to Bottle washer		12 25 652	130 50 038
Darwin Harbour	Bottle Washer		12 18 400	130 51 795
Darwin Harbour	Bouy off Ski Club		12 25 980	130 49 369
Darwin Harbour	Brolga/Eagle		12 10 999	130 39 529
Darwin Harbour	Brolga/Eagle		12 29 080	130 50 310
Darwin Harbour	Bus Stop	Fish haven	12 11 000	130 39 500
Darwin Harbour	Bus Stop		12 11 090	130 41 238
Darwin Harbour	Catalina (1)	Fish haven	12 11 110	130 41 240
Darwin Harbour	Catalina (5)		12 30 800	130 53 725
Darwin Harbour	Chang 1028		12 30 800	130 54 200
Darwin Harbour	Con Dao 3	30 m	12 10 200	130 34 700
Darwin Harbour	Dariba Rock		12 20 769	130 51 342
Darwin Harbour	Dieman		12 25 596	130 45 917
Darwin Harbour	Ellengowan	11 m	12 24 800	130 48 150
Darwin Harbour	Galah/Heron	Fish haven	12 09 700	130 40 800
Darwin Harbour	Galah/Heron		12 10 376	130 40 764
Darwin Harbour	Ham Luong		12 32 460	130 51 940
Darwin Harbour	J Holland Barge		12 28 650	130 47 900
Darwin Harbour	Jabiru/ Kookaburra		12 10 380	130 40 922
Darwin Harbour	Kelat		12 30 118	130 52 603
Darwin Harbour	Landing Barge		12 29 000	130 50 700
Darwin Harbour	Mandorah Queen		12 26 780	130 46 750
Darwin Harbour	Marchant/Albatross/Grevilia		12 10 288	130 40 578
Darwin Harbour	Marchart 3		12 10 400	130 40 600
Darwin Harbour	Mauna Loa		12 29 815	130 49 162
Darwin Harbour	Mudlark/Cockatoo		12 10 300	130 39 593
Darwin Harbour	Neptuna	Fish haven	12 28 240	130 50 970
Darwin Harbour	Nightcliff (off ramp)		12 22 763	130 50 395
Darwin Harbour	Nightcliff Ramp Approach		12 22 675	130 50 379
Darwin Harbour	No Name		12 20 266	130 50 837
Darwin Harbour	No Name		12 20 692	130 51 185

Locality	Description	Comments	Latitude	Latitude
Darwin Harbour	No Name		12 20 738	130 50 561
Darwin Harbour	No Name		12 21 204	130 50 213
Darwin Harbour	No Name		12 21 844	130 49 918
Darwin Harbour	No Name		12 23 411	130 49 107
Darwin Harbour	No Name		12 24 161	130 48 521
Darwin Harbour	No Name		12 24 702	130 48 587
Darwin Harbour	No Name		12 25 075	130 48 913
Darwin Harbour	No Name		12 25 571	130 49 935
Darwin Harbour	Nr Diemen	14 m	12 25 380	130 45 720
Darwin Harbour	Off Ski Club		12 26 131	130 49 851
Darwin Harbour	Pipeline		12 11 653	130 40 410
Darwin Harbour	Pipeline Reef	Fish haven	12 11 690	130 40 360
Darwin Harbour	Six Mile		12 24 796	130 47 758
Darwin Harbour	Six Mile Grounds		12 24 478	130 47 455
Darwin Harbour	Song Saigon		12 28 590	130 47 970
Darwin Harbour	Tipper Reef		12 18 218	130 50 478
Darwin Harbour	Tipper Reef 2nd Part		12 17 995	130 50 409
Darwin Harbour	Usat Mauna Loa		12 29 481	130 49 100
Darwin Harbour	Usat Meigs		12 29 500	130 49 072
Darwin Harbour	Uss Peary		12 28 600	130 49 750
Darwin Harbour	Zealandia		12 28 950	130 50 980
Darwin surrounds	2nm off mouth		12 08 190	131 07 533
Darwin surrounds	Bass Reef		12 29 986	130 19 993
Darwin surrounds	Blue Hole		12 02 683	131 05 189
Darwin surrounds	Bottom fishing spots		12 28 766	130 28 932
Darwin surrounds	Bowra Shoal		12 50 712	130 09 033
Darwin surrounds	Bowra Shoal		12 52 217	130 08 983
Darwin surrounds	Cape Hotham		12 02 011	131 17 735
Darwin surrounds	Catalina (East Arm)		12 30 625	130 53 893
Darwin surrounds	Charles Patches		12 20 324	130 32 177
Darwin surrounds	Charles Patches		12 20 482	130 31 539
Darwin surrounds	Fish Reef		12 26 316	130 26 749
Darwin surrounds	Harris Reef		11 59 740	130 58 103
Darwin surrounds	Henry Ellis Reef		12 05 400	131 00 638

Locality	Description	Comments	Latitude	Latitude
Darwin surrounds	Indian Island (Top end)		12 33 983	130 31 566
Darwin surrounds	Kellaway Reef (near Tapa)		12 25 850	130 33 127
Darwin surrounds	Knight Reef		12 00 240	131 08 164
Darwin surrounds	Loee Patches (Dundee/Bynoe)		12 32 429	130 16 476
Darwin surrounds	Lyne Reef (off Vernons)		12 06 420	130 59 397
Darwin surrounds	Middle reef		12 29 450	130 28 741
Darwin surrounds	Moira Reef	Take care	12 30 711	130 30 561
Darwin surrounds	near fish reef		12 27 135	130 26 405
Darwin surrounds	No Name		12 33 350	130 31 483
Darwin surrounds	Off Draytons Reef		12 02 286	131 21 354
Darwin surrounds	Off Native Point		12 43 671	130 19 998
Darwin surrounds	Off Unjin Point	4 different spots near each other	12 33 501	130 31 603
Darwin surrounds	Oliver Reef		12 01 663	130 59 382
Darwin surrounds	Price Knoll		12 00 840	131 01 816
Darwin surrounds	reef near Simms		12 34 830	130 26 166
Darwin surrounds	Roche Reef (b)		12 40 998	130 19 998
Darwin surrounds	Roche Reef (c)		12 39 303	130 20 165
Darwin surrounds	Roche Reef (c)		12 39 500	130 20 365
Darwin surrounds	Simms Reef (Bynoe/Indian Is)		12 34 065	130 27 239
Darwin surrounds	Smith Reef		12 00 492	131 00 660
Darwin surrounds	SS Brisbane		12 26 000	130 26 300
Darwin surrounds	To sea from Moira and near		12 29 249	130 28 744
Darwin surrounds	To sea from Moira and near		12 29 435	130 28 782
Darwin surrounds	Van Waerwyck Reef		12 05 297	131 00 638
Darwin surrounds	West of Bass Reef		12 28 750	130 18 233
Darwin surrounds	West of Middle Reef		12 29 285	130 28 783
Darwin surrounds	Wood Rock		12 03 741	130 57 767
Tiwi Islands	Cape Fourcroy	Ledges and reefs	11 48 200	130 01 000
Tiwi Islands	Shallow reef	Snapper	11 30 393	130 10 231

TASMANIA

Locality	Description	Comments	Latitude	Latitude
Bruny Island	Dennes Point	20+ m	43 03 298	147 21 556
Bruny Island	Bull Bay	11 m	43 05 016	147 22 051
Bruny Island	Barnes Bay	15 m	43 07 813	147 20 975
Bruny Island	Great Bay	12–15 m	43 12 025	147 21 218
Bruny Island	Cape Queen Elizabeth		43 15 237	147 25 982
Bruny Island	Moorina Bay	16.2 m	43 15 941	147 23 904
Bruny Island	Isthmus Bay	12–15 m	43 15 976	147 19 213
Bruny Island	Satellite Island	Shallow	43 18 873	147 13 328
Bruny Island	Adventure Bay	18 m	43 20 333	147 20 853
Bruny Island	Ventenat Point	11 m	43 20 674	147 10 520
Bruny Island	Partridge Island	11 m	43 23 922	147 05 548
Bruny Island	Hopwood point	36.6 m	43 25 480	147 03 215
Bruny Island	Great Taylors Bay	38 m	43 26 257	147 09 559
Bruny Island	Cloudy Bay	17+ m	43 28 114	147 12 969
Bruny Island	West Cloudy Head	18.3+ m	43 29 866	147 10 748
Bruny Island	Boreel Head	36.6 m	43 30 022	147 20 012
Bruny Island	Cape Bruny	18.3+ m	43 30 207	147 07 693
Bruny Island	Tasman Head (Friar's area)	36.6 m	43 33 308	147 17 120
Bruny Island	Bridge Rock	43 m	43 33 433	147 16 821
D'Entrecasteaux Channel	North West Bay		43 03 197	147 17 234
D'Entrecasteaux Channel	Green Island	15 m	43 11 808	147 17 118
D'Entrecasteaux Channel	Garden Island	10 m	43 15 878	147 07 599
D'Entrecasteaux Channel	Huon Island	20 m	43 17 568	147 08 236
D'Entrecasteaux Channel	Huon River Entrance		43 17 651	147 07 236
D'Entrecasteaux Channel	Rabbit Island	5 m, Atlantic salmon	43 20 285	147 00 287
D'Entrecasteaux Channel	Hope Island	30 m	43 20 434	147 02 628
D'Entrecasteaux Channel	Entrance Port Esperance	18.3 m	43 20 532	147 03 590
D'Entrecasteaux Channel	Lune River entrance	2 m variable	43 26 835	146 57 624
D'Entrecasteaux Channel	Pelican Island	5 m	43 26 924	146 58 464

Locality	Description	Comments	Latitude	Latitude
D'Entrecasteaux Channel	Entrance Southport	18.3 m	43 27 511	147 00 268
D'Entrecasteaux Channel	Actaeon Island	18.3 m	43 32 317	147 00 471
D'Entrecasteaux Channel	The Images		43 32 753	146 55 398
D'Entrecasteaux Channel	Recherche Bay		43 33 027	147 54 598
D'Entrecasteaux Channel	Catamaran River	5 m	43 33 114	146 53 584
D'Entrecasteaux Channel	Obelisk Rock		43 33 393	147 00 748
D'Entrecasteaux Channel	Cockle Creek	5 m	43 34 838	146 53 568
Derwent River	Kangaroo Bluff	20 m	42 52 565	147 21 053
Derwent River	Bellerieve Bluff	20 m	42 53 095	147 21 939
Derwent River	Sandy Bay Point	15 m	42 54 506	147 21 514
Derwent River	Transmere Bluff	15 m	42 56 467	147 24 347
Derwent River	Opossum Bay Beach	2 m	42 59 468	147 23 897
Derwent River	The Pigeon Holes	10 m	43 00 430	147 23 757
Derwent River	Sth Arm Beach / Jetty	5 m	43 01 793	147 24 484
Derwent River Entrance	Cape Contrariety	11 m	43 01 359	147 31 165
Derwent River Entrance	Tinderbox area	18.3 m	43 02 357	147 21 539
Derwent River Entrance	Marine reserve	18.3 m	43 02 647	147 22 519
Derwent River Entrance	Cape Direction	5 m	43 03 230	147 25 249
Derwent River Entrance	Betsey Island	18.3 m	43 03 302	147 28 590
Derwent River Entrance	Iron Pot	5 m	43 03 535	147 24 914
Derwent River Entrance	Little Betsy Island	18.3 m	43 04 320	147 29 486
Devonport	Point Sorrell	27 m hump. Also Local magnetic anomaly.	41 03 839	146 32 846
Devonport	Wreck	26 m.	41 07 443	146 19 587
Flinders Island	Lady Barron (Flinders Island)	Australian salmon, trevally, barracouta, sweep, wrasse, parrotfish, flathead, whiting, mullet	40 14 174	148 20 860
Fredrick Henry Bay	Tiger Head Point	Channel Way 5 m	42 51 259	147 36 397

Locality	Description	Comments	Latitude	Latitude
Fredrick Henry Bay	Seven Mile Beach	4–10 m	42 51 401	147 32 249
Fredrick Henry Bay	Spectacle Head / Spectacle Island	2–5 m	42 52 037	147 36 264
Fredrick Henry Bay	Carlton Beach	5 m	42 52 341	147 37 477
Fredrick Henry Bay	Carlton River mouth	Exposed surf 5 m	42 52 598	147 38 379
Fredrick Henry Bay	Lauderdale Beach	5 m	42 54 303	147 30 525
Fredrick Henry Bay	Dunalley Sand Flats	5 m	42 54 445	147 48 831
Fredrick Henry Bay	Fulham Island	5 m	42 54 730	147 46 909
Fredrick Henry Bay	Cremorne Canal Barway	5.5 m	42 57 269	147 32 351
Fredrick Henry Bay	Pipeclay Lagoon	9.1 m	42 58 151	147 31 132
Fredrick Henry Bay	Cape Deslacs	Nth Clifton Bluff 11 m	42 59 351	147 33 351
Fredrick Henry Bay	Clifton Bay	11 m	43 00 012	147 32 381
Georgetown	Hole	41 m.	40 59 015	146 50 904
Georgetown	Holes	31 m. Additional holes west.	40 59 593	146 54 058
Georgetown	Humps	14 m. Additional humps east.	41 00 992	146 47 112
Georgetown	Hump	19 m.	41 02 326	146 44 960
Georgetown	West Reef (2)	5 m hole. Australian salmon, barracuda, trevally, snapper, bream, mullet, flathead	41 03 692	146 46 068
Georgetown	West Reef	Australian salmon, barracuda, trevally, snapper, bream, mullet, flathead	41 03 722	146 45 621
Georgetown	Shear Rock	2 m. Australian salmon, barracuda, trevally, snapper, bream, mullet, flathead	41 04 016	146 46 860
Georgetown	West Head	Australian salmon, barracuda, trevally, snapper, bream, mullet, flathead	41 04 100	146 43 693
Georgetown	Greens Beach	Australian salmon, barracuda, trevally, snapper, bream, mullet, flathead	41 04 508	146 44 885
Launceston	Beauty Point (Tamar River)	Australian salmon, trevally, brown trout, rainbow trout	41 08 960	146 49 800
Launceston	Gravelly Beach (Tamar River)	Australian Salmon, Trevally, Snapper, Bream, Mullet, Flathead	41 17 415	146 58 800
Launceston	Rosevears (Tamar River)	Australian salmon, trevally, snapper, bream, mullet, flathead, brown trout	41 19 192	147 00 327

Locality	Description	Comments	Latitude	Latitude
Launceston	North Esk River	Rainbow trout, brown trout	41 25 980	147 07 898
Penguin Point	Hump	12 m.	41 04 473	146 05 589
Smithton	Eastern Inlet	Australian salmon, trevally, barracouta, shark, snook, bream, sweep, luderick, mullet, flathead, cod	40 47 312	145 17 500
Smithton	Black River Estuary	Australian salmon, trevally, barracouta, shark, snook, bream, sweep, luderick, mullet, flathead, cod	40 50 128	145 19 269
St Helens	Binalong Patch	Reef.	41 09 228	148 38 497
St Helens	Drop off	Stripey trumpeter, morwong, flathead, red rock cod and other reef fish	41 11 205	148 37 127
St Helens	Sloop Rock	Stripey trumpeter, morwong, flathead, red rock cod and other reef fish	41 12 616	148 17 630
St Helens	Sloop Rock S	Stripey trumpeter, morwong, flathead, red rock cod and other reef fish	41 13 158	148 17 395
St Helens	The Cliff	Stripey trumpeter, morwong, flathead, red rock cod and other reef fish	41 14 550	148 39 320
St Helens	Merricks Rock 1	Stripey trumpeter, morwong, flathead, red rock cod and other reef fish	41 15 811	148 24 701
St Helens	Merricks Rock 2	Stripey trumpeter, morwong, flathead, red rock cod and other reef fish	41 15 828	148 24 627
St Helens	Merricks Rock 3	Stripey trumpeter, morwong, flathead, red rock cod and other reef fish	41 16 286	148 24 489
St Helens	Merricks Rock 4	Stripey trumpeter, morwong, flathead, red rock cod and other reef fish	41 16 585	148 22 997
St Helens	Merricks Rock 5	5 m.	41 16 764	148 22 963
St Helens	Merricks Rock 6	Stripey trumpeter, morwong, flathead, red rock cod and other reef fish	41 16 856	148 23 341
St Helens	East Merricks Rock	Stripey trumpeter, morwong, flathead, red rock cod and other reef fish	41 17 030	148 24 313
St Helens	Merricks Rock 7	Stripey trumpeter, morwong, flathead, red rock cod and other reef fish	41 17 071	148 24 317
St Helens	North Merricks Rock	Stripey trumpeter, morwong, flathead, red rock cod and other reef fish	41 17 168	148 23 385
St Helens	South East Merricks	Stripey trumpeter, morwong, flathead, red rock cod and other reef fish	41 17 237	148 23 354
St Helens	Middle Ground	St Helens. Deep steep dropoff. Water depth 11–300 m. Reef species, crayfish.	41 18 587	148 21 886
St Helens	Drop off	Stripey trumpeter, morwong, flathead, red rock cod and other reef fish	41 21 646	148 37 723
St Helens	Ansons Hump 3	Reef Fish	41 22 010	148 39 030
St Helens	Paddy's Island East	8 m patch.	41 24 012	148 18 802

Locality	Description	Comments	Latitude	Latitude
St Helens	Pulfers Break	7 m hump. Take care.	41 26 249	148 21 614
Table Cape	FAD	40 m.	40 55 775	145 44 595
Tasman Peninsula	Marion Bay Beach		42 48 067	147 52 837
Tasman Peninsula	Cape Paul Lamanon		42 50 319	147 55 237
Tasman Peninsula	Marion Bay Barway		42 50 447	147 53 201
Tasman Peninsula	Visscher Island		42 50 938	147 58 586
Tasman Peninsula	North Bay		42 52 052	147 56 001
Tasman Peninsula	Cape Fredrick Hendrick		42 52 093	147 58 918
Tasman Peninsula	High Yellow Bluff		42 54 741	148 00 122
Tasman Peninsula	Yellow Bluff		42 55 666	147 59 821
Tasman Peninsula	Sloping Island	36.6 m	42 56 878	147 37 377
Tasman Peninsula	Cape Surville		42 57 002	147 59 865
Tasman Peninsula	Sisters Rocks	24 m	42 57 559	148 00 205
Tasman Peninsula	Deep Glen Bay	18 m	42 58 305	147 59 490
Tasman Peninsula	Sloping Main Beach	5.5 m	42 59 150	147 40 09?
Tasman Peninsula	Pirates Bay	22 m	43 01 209	147 57 380
Tasman Peninsula	Waterfall Bay entrance	28 m	43 03 525	147 57 343
Tasman Peninsula	Ohara Bluff	21 m	43 05 004	147 58 391
Tasman Peninsula	The Thumbs	9.1 m	43 06 452	147 59 086
Tasman Peninsula	Nubeena Bay Mouth		43 07 027	147 41 388
Tasman Peninsula	Fortescue Bay entrance	22 m	43 07 747	147 59 040
Tasman Peninsula	Wedge Island	5.5 m	43 07 955	147 40 661
Tasman Peninsula	The Lanterns	35 m	43 08 257	148 00 728
Tasman Peninsula	The Monument	9.1 m	43 08 815	148 00 188
Tasman Peninsula	Munroe Bight		43 11 123	147 58 916
Tasman Peninsula	Port Arthur Bay	36.6 m	43 11 936	147 52 964
Tasman Peninsula	West Arthur Head	18.3 m	43 12 475	147 52 421
Tasman Peninsula	Cape Pillar	72 m	43 13 030	148 00 629
Tasman Peninsula	The Landing Stage	91.4 m	43 13 880	148 00 571
Tasman Peninsula	Cape Raoul	91.4 m	43 14 632	147 47 807
Tasman Peninsula	Tasman Island		43 14 781	148 00 012
Tourville	The Friendly Beaches	40 m.	42 02 073	148 18 503
Tourville	The Nuggets	50 m.	42 07 196	148 22 019
Tourville	Touin Bay	30 m.	42 09 661	148 19 377

WESTERN AUSTRALIA GPS MARKS

Locality	Description	Comments	Latitude	Latitude
Broome	99		16 59 247	122 08 808
Broome	Awong Patch	Threadfin salmon, blue salmon, queenfish, trevally, sharks, barramundi, mangrove jacks, fingermark bream	16 59 740	122 15 170
Broome	Blue hump		17 54 991	121 11 710
Broome	Bluebone		17 54 886	121 11 773
Broome	Broome ramp approach		18 00 725	122 12 866
Broome	Cable Beach–Beach Launch-ing		17 55 850	122 12 300
Broome	Cape Frezier	Spanish mackerel, wahoo, barracuda, trevally, queenfish, tuna, sharks, mulloway, whiting, mullet, garfish	18 52 090	121 36 060
Broome	Cape Gourdon	Spanish mackerel, wahoo, barracuda, trevally, queenfish, tuna, sharks, mulloway, whiting, mullet, garfish	18 24 561	121 58 853
Broome	Cape Jaubert	Spanish mackerel, wahoo, barracuda, trevally, queenfish, tuna, sharks, mulloway, whiting, mullet, garfish	18 56 400	121 33 580
Broome	Cape Latouche Treville	Spanish mackerel, wahoo, barracuda, trevally, queenfish, tuna, sharks, mulloway, whiting, mullet, garfish	18 26 315	121 49 441
Broome	Cape Villaret	Threadfin salmon, blue salmon, queenfish, trevally, black mulloway, bluebone groper, fingermark bream	18 19 398	122 03 762
Broome	Casuarina Reef E	2 m. Spanish mackerel, wahoo, barracuda, trevally, queenfish, tuna, sharks, mulloway, whiting, mullet, garfish	18 41 981	121 36 166
Broome	Declaration Rock #1	Threadfin salmon, blue salmon, queenfish, trevally, sharks, barramundi, mangrove jacks, fingermark bream	17 57 300	122 10 640
Broome	Declaration Rock #2	Threadfin salmon, blue salmon, queenfish, trevally, sharks, barramundi, mangrove jacks, fingermark bream	17 57 222	122 09 970
Broome	Declaration Rock #3	Threadfin salmon, blue salmon, queenfish, trevally, black mulloway, bluebone groper, fingermark bream	17 57 447	122 09 698
Broome	Disaster Rock	Threadfin salmon, blue salmon, queenfish, trevally, sharks, barramundi, mangrove jacks, fingermark bream	18 04 149	122 04 898
Broome	East Rock	Threadfin salmon, blue salmon, queenfish, trevally, black mulloway, bluebone groper, fingermark bream	18 01 443	122 09 786
Broome	Entrance		16 46 786	122 34 023
Broome	Escape Rocks		17 59 830	122 09 640
Broome	False Cape Bossut	Spanish mackerel, wahoo, barracuda, trevally, queenfish, tuna, sharks, mulloway, whiting, mullet, garfish	18 34 109	121 43 148

Locality	Description	Comments	Latitude	Latitude
Broome	Five		17 45 796	121 58 295
Broome	Gantheume		17 58 219	121 11 230
Broome	Gantheume Point #1	Sailfish, mackerel, threadfin salmon, blue salmon, queenfish, barramundi, mangrove jacks, fingermark bream	17 58 688	122 09 730
Broome	Gourdon Bay	9 m. Threadfin salmon, blue salmon, queenfish, trevally, sharks, barramundi, mangrove jacks, fingermark bream	18 26 348	121 48 424
Broome	Grey Shoal	9 m. Threadfin salmon, blue salmon, queenfish, trevally, sharks, barramundi, mangrove jacks, fingermark bream	17 39 123	122 02 580
Broome	Gunuru Creek	Spanish mackerel, wahoo, barracuda, trevally, queenfish, tuna, sharks, mulloway, whiting, mullet, garfish	18 39 560	121 46 956
Broome	High Tide Launching		18 42 000	121 41 000
Broome	Inner Anchorage	Threadfin salmon, blue salmon, queenfish, trevally, black mulloway, bluebone groper, fingermark bream	17 59 409	122 14 526
Broome	Justice Shoal	4 m. Spanish mackerel, wahoo, barracuda, trevally, queenfish, tuna, sharks, mulloway, whiting, mullet, garfish	18 26 615	121 40 792
Broome	Lacepede Is 1		16 50 803	122 10 228
Broome	Lacepede Is 2	Sloper Shoal	16 50 523	122 17 847
Broome	Lombadina	6 m. Threadfin salmon, blue salmon, queenfish, trevally, sharks, barramundi, mangrove jacks, fingermark bream	16 27 761	122 52 319
Broome	Lord Mayor Shoal	Threadfin salmon, blue salmon, queenfish, trevally, sharks, barramundi, mangrove jacks, fingermark bream	16 31 010	122 36 950
Broome	Mack's		17 56 334	122 02 877
Broome	Marlin 1		17 44 382	121 51 218
Broome	Marlin 2		17 45 060	121 51 340
Broome	Middle Creek	Spanish mackerel, wahoo, barracuda, trevally, queenfish, tuna, sharks, mulloway, whiting, mullet, garfish	18 42 683	121 40 298
Broome	Middle Lagoon Deep #1	Threadfin salmon, blue salmon, queenfish, trevally, sharks, barramundi, mangrove jacks, fingermark bream	16 28 879	122 05 276
Broome	Middle Lagoon Deep #2	14 m. Threadfin salmon, blue salmon, queenfish, trevally, sharks, barramundi, mangrove jacks, fingermark bream	16 45 650	122 12 240
Broome	Middle Lagoon Deep #3	15 m. Threadfin salmon, blue salmon, queenfish, trevally, sharks, barramundi, mangrove jacks, fingermark bream	16 45 350	122 24 490
Broome	Middle Lagoon Deep #4	Threadfin salmon, blue salmon, queenfish, trevally, sharks, barramundi, mangrove jacks, fingermark bream	16 31 821	122 23 582

Locality	Description	Comments	Latitude	Latitude
Broome	Nab Rock	Threadfin salmon, blue salmon, queenfish, trevally, sharks, barramundi, mangrove jacks, fingermark bream	17 59 500	122 10 640
Broome	Nandanarr Rocks	Spanish mackerel, wahoo, barracuda, trevally, queenfish, tuna, sharks, mulloway, whiting, mullet, garfish	18 40 110	121 45 369
Broome	Naringla Shoal		17 39 320	122 03 493
Broome	No name		17 58 153	121 11 188
Broome	No name		17 41 523	121 50 544
Broome	No name		17 43 215	121 50 667
Broome	No name		17 54 856	121 53 757
Broome	No name		17 37 811	122 00 027
Broome	No name		17 36 761	122 00 510
Broome	No name		18 00 460	122 13 210
Broome	No name		16 30 350	122 37 973
Broome	Peanut		17 32 063	121 56 630
Broome	Pearl Shoals	Threadfin salmon, blue salmon, queenfish, trevally, sharks, barramundi, mangrove jacks, fingermark bream	17 59 704	122 09 524
Broome	Pearling North #1	Threadfin salmon, blue salmon, queenfish, trevally, sharks, barramundi, mangrove jacks, fingermark bream	17 46 135	121 58 311
Broome	Pearling North #2	Threadfin salmon, blue salmon, queenfish, trevally, sharks, barramundi, mangrove jacks, fingermark bream	17 44 020	121 58 931
Broome	Pearling North #3	18 m. Threadfin salmon, blue salmon, queenfish, trevally, sharks, barramundi, mangrove jacks, fingermark bream	17 31 981	121 56 709
Broome	Pearling South #1	Threadfin salmon, blue salmon, queenfish, trevally, sharks, barramundi, mangrove jacks, fingermark bream	17 55 380	121 56 319
Broome	Pinnacle Rock	Spanish mackerel, wahoo, barracuda, trevally, queenfish, tuna, sharks, mulloway, whiting, mullet, garfish	18 48 600	121 38 380
Broome	Pitt Shoals	Threadfin salmon, blue salmon, queenfish, trevally, sharks, barramundi, mangrove jacks, fingermark bream	16 16 350	122 52 651
Broome	Rocky Point	Spanish mackerel, wahoo, barracuda, trevally, queenfish, tuna, sharks, mulloway, whiting, mullet, garfish	18 41 779	121 44 414
Broome	Roebuck Deep		18 01 119	122 11 946
Broome	Roebuck Deep Drop-off #1	Threadfin salmon, blue salmon, queenfish, trevally, sharks, barramundi, mangrove jacks, fingermark bream	18 00 920	122 11 040
Broome	Roebuck Deep Drop-off #2	Threadfin salmon, blue salmon, queenfish, trevally, sharks, barramundi, mangrove jacks, fingermark bream	18 01 289	122 11 273

Locality	Description	Comments	Latitude	Latitude
Broome	Roebuck Deep Drop-off #3	Threadfin salmon, blue salmon, queenfish, trevally, sharks, barramundi, mangrove jacks, fingermark bream	18 01 754	122 12 524
Broome	Roebuck Deep Drop-off #4	Threadfin salmon, blue salmon, queenfish, trevally, sharks, barramundi, mangrove jacks, fingermark bream	18 01 950	122 15 172
Broome	Roebuck Deep Drop-off #5	Threadfin salmon, blue salmon, queenfish, trevally, sharks, barramundi, mangrove jacks, fingermark bream	18 01 926	122 15 435
Broome	Sailfish 1		17 44 516	122 01 632
Broome	Sailfish 2		17 44 516	121 58 774
Broome	Sailfish 3		17 48 561	122 04 820
Broome	Sailfish 4		17 45 032	122 02 249
Broome	Sails close		17 46 055	122 02 530
Broome	Sailx 2		17 39 704	122 00 637
Broome	Sandy Isle	Threadfin salmon, blue salmon, queenfish, trevally, sharks, barramundi, mangrove jacks, fingermark bream	16 51 454	122 09 527
Broome	Seven		17 55 301	121 56 256
Broome	Shark Alley Christo's		17 44 394	122 01 407
Broome	Six		17 02 536	121 53 596
Broome	Sloper Shoal	8 m. Threadfin salmon, blue salmon, queenfish, trevally, sharks, barramundi, mangrove jacks, fingermark bream	16 50 610	122 17 900
Broome	South Lacepede	Awong Patch	16 59 626	122 16 085
Broome	Three		17 43 740	121 53 987
Broome	West caves		17 43 482	121 55 421
Broome	West Disaster Rock	Threadfin salmon, blue salmon, queenfish, trevally, black mulloway, bluebone groper, fingermark bream	18 02 454	121 53 675
Broome	West Island		16 51 531	122 09 449
Broome	Weston Patch–Robber Rocks	Threadfin salmon, blue salmon, queenfish, trevally, sharks, barramundi, mangrove jacks, fingermark bream	16 47 211	122 01 347
Broome	Willie Rock		17 46 310	122 10 337
Bunbury	19 M Lump	Dhuies, snapper, sambos	33 08 092	115 32 103
Bunbury	artificial reef	pinkies	33 35 039	115 10 114
Bunbury	Harding Rock	5 m. Snapper	33 10 217	115 40 917
Dampier	Bare Rock	Spanish mackerel, wahoo, barracuda, trevally, queenfish, tuna, sharks, whiting, mullet, garfish, mulloway	20 33 299	116 26 886
Dampier	Cape Legendre	Spanish mackerel, wahoo, barracuda, trevally, queenfish, tuna, sharks, whiting, mullet, garfish, mulloway	20 20 374	116 50 827

Locality	Description	Comments	Latitude	Latitude
Dampier	Cod Bank	Spanish mackerel, wahoo, barracuda, trevally, queenfish, tuna, sharks, whiting, mullet, garfish, mulloway	20 40 332	116 17 420
Dampier	Courtenay Shoal	Spanish mackerel, wahoo, barracuda, trevally, queenfish, tuna, sharks, whiting, mullet, garfish, mulloway	20 28 310	116 42 146
Dampier	Dampier Ramp		20 39 600	116 42 243
Dampier	Delambre Island	Take care. Spanish Mackerel, wahoo, barracuda, trevally, queenfish, tuna, sharks, whiting, mullet, garfish, mulloway	20 27 123	117 01 639
Dampier	Dixon Island	Spanish mackerel, wahoo, barracuda, trevally, queenfish, tuna, sharks, whiting, mullet, garfish, mulloway	20 34 115	117 00 657
Dampier	Dockrell Reef	Spanish mackerel, wahoo, barracuda, trevally, queenfish, tuna, sharks, whiting, mullet, garfish, mulloway	20 39 675	116 31 136
Dampier	Fortescue River	Spanish mackerel, wahoo, barracuda, trevally, queenfish, tuna sharks, whiting, mullet, garfish, mulloway	20 59 726	116 06 596
Dampier	Meda Reef	Spanish mackerel, wahoo, barracuda, trevally, queenfish, tuna, sharks	21 02 660	115 46 045
Dampier	Mermaid Sound	Spanish mackerel, wahoo, barracuda, trevally, queenfish, tuna sharks, whiting, mullet, garfish, mulloway	20 34 033	116 41 345
Dampier	Mt Rough Estuary	Spanish mackerel, wahoo, barracuda, trevally, queenfish, tuna sharks, whiting, mullet, garfish, mulloway	20 53 921	116 10 474
Dampier	North Sandy Island North East Angler	Spanish mackerel, wahoo, barracuda, trevally, queenfish, tuna, sharks, whiting, mullet, garfish, mulloway	21 05 175	115 44 78
Dampier	O'Grady Shoal	Spanish mackerel, wahoo, barracuda, trevally, queenfish, tuna, sharks, whiting, mullet, garfish, mulloway	20 51 454	116 04 746
Dampier	Victoria Rock	Spanish mackerel, wahoo, barracuda, trevally, queenfish, tuna, sharks, whiting, mullet, garfish, mulloway	20 42 852	116 23 940
Dampier	West Intercourse Island North Passage	Spanish mackerel, wahoo, barracuda, trevally, queenfish, tuna, sharks, whiting, mullet, garfish, mulloway	20 41 018	116 39 200
Dampier	West Intercourse Island South Passage	Spanish mackerel, wahoo, barracuda, trevally, queenfish, tuna, sharks, whiting, mullet, garfish, mulloway	20 44 335	116 34 770
Derby	Anderdon Islands	24 m. Threadfin salmon, blue salmon, queenfish, trevally, barramundi, mangrove jacks, fingermark bream, pikey bream	14 53 371	125 12 188
Derby	August Point	Queenfish, trevally, mackerel, tuna, sharks, fingermark bream, pikey bream	14 04 551	126 12 802
Derby	Beauty Point	Queenfish, trevally, mackerel, tuna, sharks, fingermark bream, pikey bream	13 58 788	126 48 568
Derby	Beauty Point Beach Launching		13 58 775	126 46 421
Derby	Berthoud Island	Threadfin salmon, blue salmon, queenfish, trevally, barramundi, mangrove jacks, fingermark bream, pikey bream	14 17 792	125 50 104
Derby	Bigge Point	7 m. Queenfish, trevally, sharks, black mulloway, fingermark bream, pikey bream	14 15 042	125 43 685

Locality	Description	Comments	Latitude	Latitude
Derby	Bignal Reef	Queenfish, trevally, mackerel, tuna, sharks, fingermark bream, pikey bream	14 28 993	125 55 680
Derby	Bishop Island	Queenfish, trevally, mackerel, tuna, sharks, fingermark bream, pikey bream	14 25 472	125 21 694
Derby	Black Rocks	Threadfin salmon, blue salmon, queenfish, trevally, barramundi, mangrove jacks, fingermark bream, pikey bream	15 02 480	124 25 804
Derby	Bluff Point #1	Queenfish, trevally, sharks, black mulloway, fingermark bream, pikey bream	14 03 951	126 40 115
Derby	Bluff Point #2	Threadfin salmon, blue salmon, queenfish, trevally, barramundi, mangrove jacks, fingermark bream, pikey bream	14 04 101	126 38 105
Derby	Bluff Point Deep	11 m. Threadfin salmon, blue salmon, queenfish, trevally, barramundi, mangrove jacks, fingermark bream, pikey bream	14 02 102	126 37 807
Derby	Boongaree Island	Queenfish, trevally, sharks, black mulloway, fingermark bream, pikey bream	15 03 154	125 08 784
Derby	Browne Island	Hole 50 m. Queenfish, trevally, sharks, black mulloway, fingermark bream, pikey bream	15 08 228	124 29 425
Derby	Camp 1		16 31 879	123 26 739
Derby	Cape Leveque	50 m hole. Threadfin salmon, blue salmon, queenfish, trevally, black mulloway, bluebone groper, fingermark bream	16 22 430	122 55 561
Derby	Cape Pond	Queenfish, trevally, sharks, black mulloway, fingermark bream, pikey bream	14 41 592	125 06 618
Derby	Carlisle Head	9 m. Threadfin salmon, blue salmon, queenfish, trevally, black mulloway, bluebone groper, fingermark bream	16 36 640	123 12 553
Derby	Cascade		16 32 105	123 27 797
Derby	Conway Island	Queenfish, trevally, sharks, black mulloway, fingermark bream, pikey bream	15 50 991	123 40 348
Derby	Cornelia Island S #1	Hump 5 m. Queenfish, trevally, mackerel, tuna, sharks, fingermark bream, pikey bream	14 12 099	125 43 500
Derby	Cornelia Island S #2	Hump 18 m. Queenfish, trevally, mackerel, tuna, sharks, fingermark bream, pikey bream	14 13 020	125 43 770
Derby	Croc Creek		16 09 273	123 39 789
Derby	Crystal Head Access	Hole 40 m. Queenfish, trevally, mackerel, tuna, sharks, fingermark bream, pikey bream	14 28 632	125 51 816
Derby	Curran Point Central	Threadfin salmon, blue salmon, queenfish, trevally, barramundi, mangrove jacks, fingermark bream, pikey bream	13 56 762	126 47 844
Derby	D'Arcole Islands	Threadfin salmon, blue salmon, queenfish, trevally, barramundi, mangrove jacks, fingermark bream, pikey bream	15 01 515	124 36 116

Locality	Description	Comments	Latitude	Latitude
Derby	Deep Bay	Queenfish, trevally, mackerel, tuna, sharks, fingermark bream, pikey bream	14 06 100	126 35 760
Derby	Denman Shoal	Queenfish, trevally, sharks, black mulloway, fingermark bream, pikey bream	15 42 961	123 55 542
Derby	Derby		17 18 065	123 35 740
Derby	Derby Ramp	Threadfin salmon, blue salmon, queenfish, trevally, barramundi, mangrove jacks, fingermark bream, pikey bream	17 14 300	123 36 500
Derby	Derby White Island	Queenfish, trevally, sharks, black mulloway, fingermark bream, pikey bream	14 11 712	125 50 270
Derby	Dickensen Ridge	Threadfin salmon, blue salmon, queenfish, trevally, black mulloway, bluebone groper, fingermark bream	16 14 512	123 22 917
Derby	Doctor's Creek	Queenfish, trevally, mackerel, tuna, sharks, fingermark bream, pikey bream	17 10 469	123 38 317
Derby	Doubtful Bay–Foam Passage	Queenfish, trevally, mackerel, tuna, sharks, fingermark bream, pikey bream	16 02 531	124 27 158
Derby	Drysdale River	Threadfin salmon, blue salmon, queenfish, trevally, barramundi, mangrove jacks, fingermark bream, pikey bream	13 55 626	126 50 171
Derby	Dunvert Island		16 17 691	123 31 236
Derby	Eclipse Archipelago	8 m. Threadfin salmon, blue salmon, queenfish, trevally, barramundi, mangrove jacks, fingermark bream, pikey bream	13 56 271	126 22 111
Derby	Eclipse Hill Island	Queenfish, trevally, sharks, black mulloway, fingermark bream, pikey bream	13 57 124	126 17 971
Derby	Eclipse Island West	18 m. Queenfish, trevally, mackerel, tuna, sharks, fingermark bream, pikey bream	13 53 603	126 15 917
Derby	Ferret Reef	Threadfin salmon, blue salmon, queenfish, trevally, sharks, barramundi, mangrove jacks, fingermark bream	16 16 419	123 03 846
Derby	Forbin Island	Queenfish, trevally, mackerel, tuna, sharks, fingermark bream, pikey bream	15 04 905	124 43 319
Derby	Forrest Rock	Threadfin salmon, blue salmon, queenfish, trevally, barramundi, mangrove jacks, fingermark bream, pikey bream	14 06 907	125 52 233
Derby	Fury Rock	Threadfin salmon, blue salmon, queenfish, trevally, barramundi, mangrove jacks, fingermark bream, pikey bream	13 58 694	125 58 569
Derby	Hat Point	Queenfish, trevally, sharks, black mulloway, fingermark bream, pikey bream	13 54 897	125 55 531
Derby	Hells gate		16 30 584	123 25 270
Derby	Helpman Islands #1	Sailfish, mackerel, threadfin salmon, blue salmon, queenfish, barramundi, mangrove jacks, fingermark bream	16 43 316	123 31 242

Locality	Description	Comments	Latitude	Latitude
Derby	Helpman Islands #2	Sailfish, mackerel, threadfin salmon, blue salmon, queenfish, barramundi, mangrove jacks, fingermark bream	16 47 731	123 33 128
Derby	Heritage Reef	Threadfin salmon, blue salmon, queenfish, trevally, barramundi, mangrove jacks, fingermark bream, pikey bream	14 15 414	125 09 765
Derby	Hull Bank	Queenfish, trevally, sharks, black mulloway, fingermark bream, pikey bream	15 27 552	124 17 441
Derby	Hunter River	9 m. Threadfin salmon, blue salmon, queenfish, trevally, barramundi, mangrove jacks, fingermark bream, pikey bream	15 02 342	125 23 247
Derby	Inner Rip Shoal	Queenfish, trevally, sharks, black mulloway, fingermark bream, pikey bream	17 10 192	123 31 597
Derby	June Point	Queenfish, trevally, mackerel, tuna, sharks, fingermark bream, pikey bream	14 06 715	126 13 438
Derby	Lan Bay	Threadfin salmon, blue salmon, queenfish, trevally, barramundi, mangrove jacks, fingermark bream, pikey bream	14 02 882	126 44 798
Derby	Lana Reef	Threadfin salmon, blue salmon, queenfish, trevally, barramundi, mangrove jacks, fingermark bream, pikey bream	15 58 593	123 31 767
Derby	Leveque Island	Jonas Shoal	16 22 684	122 56 187
Derby	Long Reef	Threadfin salmon, blue salmon, queenfish, trevally, barramundi, mangrove jacks, fingermark bream, pikey bream	13 55 482	125 51 071
Derby	Lorikeet Shoal	Threadfin salmon, blue salmon, queenfish, trevally, barramundi, mangrove jacks, fingermark bream, pikey bream	15 39 579	124 04 604
Derby	Lorinna Shoal	Queenfish, trevally, mackerel, tuna, sharks, fingermark bream, pikey bream	14 24 309	125 09 080
Derby	Louis Island	Hole 32 m. Queenfish, trevally, mackerel, tuna, sharks, fingermark bream, pikey bream	14 00 845	126 33 457
Derby	Maia Cove	Threadfin salmon, blue salmon, queenfish, trevally, barramundi, mangrove jacks, fingermark bream, pikey bream	14 12 959	126 16 640
Derby	Mavis Reef	Queenfish, trevally, sharks, black mulloway, fingermark bream, pikey bream	15 28 684	123 33 377
Derby	Mavis Reef South	Queenfish, trevally, mackerel, tuna, sharks, fingermark bream, pikey bream	15 33 487	123 27 926
Derby	Mavis Reef W	Queenfish, trevally, mackerel, tuna, sharks, fingermark bream, pikey bream	15 28 552	123 24 003
Derby	Middle Rock	Threadfin salmon, blue salmon, queenfish, trevally, barramundi, mangrove jacks, fingermark bream, pikey bream	13 58 124	126 20 971
Derby	Montgomery Reef E	Queenfish, trevally, mackerel, tuna, sharks, fingermark bream, pikey bream	16 01 721	124 17 344

Locality	Description	Comments	Latitude	Latitude
Derby	Montgomery Reef W	Queenfish, trevally, mackerel, tuna, sharks, fingermark bream, pikey bream	16 00 160	124 03 96
Derby	Montgomery Reef West #2	Threadfin salmon, blue salmon, queenfish, trevally, barramundi, mangrove jacks, fingermark bream, pikey bream	15 50 425	124 03 499
Derby	Myres Island	Threadfin salmon, blue salmon, queenfish, trevally, barramundi, mangrove jacks, fingermark bream, pikey bream	14 34 378	125 53 256
Derby	Niblock Rocks	Threadfin salmon, blue salmon, queenfish, trevally, barramundi, mangrove jacks, fingermark bream, pikey bream	15 48 665	123 59 393
Derby	No name		16 04 928	123 35 305
Derby	No name		16 08 844	124 11 479
Derby	North Eclipse Archipelago	7 m. Queenfish, trevally, mackerel, tuna, sharks, fingermark bream, pikey bream	13 53 235	126 21 819
Derby	NW Twin Island		16 16 349	123 03 670
Derby	Oliver Rock	Threadfin salmon, blue salmon, queenfish, trevally, barramundi, mangrove jacks, fingermark bream, pikey bream	13 58 564	125 33 373
Derby	Outer Rip Shoal #1	Hole 10 m. Queenfish, trevally, mackerel, tuna, sharks, fingermark bream, pikey bream	17 08 411	123 30 688
Derby	Outer Rip Shoal #2	Threadfin salmon, blue salmon, queenfish, trevally, barramundi, mangrove jacks, fingermark bream, pikey bream	17 03 477	123 29 095
Derby	Pauline Bay	Queenfish, trevally, mackerel, tuna, sharks, fingermark bream, pikey bream	14 11 491	126 21 177
Derby	Pearl Shoal	Queenfish, trevally, mackerel, sharks, fingermark bream, pikey bream	14 05 691	126 20 506
Derby	Pickering Point	5 m. Threadfin salmon, blue salmon, queenfish, trevally, barramundi, mangrove jacks, fingermark bream, pikey bream	14 21 973	125 47 010
Derby	Point Torment	Queenfish, trevally, mackerel, tuna, sharks, fingermark bream, pikey bream	16 57 167	123 33 228
Derby	Prince Frederick Harbour	26 m. Queenfish, trevally, sharks, black mulloway, fingermark bream, pikey bream	14 58 994	125 08 847
Derby	Racine Island	Hump 5 m. Queenfish, trevally, mackerel, tuna, sharks, fingermark bream, pikey bream	14 14 343	125 51 830
Derby	Reyne Shoal	Queenfish, trevally, mackerel, tuna, sharks, fingermark bream, pikey bream	15 41 939	124 10 226
Derby	Rip Reef	Threadfin salmon, blue salmon, queenfish, trevally, sharks, barramundi, mangrove jacks, fingermark bream	16 38 900	123 26 900
Derby	Robinson River	Threadfin salmon, blue salmon, queenfish, trevally, barramundi, mangrove jacks, fingermark bream, pikey bream	16 55 530	123 49 073

Locality	Description	Comments	Latitude	Latitude
Derby	Robinson River Mouth	Threadfin salmon, blue salmon, queenfish, trevally, barramundi, mangrove jacks, fingermark bream, pikey bream	16 58 226	123 49 269
Derby	Rocky Cove	Queenfish, trevally, sharks, black mulloway, fingermark bream, pikey bream	14 13 720	126 13 562
Derby	Roe River	Queenfish, trevally, mackerel, tuna, sharks, fingermark bream, pikey bream	15 08 101	125 23 179
Derby	Rosella Shoal	Queenfish, trevally, sharks, black mulloway, fingermark bream, pikey bream	15 35 351	123 50 493
Derby	Scorpion Island NW	Queenfish, trevally, mackerel, tuna, sharks, fingermark bream, pikey bream	13 49 161	126 35 762
Derby	Sir Frederick Island	Queenfish, trevally, sharks, black mulloway, fingermark bream, pikey bream	16 07 979	123 54 807
Derby	Sir Graham Moore Islands	10 m. Threadfin salmon, blue salmon, queenfish, trevally, barramundi, mangrove jacks, fingermark bream, pikey bream	13 49 105	126 33 327
Derby	South Eclipse Archipelago	Queenfish, trevally, sharks, black mulloway, fingermark bream, pikey bream	14 02 589	126 23 076
Derby	South Meda Shoal #1	Threadfin salmon, blue salmon, queenfish, trevally, barramundi, mangrove jacks, fingermark bream, pikey bream	16 54 480	123 20 640
Derby	South Meda Shoal #2	12 m. Threadfin salmon, blue salmon, queenfish, trevally, sharks, barramundi, mangrove jacks, fingermark bream	16 55 326	123 17 420
Derby	Steamer Rock	Queenfish, trevally, mackerel, tuna, sharks, fingermark bream, pikey bream	13 55 514	126 42 683
Derby	Steamer Rock North–mound	Queenfish, trevally, mackerel, tuna, sharks, fingermark bream, pikey bream	13 52 883	126 41 741
Derby	Stokes Bay	Threadfin salmon, blue salmon, queenfish, trevally, barramundi, mangrove jacks, fingermark bream, pikey bream	17 02 321	123 45 741
Derby	Stokes Bay North #1	Hump 2 m. Queenfish, trevally, mackerel, tuna, sharks, fingermark bream, pikey bream	16 53 480	123 40 936
Derby	Stokes Bay North #2	Queenfish, trevally, mackerel, tuna, sharks, fingermark bream, pikey bream	16 50 399	123 45 355
Derby	Swift Bay	Threadfin salmon, blue salmon, queenfish, trevally, barramundi, mangrove jacks, fingermark bream, pikey bream	14 30 707	125 34 126
Derby	Symonds Point	Threadfin salmon, blue salmon, queenfish, trevally, barramundi, mangrove jacks, fingermark bream, pikey bream	14 13 545	126 17 860
Derby	Tancred Bank	10 m. Threadfin salmon, blue salmon, queenfish, trevally, barramundi, mangrove jacks, fingermark bream, pikey bream	14 05 152	125 54 252

Locality	Description	Comments	Latitude	Latitude
Derby	The Funnel	Threadfin salmon, blue salmon, queenfish, trevally, barramundi, mangrove jacks, fingermark bream, pikey bream	16 25 052	124 19 849
Derby	Thorne Reef	Queenfish, trevally, sharks, black mulloway, fingermark bream, pikey bream	15 43 665	124 08 990
Derby	Tooth Rocks	Queenfish, trevally, mackerel, tuna, sharks, fingermark bream, pikey bream	14 36 860	125 01 772
Derby	Traverse		16 15 242	124 07 772
Derby	Valentine Island	4 m. Threadfin salmon, blue salmon, queenfish, trevally, sharks, barramundi, mangrove jacks, fingermark bream	17 00 283	123 21 732
Derby	Vickers Reef	Threadfin salmon, blue salmon, queenfish, trevally, sharks, barramundi, mangrove jacks, fingermark bream	16 19 367	123 29 550
Derby	Walmesly Bay	Threadfin salmon, blue salmon, queenfish, trevally, barramundi, mangrove jacks, fingermark bream, pikey bream	14 28 632	125 41 897
Derby	Walsh Point Access	Threadfin salmon, blue salmon, queenfish, trevally, barramundi, mangrove jacks, fingermark bream, pikey bream	14 34 378	125 50 104
Derby	Waratah Shoal	Queenfish, trevally, sharks, black mulloway, fingermark bream, pikey bream	14 08 850	126 15 780
Derby	West Montalivet Island	Queenfish, trevally, mackerel, tuna, sharks, fingermark bream, pikey bream	14 18 002	125 07 440
Derby	Yule Entrance	Queenfish, trevally, mackerel, tuna, sharks, fingermark bream, pikey bream	16 20 453	124 23 521
Exmouth	Arlie Is. Taunton Reef	Spanish mackerel, wahoo, barracuda, trevally, queenfish, tuna, sharks, whiting, mullet, garfish, mulloway	21 18 649	115 09 50
Exmouth	Baylis Patches	Spanish mackerel, wahoo, barracuda, trevally, queenfish, tuna, sharks, whiting, mullet, garfish, mulloway	21 43 724	114 42 306
Exmouth	Bennet Shoal	Spanish mackerel, wahoo, barracuda, trevally, queenfish, tuna, sharks, whiting, mullet, garfish, mulloway	22 05 659	114 10 142
Exmouth	Beryl Reef	Spanish mackerel, wahoo, barracuda, trevally, queenfish, tuna, sharks, whiting, mullet, garfish, mulloway	21 53 274	114 24 362
Exmouth	Burnside Island N	Spanish mackerel, wahoo, barracuda, trevally, queenfish, tuna, sharks, whiting, mullet, garfish, mulloway	22 04 108	114 29 930
Exmouth	Campbell Shoal	Spanish mackerel, wahoo, barracuda, trevally, queenfish, tuna, sharks, whiting, mullet, garfish, mulloway	22 07 891	114 20 715
Exmouth	Camplin Shoal	Spanish mackerel, wahoo, barracuda, trevally, queenfish, tuna, sharks, whiting, mullet, garfish, mulloway	22 03 881	114 11 888
Exmouth	Cody Shoal	Spanish mackerel, wahoo, barracuda, trevally, queenfish, tuna, sharks, whiting, mullet, garfish, mulloway	22 06 834	114 21 775
Exmouth	Combe Reef	3 m. Spanish mackerel, wahoo, barracuda, trevally, queenfish, tuna, sharks, whiting, mullet, garfish, mulloway	21 47 097	114 25 018

Locality	Description	Comments	Latitude	Latitude
Exmouth	Concrete ramp		21 49 000	114 10 140
Exmouth	Coolgra Point–Bank Launch-ing	Spanish mackerel, wahoo, barracuda, trevally, queenfish, tuna, sharks, whiting, mullet, garfish, mulloway	21 34 403	115 14 894
Exmouth	Coopers-Camplin Shoal	Spanish mackerel, wahoo, barracuda, trevally, queenfish, tuna, sharks, whiting, mullet, garfish, mulloway	22 03 289	114 13 379
Exmouth	Direction Island NW	Lump 2 m. Spanish mackerel, wahoo, barracuda, trevally, queenfish, tuna, sharks, whiting, mullet, garfish, mulloway	21 31 185	115 05 656
Exmouth	Exmouth Reef	Spanish mackerel, wahoo, barracuda, trevally, queenfish, tuna, sharks, whiting, mullet, garfish, mulloway	21 51 305	114 22 344
Exmouth	Fairway Reef	2.5 m. Spanish mackerel, wahoo, barracuda, trevally, queenfish, tuna, sharks, whiting, mullet, garfish, mulloway	21 42 227	114 35 381
Exmouth	Glennie Patches	Spanish mackerel, wahoo, barracuda, trevally, queenfish, tuna, sharks, whiting, mullet, garfish, mulloway	21 36 672	114 54 518
Exmouth	Gorgon Patch	Spanish mackerel, wahoo, barracuda, trevally, queenfish, tuna, sharks, whiting, mullet, garfish, mulloway	21 32 750	115 04 747
Exmouth	Herald Reef	Spanish mackerel, wahoo, barracuda, trevally, queenfish, tuna, sharks, whiting, mullet, garfish, mulloway	21 29 301	115 13 51
Exmouth	Hood Reef	Nodules 5 m. Spanish mackerel, wahoo, barracuda, trevally, queenfish, tuna, sharks, whiting, mullet, garfish, mulloway	21 39 543	114 36 635
Exmouth	Islam Islands	Spanish mackerel, wahoo, barracuda, trevally, queenfish, tuna, sharks, whiting, mullet, garfish, mulloway	22 14 958	114 20 347
Exmouth	Larkin Shoal	Spanish mackerel, wahoo, barracuda, trevally, queenfish, tuna, sharks, whiting, mullet, garfish, mulloway	22 08 645	114 18 318
Exmouth	Little Shoals	Spanish mackerel, wahoo, barracuda, trevally, queenfish, tuna, sharks, whiting, mullet, garfish, mulloway	21 24 162	115 14 837
Exmouth	Locker Reef	4 m. Spanish mackerel, wahoo, barracuda, trevally, queenfish, tuna, sharks, whiting, mullet, garfish, mulloway	21 41 499	114 43 978
Exmouth	Manicom Bank	5 m. Spanish mackerel, wahoo, barracuda, trevally, queenfish, tuna, sharks, whiting, mullet, garfish, mulloway	21 40 684	114 50 648
Exmouth	Miles Shoal	5 m. Spanish mackerel, wahoo, barracuda, trevally, queenfish, tuna, sharks, whiting, mullet, garfish, mulloway	21 33 953	114 57 673
Exmouth	Nares Rock	Spanish mackerel, wahoo, barracuda, trevally, queenfish, tuna, sharks, whiting, mullet, garfish, mulloway	21 25 712	115 17 727
Exmouth	Oil Line	3 m. Spanish mackerel, wahoo, barracuda, trevally, queenfish, tuna, sharks, whiting, mullet, garfish, mulloway	21 33 938	115 00 528
Exmouth	Otway Reef	Spanish mackerel, wahoo, barracuda, trevally, queenfish, tuna, sharks, whiting, mullet, garfish, mulloway	21 43 872	114 28 163

Locality	Description	Comments	Latitude	Latitude
Exmouth	Penguin Bank	Spanish mackerel, wahoo, barracuda, trevally, queenfish, tuna, sharks, whiting, mullet, garfish, mulloway	21 12 338	115 03 831
Exmouth	Point Lefroy North East Angler	Spanish mackerel, wahoo, barracuda, trevally, queenfish, tuna, sharks, whiting, mullet, garfish, mulloway	22 15 628	114 13 379
Exmouth	Rosily Cays	Spanish mackerel, wahoo, barracuda, trevally, queenfish, tuna, sharks, whiting, mullet, garfish, mulloway	21 15 779	115 01 393
Exmouth	Rosily Islands	10 m. Spanish mackerel, wahoo, barracuda, trevally, queenfish, tuna, sharks, whiting, mullet, garfish, mulloway	21 17 484	115 05 789
Exmouth	Schofield Shoal	Spanish mackerel, wahoo, barracuda, trevally, queenfish, tuna, sharks, whiting, mullet, garfish, mulloway	22 15 578	114 11 518
Exmouth	Snapper Shoal	Spanish mackerel, wahoo, barracuda, trevally, queenfish, tuna, sharks, whiting, mullet, garfish, mulloway	22 12 393	114 18 025
Exmouth	South Murion Island	8 m. Spanish mackerel, wahoo, barracuda, trevally, queenfish, tuna, sharks, whiting, mullet, garfish, mulloway	21 44 293	114 19 365
Exmouth	Stewart Shoal	Spanish mackerel, wahoo, barracuda, trevally, queenfish, tuna, sharks, whiting, mullet, garfish, mulloway	22 08 350	114 07 16
Exmouth	Sultan Reef	5 m. Spanish mackerel, wahoo, barracuda, trevally, queenfish, tuna, sharks, whiting, mullet, garfish, mulloway	21 24 703	115 05 84
Exmouth	Table Island E	Spanish mackerel, wahoo, barracuda, trevally, queenfish, tuna, sharks, whiting, mullet, garfish, mulloway	21 37 924	114 46 722
Exmouth	The Lumps	To 4.5 m. Spanish mackerel, wahoo, barracuda, trevally, queenfish, tuna, sharks, whiting, mullet, garfish, mulloway	21 49 404	114 21 709
Exmouth	Tongue Shoals	4 m. Spanish mackerel, wahoo, barracuda, trevally, queenfish, tuna, sharks, whiting, mullet, garfish, mulloway	21 38 917	114 50 738
Exmouth	Trap Reef	Spanish mackerel, wahoo, barracuda, trevally, queenfish, tuna, sharks, whiting, mullet, garfish, mulloway	21 23 986	115 00 823
Exmouth	Wapet Shoal	Spanish mackerel, wahoo, barracuda, trevally, queenfish, tuna, sharks, whiting, mullet, garfish, mulloway	22 11 498	114 07 068
Exmouth	Ward Reef	Spanish mackerel, wahoo, barracuda, trevally, queenfish, tuna, sharks, whiting, mullet, garfish, mulloway	21 36 575	115 04 547
Exmouth	Ward Reef N	2 m. Spanish mackerel, wahoo, barracuda, trevally, queenfish, tuna, sharks, whiting, mullet, garfish, mulloway	21 34 244	115 01 855
Exmouth	Web Reef	4 m. Spanish mackerel, wahoo, barracuda, trevally, queenfish, tuna, sharks, whiting, mullet, garfish, mulloway	21 46 659	114 33 253
Fremantle	Ben 1	5 m. Snapper	32 08 056	115 39 337
Fremantle	Casuarina Shoal	Snapper, dhufish	32 09 397	115 36 581
Fremantle	D9—Bulldozer	14 m. Snapper	32 11 645	115 44 524

Locality	Description	Comments	Latitude	Latitude
Fremantle	FAD		32 00 000	115 20 500
Fremantle	FAD–Alec's Marine	Water depth approx. 142 m	31 57 350	115 15 730
Fremantle	FAD–Club Marine	Water depth approx. 100 m	32 03 200	115 19 500
Fremantle	FAD–Fremantle Sailing Club	Water depth approx. 220 m	32 05 000	115 11 000
Fremantle	FAD–Hillarys Yacht Club	Water depth approx. 175 m	31 54 500	115 12 000
Fremantle	FAD–Perth Game Fishing Club	Water depth approx. 185 m	32 00 000	115 13 500
Fremantle	FAD–Yamaha	Water depth approx. 190 m	32 08 500	115 10 500
Fremantle	Five Fathoms Bank	Sampson, snapper, dhufish–reef-drop-off	32 08 000	115 35 150
Fremantle	Harding Rock	5 m. Snapper	32 10 217	115 40 917
Fremantle	Mewstone	KG whiting, herring, dhufish–reef	32 05 070	115 39 180
Fremantle	Rizabar Wreck	7 m. Snapper	32 16 882	115 37 659
Fremantle	Seaward Reef	Snapper, dhufish	32 06 959	115 36 340
Fremantle	Star Wreck	3 m. Snapper, fish on drift	32 22 590	115 41 300
Fremantle	Sulphur Rock	10 m. Snapper, dhufish	32 11 087	115 40 941
Fremantle	Trigg	29 m. Snapper, herring, West Australian Dhufish	31 55 490	115 35 100
Ningaloo Reef	Alison Point	Spanish mackerel, wahoo, barracuda, trevally, queenfish, tuna, sharks, whiting, mullet, garfish, mulloway	23 28 941	113 45 369
Ningaloo Reef	Bateman Bay Reefs	Caution. Spanish mackerel, wahoo, barracuda, trevally, queenfish, tuna, sharks, whiting, mullet, garfish, mulloway	23 03 384	113 45 67
Ningaloo Reef	Bulbari Point	Spanish mackerel, wahoo, barracuda, trevally, queenfish, tuna, sharks, whiting, mullet, garfish, mulloway	23 32 226	113 43 151
Ningaloo Reef	Cape Farquhar	Spanish mackerel, wahoo, barracuda, trevally, queenfish, tuna, sharks, whiting, mullet, garfish, mulloway	23 36 952	113 35 99
Ningaloo Reef	Gnarraloo Beach	Spanish mackerel, wahoo, barracuda, trevally, queenfish, tuna, sharks, whiting, mullet, garfish, mulloway	23 44 885	113 32 97
Ningaloo Reef	Helby Bank	Spanish mackerel, wahoo, barracuda, trevally, queenfish, tuna, sharks, whiting, mullet, garfish, mulloway	21 48 544	114 01 054
Ningaloo Reef	Jurabi Point	Spanish mackerel, wahoo, barracuda, trevally, queenfish, tuna, sharks, whiting, mullet, garfish, mulloway	21 52 456	113 57 74
Ningaloo Reef	Ningaloo South Passage	Spanish mackerel, wahoo, barracuda, trevally, queenfish, tuna, sharks, whiting, mullet, garfish, mulloway	23 11 891	113 45 267
Ningaloo Reef	North West Reef	Spanish mackerel, wahoo, barracuda, trevally, queenfish, tuna, sharks, whiting, mullet, garfish, mulloway	21 45 642	114 10 305

Locality	Description	Comments	Latitude	Latitude
Ningaloo Reef	Sandy Bay	Spanish mackerel, wahoo, barracuda, trevally, queenfish, tuna, sharks, whiting, mullet, garfish, mulloway	22 11 426	113 50 496
Ningaloo Reef	T-bone Bay	Spanish mackerel, wahoo, barracuda, trevally, queenfish, tuna, sharks, whiting, mullet, garfish, mulloway	22 00 811	113 54 062
Onslow	Barrow Island	10 m. Spanish mackerel, wahoo, barracuda, trevally, queenfish, tuna, sharks, whiting, mullet, garfish, mulloway	20 54 428	115 32 480
Onslow	Barrow Island SE	Spanish mackerel, wahoo, barracuda, trevally, queenfish, tuna, sharks, whiting, mullet, garfish, mulloway	20 51 574	115 31 919
Onslow	Barrow Island Shoals	Spanish mackerel, wahoo, barracuda, trevally, queenfish, tuna, sharks, whiting, mullet, garfish, mulloway	21 07 446	115 29 559
Onslow	Boat ramp		21 37 924	115 05 855
Onslow	Cape Dupuv	Spanish mackerel, wahoo, barracuda, trevally, queenfish, tuna, sharks, whiting, mullet, garfish, mulloway	20 37 929	115 26 140
Onslow	Cowie Island Estuary	Spanish mackerel, wahoo, barracuda, trevally, queenfish, tuna, sharks, whiting, mullet, garfish, mulloway	21 15 170	115 47 033
Onslow	Cowie Island South Estuary	Spanish mackerel, wahoo, barracuda, trevally, queenfish, tuna, sharks, whiting, mullet, garfish, mulloway	21 15 682	115 45 610
Onslow	Cowie Island West	1.5 m. Spanish mackerel, wahoo, barracuda, trevally, queenfish, tuna, sharks, whiting, mullet, garfish, mulloway	21 13 877	115 42 329
Onslow	Fairway Shoals	Spanish mackerel, wahoo, barracuda, trevally, queenfish, tuna, sharks, whiting, mullet, garfish, mulloway	21 05 977	115 34 788
Onslow	Great Sandy Island SE	Spanish mackerel, wahoo, barracuda, trevally, queenfish, tuna, sharks, whiting, mullet, garfish, mulloway	21 14 355	115 41 112
Onslow	Inner Mary Group Estuaries	Spanish mackerel, wahoo, barracuda, trevally, queenfish, tuna, sharks, whiting, mullet, garfish, mulloway	21 29 202	115 28 108
Onslow	Lightfoot Reef	Spanish mackerel, wahoo, barracuda, trevally, queenfish, tuna, sharks, whiting, mullet, garfish, mulloway	21 15 276	115 30 684
Onslow	Mary Anne Group North	Spanish mackerel, wahoo, barracuda, trevally, queenfish, tuna, sharks, whiting, mullet, garfish, mulloway	21 15 429	115 36 625
Onslow	Mary Anne Passage North	Spanish mackerel, wahoo, barracuda, trevally, queenfish, tuna, sharks, whiting, mullet, garfish, mulloway	21 08 708	115 24 58

Locality	Description	Comments	Latitude	Latitude
Onslow	Mary Anne Passage South / Flinders Shoal	Spanish mackerel, wahoo, barracuda, trevally, queenfish, tuna, sharks, whiting, mullet, garfish, mulloway	21 14 067	115 28 559
Onslow	Mary Anne Reef	9 m. Spanish mackerel, wahoo, barracuda, trevally, queenfish, tuna, sharks, whiting, mullet, garfish, mulloway	21 16 093	115 22 508
Onslow	Middle Mary Anne Estuary	Spanish mackerel, wahoo, barracuda, trevally, queenfish, tuna, sharks, whiting, mullet, garfish, mulloway	21 20 811	115 36 844
Onslow	Middle Mary Anne Island South	Spanish mackerel, wahoo, barracuda, trevally, queenfish, tuna, sharks, whiting, mullet, garfish, mulloway	21 19 649	115 32 847
Onslow	Montebello Island East	9 m. Spanish mackerel, wahoo, barracuda, trevally, queenfish, tuna, sharks, whiting, mullet, garfish, mulloway	20 29 953	115 39 368
Onslow	Polyre Reef	Spanish mackerel, wahoo, barracuda, trevally, queenfish, tuna, sharks, whiting, mullet, garfish, mulloway	20 59 639	115 16 728
Onslow	Ripple Shoals	Spanish mackerel, wahoo, barracuda, trevally, queenfish, tuna, sharks, whiting, mullet, garfish, mulloway	21 10 214	115 20 294
Onslow	Robe River Estuary	Spanish mackerel, wahoo, barracuda, trevally, queenfish, tuna, sharks, whiting, mullet, garfish, mulloway	21 18 716	115 40 495
Onslow	Robe River North Estuary	Spanish mackerel, wahoo, barracuda, trevally, queenfish, tuna, sharks, whiting, mullet, garfish, mulloway	21 16 961	115 42 438
Onslow	Robe River South	Spanish mackerel, wahoo, barracuda, trevally, queenfish, tuna, sharks, whiting, mullet, garfish, mulloway	21 19 653	115 38 751
Onslow	Rough ramp		21 38 917	115 05 656
Onslow	South Pepper	Spanish mackerel, wahoo, barracuda, trevally, queenfish, tuna, sharks, whiting, mullet, garfish, mulloway	21 05 719	115 15 859
Onslow	Trimouille Island	Spanish mackerel, wahoo, barracuda, trevally, queenfish, tuna, sharks, whiting, mullet, garfish, mulloway	20 21 692	115 34 353
Onslow	Weld Island Estuary North	Spanish mackerel, wahoo, barracuda, trevally, queenfish, tuna, sharks, whiting, mullet, garfish, mulloway	21 22 957	115 35 174
Port Hedland	Beagle Reef West	Spanish mackerel, wahoo, barracuda, trevally, queenfish, tuna, sharks, mulloway, whiting, mullet, garfish	20 23 425	117 38 661
Port Hedland	Beagle Reef West–Pilbara	Spanish mackerel, wahoo, barracuda, trevally, queenfish, tuna, sharks, mulloway, whiting, mullet, garfish	20 23 603	117 48 150

Locality	Description	Comments	Latitude	Latitude
Port Hedland	Bedout Island	Spanish mackerel, wahoo, barracuda, trevally, queenfish, tuna, sharks, mulloway, whiting, mullet, garfish	19 35 391	119 06 590
Port Hedland	Breaker Inlet	Spanish mackerel, wahoo, barracuda, trevally, queenfish, tuna, sharks, mulloway, whiting, mullet, garfish	19 57 227	119 09 002
Port Hedland	Cape Keraudren E	Spanish mackerel, wahoo, barracuda, trevally, queenfish, tuna, sharks, mulloway, whiting, mullet, garfish	19 59 142	119 42 931
Port Hedland	Channel	Spanish mackerel, wahoo, barracuda, trevally, queenfish, tuna, sharks, mulloway, whiting, mullet, garfish	20 16 450	118 35 051
Port Hedland	Cornellisse Shoal South	10 m. Spanish mackerel, wahoo, barracuda, trevally, queenfish, tuna, sharks, mulloway, whiting, mullet, garfish	20 06 386	118 15 975
Port Hedland	Cornellisse Shoals	10 m. Spanish mackerel, wahoo, barracuda, trevally, queenfish, tuna, sharks, mulloway, whiting, mullet, garfish	20 02 096	118 22 327
Port Hedland	Cossack Beach Ramp		20 40 696	117 11 752
Port Hedland	Coxon Shoals East	Spanish mackerel, wahoo, barracuda, trevally, queenfish, tuna, sharks, mulloway, whiting, mullet, garfish	20 01 925	118 35 507
Port Hedland	Delambre Reef	5 m. Spanish mackerel, wahoo, barracuda, trevally, queenfish, tuna, sharks, mulloway, whiting, mullet, garfish	20 26 359	117 14 451
Port Hedland	Depuch Island	Spanish mackerel, wahoo, barracuda, trevally, queenfish, tuna, sharks, mulloway, whiting, mullet, garfish	20 36 144	117 43 569
Port Hedland	Geographe Shoals	Spanish mackerel, wahoo, barracuda, trevally, queenfish, tuna, sharks, mulloway, whiting, mullet, garfish	20 15 785	117 54 076
Port Hedland	Geographe Shoals South	5 m. Spanish mackerel, wahoo, barracuda, trevally, queenfish, tuna, sharks, mulloway, whiting, mullet, garfish	20 21 104	117 55 457
Port Hedland	Maniliya Bank	7 m. Spanish mackerel, wahoo, barracuda, trevally, queenfish, tuna, sharks, mulloway, whiting, mullet, garfish	20 08 897	118 38 070
Port Hedland	North Turtle Islet Shoals	11 m. Spanish mackerel, wahoo, barracuda, trevally, queenfish, tuna, sharks, mulloway, whiting, mullet, garfish	19 46 166	118 53 593
Port Hedland	Port Hedland Public Ramp		20 19 126	118 35 000
Port Hedland	Port Walcott	Spanish mackerel, wahoo, barracuda, trevally, queenfish, tuna, sharks, mulloway, whiting, mullet, garfish	20 33 931	117 13 106
Port Hedland	Reef Island	5 m. Spanish mackerel, wahoo, barracuda, trevally, queenfish, tuna, sharks, mulloway, whiting, mullet, garfish	20 29 709	117 53 494

Locality	Description	Comments	Latitude	Latitude
Port Hedland	Rocky Patches	Spanish mackerel, wahoo, barracuda, trevally, queenfish, tuna, sharks, mulloway, whiting, mullet, garfish	19 50 261	120 21 763
Port Hedland	Ronsard Islands	5 m. Spanish mackerel, wahoo, barracuda, trevally, queenfish, tuna, sharks, mulloway, whiting, mullet, garfish	20 33 407	117 48 658
Port Hedland	Tessa Shoals	9 m. Spanish mackerel, wahoo, barracuda, trevally, queenfish, tuna, sharks, mulloway, whiting, mullet, garfish	20 29 482	117 22 557
Port Hedland	Weerdee Island	Spanish mackerel, wahoo, barracuda, trevally, queenfish, tuna, sharks, mulloway, whiting, mullet, garfish	20 19 126	118 27 561
Port Hedland	Yule River	Hump 3 m. Spanish mackerel, wahoo, barracuda, trevally, queenfish, tuna, sharks, mulloway, whiting, mullet, garfish	20 16 650	118 05 565
Port Hedland	Yule River North	4 m. Spanish mackerel, wahoo, barracuda, trevally, queenfish, tuna, sharks, mulloway, whiting, mullet, garfish	20 12 122	118 11 382
Rottnest Island	City of York	Wreck. 12 m.	31 59 645	115 29 300
Rottnest Island	Coesy Point	Pelagic fish. 18 m	31 59 330	115 29 300
Rottnest Island	Crystal Palace	Reef and ledge bottom. 18 m.	32 01 550	115 32 700
Rottnest Island	Dyer Island	Wreck. Reef bottom. 14 m.	32 01 350	115 33 070
Rottnest Island	Horse Shoe Reef 1	Reef bottom. 18 m.	32 00 345	115 27 710
Rottnest Island	Horse Shoe Reef 2	Reef bottom.	32 00 180	115 27 270
Rottnest Island	Horse Shoe Reef 3	Reef bottom.	32 00 300	115 27 160
Rottnest Island	Jacksons RKS	10 m. Reef bottom.	32 01 550	115 35 000
Rottnest Island	Jeannies drop-off	Drop-off. 24 m.	32 01 955	115 31 490
Rottnest Island	Kitson Point	Reef bottom. 18 m.	32 01 420	115 29 610
Rottnest Island	Lady Elizabeth	Wreck. 6 m.	32 01 080	115 32 960
Rottnest Island	Mirp Flores	Jewfish. 15 m.	32 00 345	115 28 240
Rottnest Island	Monday WK	12 m.	31 59 050	115 32 210
Rottnest Island	N/E Roe Reef	Reef bottom. 25 m.	31 58 110	115 33 220
Rottnest Island	North Point	Reef bottom. 10 m	31 59 050	115 30 680
Rottnest Island	North Point Deep	Canyon. 14–26 m.	31 58 580	115 29 850
Rottnest Island	North West Patch 1	Reef bottom.	32 00 860	115 26 850
Rottnest Island	North West Patch 2	Reef bottom. 18 m.	32 00 750	115 26 930
Rottnest Island	North West Patch 3	Reef bottom.	32 00 795	115 26 495
Rottnest Island	Outer Armstrong	Drop-off 11–25 m.	31 58 910	115 29 905
Rottnest Island	Outer Parrakeet	Sharks. 16 m.	31 58 720	115 31 080

Locality	Description	Comments	Latitude	Latitude
Rottnest Island	Parker Point	Coral bottom. 25 m.	32 01 840	115 31 780
Rottnest Island	Parrakeet Bay	6 m.	31 59 030	115 31 190
Rottnest Island	Point Clune	Reef bottom. 12 m	31 58 750	115 31 400
Rottnest Island	Radar Reef	Stingray. Coral bottom. 18 m.	32 01 700	115 27 625
Rottnest Island	Roe Reef	Reef bottom. 8 m.	31 58 420	115 32 210
Rottnest Island	Salmon Point	Bream. Coral bottom. 21 m.	32 01 880	115 31 00
Rottnest Island	South Point	18 m.	32 01 450	115 28 400
Rottnest Island	Strickland Bay	Reef bottom. 18 m.	32 01 330	115 28 790
Rottnest Island	Swirl Reef	Coral bottom. 21 m.	31 59 970	115 28 130
Rottnest Island	The Count	Reef bottom. 10 m.	32 00 915	115 33 500
Shark Bay–Carnarvon	Ballast Ground	6 m. Snapper, Norwest snapper, black snapper, emperor, whiting, mullet, garfish	24 53 767	113 36 027
Shark Bay–Carnarvon	Bejaling Shoals	3.5 m. Spanish mackerel, wahoo, barracuda, trevally, queenfish, tuna, sharks, snapper, coral trout, spangled emperor, Sweetlip, whiting, mullet, garfish	24 38 588	113 28 436
Shark Bay–Carnarvon	Cape Boullanger	Spanish mackerel, wahoo, barracuda, tailor, sharks, snapper, emperor, Sweetlip, whiting, mullet, garfish	24 59 299	113 06 814
Shark Bay–Carnarvon	Cape Ronsard, Koks Island	Spanish mackerel, wahoo, barracuda, trevally, queenfish, tuna, sharks, snapper, coral trout, spangled emperor, Sweetlip, whiting, mullet, garfish	24 44 812	113 09 618
Shark Bay–Carnarvon	Carnarvon Ramp		24 52 289	113 37 362
Shark Bay–Carnarvon	Dampier Reef	4 m. Marlin, Spanish mackerel, amberjack, wahoo, barracuda, tailor, snapper, black snapper, Norwest snapper, mulloway, bluebone groper, coral trout, parrotfish, whiting, mullet, garfish, flathead	25 21 967	113 04 587
Shark Bay–Carnarvon	Darwin Reefs	Spanish mackerel, wahoo, barracuda, trevally, queenfish, tuna, sharks, snapper, coral trout, spangled emperor, Sweetlip, whiting, mullet, garfish	24 35 667	113 26 108
Shark Bay–Carnarvon	Dorre Island South Tip	Marlin, Spanish mackerel, amberjack, wahoo, barracuda, tailor, snapper, black snapper, Norwest snapper, mulloway, bluebone groper, coral trout, parrotfish, whiting, mullet, garfish, flathead	25 16 765	113 04 290
Shark Bay–Carnarvon	Fitzroy Reefs	Spanish mackerel, wahoo, barracuda, trevally, queenfish, tuna, sharks, snapper, coral trout, spangled emperor, Sweetlip, whiting, mullet, garfish	24 32 635	113 25 532
Shark Bay–Carnarvon	Garth's Rock	Spanish mackerel, wahoo, barracuda, trevally, queenfish, tuna, sharks, snapper, coral trout, spangled emperor, Sweetlip	24 13 523	113 22 762

Locality	Description	Comments	Latitude	Latitude
Shark Bay–Carnarvon	Gnaraloo	Spanish mackerel, wahoo, barracuda, trevally, queenfish, tuna, sharks, snapper, coral trout, spangled emperor, Sweetlip, whiting, mullet, garfish	23 48 665	113 30 026
Shark Bay–Carnarvon	Greenough Point	Marlin, Spanish mackerel, amberjack, wahoo, barracuda, tailor, snapper, black snapper, Norwest snapper, mulloway, bluebone groper, coral trout, parrotfish, whiting, mullet, garfish, flathead	25 15 281	113 49 937
Shark Bay–Carnarvon	Point Quobba	Spanish mackerel, wahoo, barracuda, trevally, queenfish, tuna, sharks, snapper, coral trout, spangled emperor, Sweetlip, whiting, mullet, garfish	24 29 555	113 24 217
Shark Bay–Carnarvon	Red Bluff–Small Beach Launching	Spanish mackerel, wahoo, barracuda, trevally, queenfish, tuna, sharks, snapper, coral trout, spangled emperor, Sweetlip, whiting, mullet, garfish	24 01 327	113 25 153
Shark Bay–Carnarvon	The Banks	Spanish mackerel, tailor, snapper, emperor, mulloway, whiting	25 00 060	112 28 419
Shark Bay–Carnarvon	The Tyres	Spanish mackerel, tailor, trevally, mulloway, pink snapper, emperor, parrotfish	25 02 760	113 32 254
Shark Bay–Carnarvon	Uranie Bank	Spanish mackerel, tailor, snapper, emperor, mulloway, whiting	25 10 510	113 10 700
Shark Bay–Carnarvon	Uranie Bank South	9.5 m. Marlin, Spanish mackerel, amberjack, wahoo, barracuda, tailor, snapper, black snapper, Norwest snapper, mulloway, bluebone groper, coral trout, parrotfish, whiting, mullet, garfish, flathead	25 14 847	113 10 741
Shark Bay–Carnarvon	Whaling Barge	Spanish mackerel, wahoo, barracuda, trevally, queenfish, tuna sharks, mulloway, pink snapper, whiting, mullet, garfish	24 54 442	113 37 085
Shark Bay–Denham	Bar Flats	2 m. Spanish mackerel, tailor, snapper, bluebone, coral trout, sea perch, garfish, mullet, whiting	25 53 578	113 18 509
Shark Bay–Denham	Belefin Flats	1 m. Spanish mackerel, tailor, snapper, bluebone, coral trout, sea perch, garfish, mullet, whiting	26 02 581	113 20 218
Shark Bay–Denham	Cape Bellefin	9 m. Spanish mackerel, tailor, sharks, snapper, Norwest snapper, garfish, mullet	26 02 793	113 15 291
Shark Bay–Denham	Cape Inscription	9 m. Marlin, Spanish mackerel, amberjack, wahoo, barracuda, tailor, snapper, black snapper, Norwest snapper, mulloway, bluebone groper, coral trout, parrotfish, whiting, mullet, garfish, flathead	25 27 756	112 57 268
Shark Bay–Denham	Denham Sound	Marlin, Spanish mackerel, amberjack, wahoo, barracuda, tailor, snapper, black snapper, Norwest snapper, mulloway, bluebone groper, coral trout, parrotfish, whiting, mullet, garfish, flathead	25 27 050	113 11 130
Shark Bay–Denham	Dirk Hartog Island East	Marlin, Spanish mackerel, amberjack, wahoo, barracuda, tailor, snapper, black snapper, Norwest snapper, mulloway, bluebone groper, coral trout, parrotfish, whiting, mullet, garfish, flathead	25 42 274	113 05 657

Locality	Description	Comments	Latitude	Latitude
Shark Bay–Denham	Eagle Island	Marlin, Spanish mackerel, amberjack, wahoo, barracuda, tailor, snapper, black snapper, Norwest snapper, mulloway, bluebone groper, coral trout, parrotfish, whiting, mullet, garfish, flathead	26 05 702	113 34 512
Shark Bay–Denham	Heirisson Prong	Spanish mackerel, tailor, snapper, bluebone, coral trout, sea perch, garfish, mullet, whiting	26 02 581	113 21 673
Shark Bay–Denham	Lagoon Point	Marlin, Spanish mackerel, amberjack, wahoo, barracuda, tailor, snapper, black snapper, Norwest snapper, mulloway, bluebone groper, coral trout, parrotfish, whiting, mullet, garfish, flathead	25 55 110	113 30 774
Shark Bay–Denham	Levillain Shoal	5 m. Marlin, Spanish mackerel, amberjack, wahoo, barracuda, tailor, snapper, black snapper, Norwest snapper, mulloway, bluebone groper, coral trout, parrotfish, whiting, mullet, garfish, flathead	25 30 823	113 02 438
Shark Bay–Denham	Middle Flat	4 m. Marlin, Spanish mackerel, amberjack, wahoo, barracuda, tailor, snapper, black snapper, Norwest snapper, mulloway, bluebone groper, coral trout, parrotfish, whiting, mullet, garfish, flathead	26 03 533	113 28 592
Shark Bay–Denham	Naturaliste Channel	11 m. Marlin, Spanish mackerel, amberjack, wahoo, barracuda, tailor, snapper, black snapper, Norwest snapper, mulloway, bluebone groper, coral trout, parrotfish, whiting, mullet, garfish, flathead	25 29 108	113 06 928
Shark Bay–Denham	Shaoling Rep 1	Spanish mackerel, tailor, sharks, snapper, Norwest snapper, garfish, mullet	25 29 624	113 30 512
Shark Bay–Denham	Shoaling Rep	2 m. Marlin, Spanish mackerel, amberjack, wahoo, barracuda, tailor, snapper, black snapper, Norwest snapper, mulloway, bluebone groper, coral trout, parrotfish, whiting, mullet, garfish, flathead	25 46 423	113 21 673
Shark Bay–Denham	Useless Loop	Marlin, Spanish mackerel, amberjack, wahoo, barracuda, tailor, snapper, black snapper, Norwest snapper, mulloway, bluebone groper, coral trout, parrotfish, whiting, mullet, garfish, flathead	25 53 364	113 14 947
Shark Bay–Denham	Withnell Point	9 m. Marlin, Spanish mackerel, amberjack, wahoo, barracuda, tailor, snapper, black snapper, Norwest snapper, mulloway, bluebone groper, coral trout, parrotfish, whiting, mullet, garfish, flathead	25 31 647	113 05 602
Shark Bay–Monkey Mia	80 Acres	15 m. Spanish mackerel, trevally, tailor, snapper, black snapper, Norwest snapper, parrotfish	25 29 110	113 37 360
Shark Bay–Monkey Mia	Bibra Landing	Snapper, parrotfish, whiting, mullet, garfish	25 57 134	114 14 658
Shark Bay–Monkey Mia	Briggs Rocks	Marlin, Spanish mackerel, amberjack, wahoo, barracuda, tailor, snapper, black snapper, Norwest snapper, mulloway, bluebone groper, coral trout, parrotfish, whiting, mullet, garfish, flathead	26 16 408	113 29 690
Shark Bay–Monkey Mia	Dubaut Point	1 m. Marlin, Spanish mackerel, amberjack, wahoo, barracuda, tailor, snapper, black snapper, Norwest snapper, mulloway, bluebone groper, coral trout, parrotfish, whiting, mullet, garfish, flathead	25 52 572	113 45 963

Locality	Description	Comments	Latitude	Latitude
Shark Bay–Monkey Mia	Fork Flat	1 m. Marlin, Spanish mackerel, amberjack, wahoo, barracuda, tailor, snapper, black snapper, Norwest snapper, mulloway, bluebone groper, coral trout, parrotfish, whiting, mullet, garfish, flathead	26 17 247	113 38 017
Shark Bay–Monkey Mia	Giraud Point W	Marlin, Spanish mackerel, amberjack, wahoo, barracuda, tailor, snapper, black snapper, Norwest snapper, mulloway, bluebone groper, coral trout, parrotfish, whiting, mullet, garfish, flathead	26 29 947	113 35 535
Shark Bay–Monkey Mia	Goulet Bluff	Marlin, Spanish mackerel, amberjack, wahoo, barracuda, tailor, snapper, black snapper, Norwest snapper, mulloway, bluebone groper, coral trout, parrotfish, whiting, mullet, garfish, flathead	26 12 951	113 41 100
Shark Bay–Monkey Mia	Pelican Island	Marlin, Spanish mackerel, amberjack, wahoo, barracuda, tailor, snapper, black snapper, Norwest snapper, mulloway, bluebone groper, coral trout, parrotfish, whiting, mullet, garfish, flathead	25 50 931	114 00 505
Shark Bay–Monkey Mia	Shaoling Rep 2	8 m. Marlin, Spanish mackerel, amberjack, wahoo, barracuda, tailor, snapper, black snapper, Norwest snapper, mulloway, bluebone groper, coral trout, parrotfish, whiting, mullet, Garfish, Flathead	25 22 151	113 31 122
Shark Bay–Monkey Mia	Smith Island	Marlin, Spanish mackerel, amberjack, wahoo, barracuda, tailor, snapper, black snapper, Norwest snapper, mulloway, bluebone groper, coral trout, parrotfish, whiting, mullet, garfish, flathead	26 34 705	113 43 211
Shark Bay–Monkey Mia	Three Bays Island	5 m. Marlin, Spanish mackerel, amberjack, wahoo, barracuda, tailor, snapper, black snapper, Norwest snapper, mulloway, bluebone groper, coral trout, parrotfish, whiting, mullet, garfish, flathead	26 33 385	113 39 049
Shark Bay–Monkey Mia	White Island S	Marlin, Spanish mackerel, amberjack, wahoo, barracuda, tailor, snapper, black snapper, Norwest snapper, mulloway, bluebone groper, coral trout, parrotfish, whiting, mullet, garfish, flathead	26 28 947	113 45 963
Shark Bay–Nanga	Petit Point	Marlin, Spanish mackerel, amberjack, wahoo, barracuda, tailor, snapper, black snapper, Norwest snapper, mulloway, bluebone groper, coral trout, parrotfish, whiting, mullet, garfish, flathead	25 56 438	113 52 487
Shark Bay–Steep Point	South Passage	Marlin, Spanish mackerel, amberjack, wahoo, barracuda, tailor, snapper, black snapper, Norwest snapper, mulloway, bluebone groper, coral trout, parrotfish, whiting, mullet, garfish, flathead	26 07 568	113 09 764
Shark Bay–Steep Point	Zuytdorp Point	Marlin, Spanish mackerel, amberjack, wahoo, barracuda, tailor, snapper, black snapper, Norwest snapper, mulloway, bluebone groper, coral trout, parrotfish, whiting, mullet, garfish, flathead	26 24 036	113 17 398
Wyndham	Berkley River	Threadfin salmon, blue salmon, queenfish, trevally, barramundi, mangrove jacks, fingermark bream, pikey bream	14 20 793	127 46 931
Wyndham	Bertram Cove	Queenfish, trevally, fingermark bream, pikey bream	14 03 568	127 27 350

Locality	Description	Comments	Latitude	Latitude
Wyndham	Buckle Head	Threadfin salmon, blue salmon, queenfish, trevally, barramundi, mangrove jacks, fingermark bream, pikey bream	14 26 323	127 50 218
Wyndham	Buckle Head E	13 m. Queenfish, trevally, fingermark bream, pikey bream	14 25 581	127 53 290
Wyndham	Buckle Head Outer	18 m. Queenfish, trevally, fingermark bream, pikey bream	14 26 399	127 58 869
Wyndham	Cambridge Gulf	10 m. Queenfish, trevally, mackerel, tuna, sharks, fingermark bream, pikey bream	14 48 779	128 16 946
Wyndham	Cape Bernier East	Queenfish, trevally, mackerel, tuna, fingermark bream, pikey bream	14 00 363	127 38 546
Wyndham	Cape Bernier South	Queenfish, trevally, mackerel, tuna, fingermark bream, pikey bream	14 01 650	127 28 951
Wyndham	Cape Domett	13 m. Queenfish, trevally, mackerel, black mulloway, fingermark bream, pikey bream	14 47 453	128 21 056
Wyndham	Cape Dussejour	Queenfish, trevally, mackerel, tuna, sharks, fingermark bream, pikey bream	14 44 851	128 11 149
Wyndham	Cape Londonderry	Queenfish, trevally, fingermark bream, pikey bream	13 44 108	126 53 382
Wyndham	Cape Rulhieres	19 m. Queenfish, trevally, mackerel, tuna, sharks, fingermark bream, pikey bream	13 52 870	127 20 524
Wyndham	Cape Rulhieres Deep	17 m. Queenfish, trevally, mackerel, tuna, sharks, fingermark bream, pikey bream	13 51 025	127 31 356
Wyndham	Cape Rulhieres North	55 m. Queenfish, trevally, mackerel, tuna, sharks, fingermark bream, pikey bream	13 51 555	127 20 524
Wyndham	Cape St Lambert	Queenfish, trevally, mackerel, fingermark bream, pikey bream	14 17 673	127 46 024
Wyndham	Cape Whiskey	Queenfish, trevally, mackerel, barramundi, mangrove jacks, fingermark bream, pikey bream	14 10 595	127 38 903
Wyndham	Cowan Patches	5 m. Queenfish, trevally, fingermark bream, pikey bream	14 51 642	128 14 460
Wyndham	Elsie Island	Threadfin salmon, blue salmon, queenfish, trevally, barramundi, mangrove jacks, fingermark bream, pikey bream	14 14 941	127 42 001
Wyndham	Faraway Bay Inner	Queenfish, trevally, fingermark bream, pikey bream	13 54 357	127 07 947
Wyndham	Faraway Bay Outer	Queenfish, trevally, fingermark bream, pikey bream	13 52 081	127 06 741
Wyndham	Fathom Rock E	3 m. Queenfish, trevally, fingermark bream, pikey bream	14 42 516	128 14 840
Wyndham	Glycosma Bay North	Queenfish, trevally, fingermark bream, pikey bream	13 48 168	127 02 247
Wyndham	Inshore Kanggurryu Island	Queenfish, trevally, mackerel, tuna, sharks, fingermark bream, pikey bream	14 47 609	128 36 092

Locality	Description	Comments	Latitude	Latitude
Wyndham	Kanggurryu Island	Queenfish, trevally, mackerel, tuna, sharks, fingermark bream, pikey bream	14 42 867	128 37 819
Wyndham	King George River	20 m. Queenfish, trevally, fingermark bream, pikey bream	13 57 312	127 19 613
Wyndham	King Shoals	Queenfish, trevally, fingermark bream, pikey bream	14 36 639	128 11 000
Wyndham	Lacrosse Island E	45 m. Threadfin salmon, blue salmon, queenfish, trevally, barramundi, mangrove jacks, fingermark bream, pikey bream	14 44 450	128 16 946
Wyndham	Leseaur Islands	14 m. Threadfin salmon, blue salmon, queenfish, trevally, barramundi, mangrove jacks, fingermark bream, pikey bream	13 50 306	127 11 513
Wyndham	Medusa Bank Deep 1	9 m. Queenfish, trevally, mackerel, sharks, fingermark bream, pikey bream	14 39 382	128 34 982
Wyndham	Medusa Bank Deep 2	10 m. Queenfish, trevally, mackerel, tuna, sharks, fingermark bream, pikey bream	14 37 383	128 32 237
Wyndham	Medusa Bank East 1	8 m. Queenfish, trevally, mackerel, fingermark bream, pikey bream	14 31 643	128 38 962
Wyndham	Medusa Bank East 2	14 m. Queenfish, trevally, mackerel, fingermark bream, pikey bream	14 26 575	128 43 577
Wyndham	Middle King Shoal	Queenfish, trevally, fingermark bream, pikey bream	14 31 769	128 08 391
Wyndham	Middle King Shoal 2	Queenfish, trevally, fingermark bream, pikey bream	14 36 711	128 13 406
Wyndham	Myrmidon Lodge	10 m. Queenfish, trevally, fingermark bream, pikey bream	14 48 531	128 14 529
Wyndham	Reveley Island	Queenfish, trevally, mackerel, tuna, sharks, fingermark bream, pikey bream	14 22 793	127 48 493
Wyndham	Sandwaves Shoal	18 m. Queenfish, trevally, fingermark bream, pikey bream	14 21 072	128 17 241
Wyndham	Shakespeare Hill	Threadfin salmon, blue salmon, queenfish, trevally, barramundi, mangrove jacks, fingermark bream, pikey bream	14 47 824	128 27 909
Wyndham	Shakespeare Hill East	Threadfin salmon, blue salmon, queenfish, trevally, barramundi, mangrove jacks, fingermark bream, pikey bream	14 47 045	128 31 528
Wyndham	Shark Rock W	Queenfish, trevally, sharks, black mulloway, fingermark bream, pikey bream	14 49 506	128 22 285
Wyndham	Stewart Islands	Queenfish, trevally, mackerel, tuna, sharks, fingermark bream, pikey bream	13 41 512	126 55 311

SHIMANO